Nonprofit Governance and Management

THIRD EDITION

Cheryl Sorokin
Judith A. Cion
Jeannie Carmedelle Frey
Richard Sevcik
Executive Editors

SOCIETY OF CORPORATE SECRETARIES
& GOVERNANCE PROFESSIONALS

AMERICAN BAR ASSOCIATION
Business Law Section

Cover design by ABA Publishing.

Page layout by Quadrum Solutions.

The materials contained herein represent the opinions of the authors and editors and should not be construed to be the views or opinions of the law firms or companies with whom such persons are in partnership with, associated with, or employed by, nor of the American Bar Association or the Business Law Section unless adopted pursuant to the bylaws of the Association.

Nothing contained in this book is to be considered as the rendering of legal advice for specific cases, and readers are responsible for obtaining such advice from their own legal counsel. This book and any forms and agreements herein are intended for educational and informational purposes only.

Printed in the United States of America.

Library of Congress Cataloging-in-Publication Data

Nonprofit governance and management / by Cheryl Sorokin .. [et al.]. — 3rd ed.

　　　p. cm.

　　Includes bibliographical references and index.

　　ISBN 978-1-61632-975-4 (alk. paper)

　　1. Nonprofit organizations—Law and legislation—United States. 2. Corporate governance—Law and legislation—United States. 3. Directors of corporations—United States—Handbooks, manuals, etc. I. Sorokin, Cheryl.

　　KF1388.N66 2011

　　658'.048—dc23

2011027286

Discounts are available for books ordered in bulk. Special consideration is given to state bars, CLE programs, and other bar-related organizations. Inquire at Book Publishing, ABA Publishing, American Bar Association, 321 N. Clark Street, Chicago, Illinois 60654-7598.

www.ababooks.org

15 14 13 12 11　　　　5 4 3 2 1

Table of Contents

Chapter 2: Dealing with Substantive Issues

This edition of Nonprofit Governance and Management *is dedicated to the memory of Judith A. Cion, whose exceptional commitment to the best practices and processes of governance will continue to enrich our communities long into the future.*

Foreword

Serving on the board of directors or as executive staff of a nonprofit organization is both a privilege and a responsibility. It is a privilege to be able to help shape the vision and mission of an organization and to guide its long-range planning. It is a responsibility to protect the interests of the organization and those it serves and to ensure that its policies and goals are carried out.

Nonprofit Governance and Management (3rd edition), a collaborative effort of the American Bar Association and the Society of Corporate Secretaries and Governance Professionals, is an invaluable guide for nonprofit board chairs, executive officers, and other directors and officers. This book provides an overview of governance basics and board structure and operations, as well as specific guidance on such key substantive issues as strategic planning, financial management, fund-raising, oversight of the executive officer, human resources management, risk management, and handling of crises. In the wake of negative publicity surrounding fiscal mismanagement in some high-profile nonprofit organizations, today's board members and executive staff face increasing scrutiny from the Internal Revenue Service as well as from their members, constituents, and donors. Both directors and executives need to be knowledgeable about the organization's tax-exempt status, internal controls, fund-raising activities, lobbying, financial reporting, intermediate sanctions, unrelated business income tax, and other fiscal management issues. *Nonprofit Governance and Management* covers each of these areas in a well-organized, easy-to-use format.

While this book is an indispensable tool for nonprofit board members, it is of particular value to executive officers and board chairs. It clearly spells out the responsibilities of these two roles and stresses the importance of mutual respect, trust, and support in promoting the organization's goals.

The "Practical Advice" section at the end of each chapter expands on the topics covered in the chapter and offers concise, cogent examples of how to apply the suggestions and recommendations. The "Sample Forms and Guidelines" contained in the Appendices are a treasure trove for any board and its management leaders and can be adapted to virtually any type of nonprofit organization.

While the commitment of time, expertise, and money required from individuals serving on a board of directors continues to mount, board members, as well as nonprofit executives, have numerous resources at their disposal. Chief among these is this edition of *Nonprofit Governance and Management*, a comprehensive publication containing timely and important insights and advice that any nonprofit board and its executive staff would do well to implement.

Annika Jaspers
Chairman of the Board
Swedish American Museum
Chicago, IL

Preface

Governance is the review and decision-making process engaged in by the individuals and boards charged with oversight and management of organizations. It involves the interaction and application of a variety of concepts, practices, procedures, expectations, legal requirements, and traditions related to the governance process.

Governance is a fundamental responsibility of an organization's board of directors and management. However, as a practical matter, the Board Chair and Executive Officer are often catalysts in shaping and improving an organization's governance practices and honing the effectiveness of board governance. Frequently, other board and management leaders, such as committee chairs and senior staff, play a critical role in improving governance as well. For this reason, this publication is designed specifically to assist such leaders, particularly Board Chairs and Executive Officers, in fulfilling their governance roles and in understanding how they may work together in shaping and improving the governance practices of the organization they serve. This publication may also be a useful reference for others involved in nonprofit governance and management issues, such those who advise nonprofit organizations as attorneys, accountants, and consultants.

Governance and management are separate but highly interrelated functions because effective governance helps ensure effective management of an organization. However, not all governance is effective or results in effective management. There is still no hard evidence that any specific governance practices or approaches yield success. Despite the fact that there is no universally accepted set of "good governance practices," current expectations for nonprofit governance are higher than in the past, reflecting similar expectations in the business world.

A major challenge to any discussion of nonprofit governance and management is the sheer variety of types and sizes of entities within the nonprofit sector. Although this publication focuses principally on nonprofit organizations that are structured as corporations, even among organizations with a corporate structure, application of governance principles will necessarily vary depending on a variety of factors. Nonetheless, there are many common principles and practices that are relevant and applicable to many types and sizes of nonprofit organizations. Periodic review of a nonprofit's governance structure and practices can help assure that the organization's governance is, and remains, effective and consistent not only with current governance trends but also with the organization's culture and operations.

Each chapter of this publication describes substantive governance issues, and includes a Practical Advice section that provides guidance on how to apply principles and address different substantive issues. The suggestions contained in the Practical Advice sections, many in bullet point or checklist format, are intended to help nonprofit management and board leadership convert principles and concepts into concrete actions to improve governance and help board members understand their responsibilities. They are based on practical experience of the authors and editors who contributed their insights from their experience in working for or advising organizations in the nonprofit sector.

Included at the end of this publication are numerous forms and guidelines relating to a wide variety of the governance topics addressed herein.

Executive Editors:
Cheryl Sorokin
Judith A. Cion
Jeannie Carmedelle Frey
Richard L. Sevcik

Acknowledgements

This work is the result of the efforts of a number of individuals who contributed ideas, text, and suggested approaches to various issues or topics, and some of whom also assisted with editing.

Much of the writing and the initial structuring of the text were done by Cheryl Sorokin and Judith A. Cion from the Society of Corporate Secretaries and Governance Professionals (Society), with significant contributions from Jeannie Carmedelle Frey and Richard Sevcik of the Nonprofit Organizations Committee of the Business Law Section of the American Bar Association (ABA).

Mses. Sorokin, Cion, and Frey and Mr. Sevcik served as Executive Editors in the final shaping and editing of the text.

The following individuals served as members of the Editorial Board and assisted with editing and shaping the overall content:

The Society of Corporate Secretaries and Governance Professionals	The American Bar Association Business Law Section
Karl Barnikol	Lawrence Beaser
Don Hager	Willard L. Boyd, III
Richard Koppes	Megan A. Christensen
Carol Strickland	Michael Malamut
Kris Veaco	Cynthia Rowland
	Lisa A. Runquist
	Patrick Sternal

This work also builds on the work of writers and contributors to two predecessor texts produced by the Society and the ABA on the topic of governance for nonprofits: *Nonprofit Governance and Management*, published in 2002, and *Nonprofit Governance: The Executive's Guide*, published in 1997. The driving force behind both these texts was Victor Futter, who was for many years a significant presence in both the Society and the ABA. Both texts helped influence the contents of this work and portions of the texts were adapted or reworked for inclusion in this publication.

The work of all these individuals is gratefully acknowledged by the Society of Corporate Secretaries and Governance Professionals and the American Bar Association.

Executive Editors:
Cheryl Sorokin
Judith A. Cion
Jeannie Carmedelle Frey
Richard L. Sevcik

Terminology

Titles and terms relating to governance matters in the nonprofit sector can be confusing. In this publication, the following terms are used as described below:

Articles of Incorporation or Articles refers to the document filed with the state by which a nonprofit (or other) corporation is organized, setting forth basic information about the organization's purpose and structure. Depending on the state, this document may be referred to by another name, such as certificate of incorporation, certificate of organization, or charter.

Board of Directors or Board refers to the governing body of a nonprofit corporation that has the primary functions of major decision-making for the organization, overseeing and advising management, and providing leadership to the organization. Other common names for this body include governing board, board of trustees, board of overseers, governing committee, and board of governors.

Board Member or Member of the Board refers to an individual elected or appointed or designated to serve on a nonprofit organization's board. A board member also may be referred to as a director and in this publication the terms director, board member, and member of the board are used interchangeably.

Chair or Board Chair refers to the person who presides over or convenes the board of directors and who usually is elected to the position by fellow board members. Typically, the Chair is a volunteer, not an employee, and not engaged full time in the organization's service. In some nonprofit organizations, the Chair also exercises managerial powers; however, in this publication, the term Chair refers to an individual's role with the board rather than as a manager.

Director refers to an individual elected or appointed to serve on a nonprofit organization's board. As noted above, in this publication the terms director, board member, and member of the board are used interchangeably. In some organizations, "Director" may be the title given to the chief managerial officer of the organization, but it is not used with that meaning in this publication.

Executive Officer refers to the chief managerial officer of the nonprofit organization. This individual is the person principally responsible for assuring the accomplishment of the organization's day-to-day and long-term activities, typically performing functions similar to those of an individual who would hold the title Chief Executive Officer, CEO, President, Chief Operating Officer, or COO in a for-profit organization. Increasingly, nonprofits are using the title Chief Executive Officer or President for the chief managerial officer, but other titles for the chief managerial officer include Executive Director, Managing Director, General Director, Director, Head of School, and Chief Administrator. In many organizations, the Executive Officer is a full-time paid employee. In others, the individual may be part-time and may or may not receive a salary. In some nonprofits, the role of Executive Officer may be divided between two persons—for example, in arts organizations the role may be divided between an Executive Director and an Artistic Director. In this publication, the term Executive Officer encompasses the Executive Officer roles assigned to both. The Executive Officer may or may not be a board member.

Member refers to a person having voting rights of any kind other than as a director (usually including, or perhaps limited to, the right to elect directors) in a nonprofit's governance structure. While many organizations, such as museums or public radio stations, refer to certain donors or supporters as "members" with certain admission or other privileges, the term "member" in this publication is limited to those individuals or organizations that hold voting rights, typically the right to vote for directors, or the right to vote on certain matters set forth under state law or in the nonprofit's bylaws or articles of incorporation. These rights are often referred to as "reserved powers."

Membership Organization refers to a nonprofit corporation with members as defined above.

Mission refers to the general purposes for which the nonprofit corporation was organized and is operated. These purposes are stated in the corporation's articles of incorporation. The mission is derived from these purposes.

Mission Statement refers to the articulation of the mission, often in a format used for internal or external marketing or fund-raising purposes.

Nonprofit Organization, Nonprofit Corporation, or Nonprofit refers to a corporation organized under its state nonprofit corporation law (or in some cases, federal law) that operates for nonprofit purposes. The fact that an organization is a nonprofit organization under state law does not necessarily mean that it is a tax-exempt organization under the Internal Revenue Code (IRC). For an organization to be exempt from federal income tax, it generally must file an application with the Internal Revenue Service (IRS) and receive a determination letter from the IRS.

There are several types of tax-exempt organizations (sometimes referred to simply as "exempt" organizations) under Section 501(c) and other sections of the IRC. These include, among others, Section 501(c)(3) charitable, educational, scientific, or religious organizations; Section 501(c)(6) trade associations, and Section 501(c)(7) social and recreational clubs. Income received by these exempt organizations in connection with their tax-exempt purposes is exempt from federal income taxation under Section 501 or other specified sections of the IRC. Revenue from activities that are not substantially related to the tax-exempt purposes of the nonprofit organization may be treated as taxable "unrelated business income."

Those nonprofit corporations that have not qualified for exempt status are subject to federal income taxes. Often such "taxable nonprofits" are affiliated with tax-exempt nonprofit organizations and are separately incorporated specifically to carry out non-tax-exempt activities. Because of their close affiliation with tax-exempt nonprofits, many of the principles discussed in this publication with respect to tax-exempt nonprofits also apply to taxable nonprofit entities. Other "taxable nonprofits" may not be affiliated with tax-exempt nonprofit organizations but have been formed for other reasons, e.g., the ability to contract with or receive grants from governmental agencies. However, the term nonprofit in this publication is intended to refer to nonprofit organizations whose primary income is exempt from federal tax.

Only donations to nonprofits meeting the requirements of Section 501(c)(3) of the IRC are deductible as charitable contributions from the donors' income for tax purposes. Donations to other tax-exempt organizations are not tax deductible as charitable contributions to the donor although, depending on the circumstances, they might be deductible as business expenses. Section 501(c)(3) organizations are organized primarily for religious, educational, charitable, scientific, or literary purposes, for public safety testing, to foster national or international amateur sports competitions, or to prevent cruelty to animals.

Private Foundation refers to an organization that is tax-exempt under Section 501(c)(3) and characterized under Section 509(a) of the IRC as a private foundation, rather than a public charity. Private foundations normally have limited or single funding sources, such as members of a family or a corporation. The IRC imposes special requirements on private foundations regarding distributions, investments, and other matters.

Secretary refers to the individual responsible for documentation of corporate actions and retention of vital corporate records. This person may be called a Corporate Secretary or Secretary to the Board or just Secretary.

The person performing these functions for a nonprofit board may be a director or a staff member. If the person serving as Secretary is a senior member of management or a director, he or she also may be the primary advisor to the organization and the board on corporate governance matters. He or she may be a focal point for communication with the board of directors, senior management, and the company's various constituencies and may occupy a key role in the administration of critical corporate matters. If the person is a more junior level staff person, he or she is likely to be limited in function to the more ministerial aspects of this role. In many nonprofits, the Secretary's functions are divided between an individual denominated Secretary of the Board or Corporate Secretary and a staff person designated as Board Liaison. In some organizations, the staff person is appointed as assistant secretary.

CHAPTER 1: Governance Basics

CHAPTER **1**

Governance Basics

The Function of Corporate Governance

Definition. Corporate governance encompasses the concepts, practices, procedures, expectations, legal requirements, and traditions used by the leadership of organizations, the boards, and the individuals charged with organizational oversight and management. At its most basic, corporate governance refers to the way an organization allocates authority and oversight responsibility for decisions and operational activities.

The governance of any corporation is the shared responsibility of management and the board. Each corporation has a legal structure mandated by law that contemplates bifurcation of responsibility for governance (major decisions and general oversight in the hands of a board) and management (implementation and operations by management). But, beyond those structural basics, it is the board and management that typically create a framework of governance policies and practices that facilitate the successful functioning of the organization.

Differences Between Nonprofits and For-Profit Organizations. Business organizations are often referred to as "for-profit" organizations because a fundamental goal of the governing bodies of these organizations is to further the economic interests of the businesses' owners by an increase in shareholder value. In fact, the success of business organizations is generally defined by financial viability, growth, and increase in shareholder (or owner) value. As a result, the business organization's shareholders or owners have a direct interest in monitoring not only the organization but also the board, which they elect.

3

By contrast, the measure of a nonprofit organization's success is usually driven not by shareholder or owner value, but by how well the organization achieves its mission. Measuring the successful fulfillment of a nonprofit organization's mission is not simply a matter of quantifying the level of profits and losses that occur—although too many losses for too long will adversely affect the organization's ability to operate. Qualitative measures are important as well. Is the organization achieving the purpose for which it was established? Is it reaching its intended beneficiaries? Is the service or program provided by the organization being delivered effectively? Is the quality of the service or program appropriate? Is the mission viable?

Some nonprofit cooperative organizations do exist to increase the value of the members' financial stake in the organization, but this is not the case for most nonprofits. Most nonprofit organizations have no shareholders, owners, or members with a direct financial interest in ensuring that the organization's mission is accomplished effectively. The role of assuring mission achievement typically falls to the nonprofit board, which is most often the guardian of the nonprofit's mission and plays an integral role in ensuring that the nonprofit's mission is accomplished. If the nonprofit has members, the board may share responsibility for accomplishing the organization's mission with the members or an assembly of members in the manner set forth in the organization's governing documents. A nonprofit board is also responsible for assuring that the organization does not violate the legal basis that enabled the organization to receive the benefits associated with nonprofit status. In short, governance for a nonprofit assists the organization in fulfilling its mission and its purposes.

Leadership of the Chair and Relationship with Executive Officer. The nonprofit Board Chair has a critical governance role, providing leadership to both the board and the organization as a whole. Additionally, an effective relationship between the Board Chair and the Executive Officer is an important element in nonprofit governance. An effective relationship does not mean that the Board Chair and Executive Officer must agree on everything, but it does require that they have mutual respect, deal forthrightly with each other, and have the ability to address issues constructively and in a manner that is in the best long-term interest of their organization.

Leadership of the Executive Officer and Relationship with the Board and the Board Chair. In overseeing the organization's operations, the Executive Officer has direct access to operational information and is able to monitor and see trends and developments relating to the organization's mission of which the board may be unaware. In addition to working to make operations effective, the Executive Officer is accountable to the board not only with respect to the matters routinely reported to the board (such as sales, profits, quality of products or services, etc.), but also with respect to opportunities, trends, challenges, and strategic issues the board needs to understand to successfully manage the organization for the future. An effective Executive Officer works closely with the board and the Board Chair to identify what information should be provided to the board regarding both current operating results and future challenges and opportunities.

The Practical Advice Section of this Chapter has specific suggestions for how board and management leaders might work together on governance issues and also lists a number of matters to keep in mind in attempting to make governance changes. See pages 23–27.

Board Basics

Role of the Board in General

Decision-Making, Oversight and Advice, Leadership. Every corporation has a board of directors with the primary functions of major decision-making, overseeing and advising, and providing leadership to management and the organization. It is by the exercise of these functions that the nonprofit board helps assure that the entity achieves its mission and fulfills its obligations under the law to its donors, its staff and volunteers, its clients, and the public.

Decision-making functions of nonprofit boards most often include:

- Shaping, and if necessary, revising the nonprofit's mission;
- Setting strategy and goals for the organization;
- Determining and approving major organizational policies;
- Hiring, evaluating, and, if necessary, terminating the Executive Officer;
- Delegating authority to board committees for specific governance oversight and decisions in certain areas (such as finance, executive compensation, or compliance);
- Delegating appropriate levels of operational and decisional authority to management;
- Approving budgets, major expenditures, and the acquisition or disposition of major assets; and
- Setting policies and procedures for enhancing and evaluating the board's own performance.

Oversight and advice functions of nonprofit boards typically include:

- Evaluating how well the nonprofit's operations fulfill its mission;
- Monitoring financial performance and projections and use of assets;
- Evaluating the adequacy of internal controls and financial reporting;
- Overseeing and reviewing management performance;

- Reviewing performance measures for the organization's programs and goals;
- Overseeing functions that support compliance with legal obligations and organizational policies;
- Evaluating risks to the organization and its mission;
- Evaluating trends that may affect the organization's ability to fulfill its mission and serve its intended class of beneficiaries;
- Making suggestions and providing advice based on experience; and
- Serving as a sounding board for management ideas.

Leadership functions of nonprofit boards include:

- Serving as an advocate for the organization and its mission;
- Bringing creativity, experience, personal good judgment, common sense, and integrity to board deliberations and other work as directors;
- Supporting and advising the Executive Officer and other senior staff without micromanaging; and
- For nonprofits that are tax-exempt charitable organizations, personal participation in fund-raising and personal donations to the organization at a leadership level.

Operating or Governing Boards. Boards are sometimes categorized as either "operating boards" or "governing boards." These terms can be misleading. All boards govern; that is their role. However, especially with smaller nonprofit organizations having minimal professional staff and resources, individual board members or other members of the organization may also assume certain managerial roles. In such cases, the governing and management roles of board members may become blurred, and members of a so-called operating board may essentially function as an executive management committee of the nonprofit, handling day-to-day decisions. Even in organizations in which the nonprofit board does function more as a governance-oriented body, a crisis may induce or require the board to become involved in operational decisions that normally would be delegated to management. In effect, board members of operating boards are playing two roles: that of management and that of board member, and it can be difficult for board members to keep separate their board/governance role and their management/operational role.

More typically, directors are not engaged in actual delivery of services, and directors do not function as members of management. Most nonprofit boards function primarily as oversight or governing boards which engage in decision-making, oversight, and leadership, but delegate implementation of board decisions, as well as day-to-day operational decision-making and management, to the nonprofit's Executive Officer and staff. The board is thereby able to focus on overseeing the nonprofit's ability to deliver its mission and sustain itself over time. While governing boards do affect the day-to-day operations of the organization, they do so by such activities as periodic review of the mission, setting strategy, approving budgets, monitoring risk, fund-raising, and hiring, evaluating, and, if necessary, removing the Executive Officer.

Importance of Understanding the Board's Role. The role distinctions between governing and operating boards are not always easy to make. Management concerns about micromanagement by the board and board perceptions of management's desire to control the organization without "interference" or guidance from board members tend to stem from misunderstandings about the appropriate role of the board and management. Frequent and candid communication between the board—in particular the Board Chair—and the Executive Officer can help reduce such misunderstanding, defuse potentially explosive situations, and strengthen the supportive functions of the board for management and of management for the board.

Member Organizations. A nonprofit may have a member or members who have various voting rights. Members may have the right to elect the directors or the right to vote on or to approve certain matters set forth under state law or in the articles of incorporation or bylaws of the nonprofit. These rights often are referred to as "reserved powers." These members may be individuals, as is common in trade associations, or other nonprofits, as is common with membership organizations formed by hospital systems and colleges and universities. With respect to nonprofits with a single nonprofit member, the nonprofit's bylaws often specify who has the authority to act on behalf of the sole member (board, committee, Executive Officer), and the mechanism for the member to take such action.

The Practical Advice Section of this Chapter suggests a number of issues for Board Chairs and Executive Officers to discuss on the topic of governance. See pages 24–26.

Collective vs. Individual Action of Directors

Collective Action. A board acts as a collective body. If a quorum is present, typically a majority vote will decide an issue, absent a state law or bylaw requirement of a greater than majority vote. A director may dissent or vote "no," but once the majority has made a decision, the organization and all its directors, staff, and other agents are bound by the decision of the majority.

Collegiality and Dissent. Collegiality and shared values can be important factors in effective governance, but collegiality does not preclude discussion and dissent. In many nonprofit organizations, there is a strong but sometimes unstated bias against decisions that are not supported at least apparently by all or substantially all board members.

One key function of the Board Chair is to make sure that all directors are comfortable articulating dissenting views and to encourage board members to consider all perspectives, even if some perspectives appear to be held by only a small percentage of voting directors. However, significant dissent, or continued actions in opposition by board members unable to support a majority decision once it has occurred, may indicate a serious problem that needs to be addressed.

Board retreats, strategic planning sessions, use of outside advisors, board self-evaluations, and individual director evaluations are all tools that can be employed to help create a more cohesive board. Nonetheless, from time to time, board and management leaders may need to consider if one or more board members are in such conflict with the other directors that the board's overall effectiveness is undermined. Addressing such situations requires courage, sensitivity, and diplomacy, especially from Board Chairs and Executive Officers. Failing to address clear or growing problems of internal board dissent may result in adverse, and occasionally devastating, effects on the organization's ability to fulfill its mission.

Apparent Authority. An individual director is not legally empowered, as a director, to sign contracts, enter into agreements, or take other individual action that is binding on the organization, unless that action has been authorized as required by law and the appropriate procedures of the nonprofit. However, there may be circumstances in which an individual board member takes action or agrees to do something on behalf of the nonprofit which the other party to the transaction believes the director has authority to undertake. In such event, the other party is said to be relying on the apparent authority of the board member holding himself or herself out as authorized to speak or act for the organization, and the nonprofit may find itself obligated to the other party even if the director's action was not appropriately authorized.

Avoiding instances of apparent authority may best be accomplished by periodically reminding board members that their governance role does not permit them to hold themselves out as representing the board or the organization unless the board has specifically delegated such authority to them. Operating boards in which directors exercise both governance and managerial authority may especially need to clarify the extent of a board member's authority when acting in a managerial capacity. Apparent authority issues often arise with a founder or "heart of gold" board member who so identifies with the organization that outside parties assume that the director has authority to speak for or bind the organization.

Basic Legal Duties of Directors

Fiduciary Duties. Directors, whether of for-profit or nonprofit organizations, are considered fiduciaries who owe two core duties to the organization: the duty of care and the duty of loyalty. While the duty of care and duty of loyalty standards have derived primarily from a long tradition of jurisprudence in the sphere of business corporations, they are equally applicable to boards and board members of nonprofits. In some states, compliance with fiduciary duty standards may be required by statute. Understanding these concepts is important for both directors and staff of nonprofits, as they are important legal standards that shape how boards and board members must act in order to fulfill their responsibilities. These standards affect what board members need to know, what they may ask for or about, and what actions they may or may not take. If a board member, or the board as a whole, fails to exercise the duty of care or duty of loyalty, or to act in good faith, there could be legal liability for the individual or the board. Failure to adhere to these standards may also adversely affect the organization's continued viability, how well it is able to fulfill its mission, and the level of trust that donors, regulators, and other constituencies have in the organization.

Duty of Care and Good Faith. The duty of care requires a director to act in a reasonable, diligent, and informed manner in preparing for and participating in board and committee actions. Directors exercise the duty of care by performing their duties in good faith with honest intent and with the care that an ordinarily prudent person would believe appropriate in a similar position and under similar circumstances. This means acting competently and using common sense, being diligent and attentive to the organization's needs, and using one's best efforts to make sound and informed decisions.

Ways in which board members exercise their duty of care and show good faith include:

- Diligence in preparing for, attending, and participating in board and committee meetings, being informed on matters coming before the board or committee for decision or review, and considering all factors relevant to a decision, including the views of management and other board members;

- Exercising independent and informed judgment in making decisions and making determinations based solely on what is in the best interest of the entity, taking into account, but not ceding to, decisions or opinions of other board members, management, or outside experts;

- Requiring (for oneself and for others on the board) complete and adequate information on which to make decisions; and

- Asking questions about how the organization assures compliance with laws and identifies and addresses operational risks.

Reliance on Committees, Officers, and Others. Directors are generally entitled to rely on information and opinions provided by board committees, management executives, and outside experts acting within their respective areas of responsibility or expertise. However, in each instance, such reliance on others must be reasonable. If relying on outside advisors, board members will want to know the advisor's credentials and evaluate whether such advisors have been diligent in their work and have furnished accurate and complete information to the board. If relying on board committees or management, board members will want to be satisfied that such bodies or the individuals have the appropriate levels of experience and have themselves exercised reasonable diligence in considering all relevant information and arriving at their conclusions.

Appendix 1 has a sample bylaw provision setting forth fundamental duties of directors.

Duty of Loyalty. The duty of loyalty means that each board member is expected to act in good faith and in the best interests of the nonprofit and in furtherance of its mission rather than in furtherance of his or her personal interests or the interests of another entity with which he or she is associated. However, a board member may share with other directors the perspectives of such other entity, to the extent that such perspective may be considered relevant to the nonprofit. For example, an individual sitting on a national board by virtue of appointment by a regional affiliate would be entitled and expected to share concerns that his or her regional organization might have about a decision being considered by the national organization and vice versa. When voting on a decision, however, the board member's fiduciary duty of loyalty is owed to the organization and the board making the decision, requiring the board member to vote based on the best interest of that organization.

To avoid legal problems or negative public reaction, conflicts of interest, whether real or apparent, are best avoided. If a board member has a personal interest in a matter coming before the board or a committee, at a minimum, such interest needs to be fully disclosed to the board or committee. A board member with a conflict of interest generally does not participate in any discussion or decision of a matter in which he or she has a conflict, although such a board member generally has the right to explain his or her personal interest.

The duty of loyalty also prohibits a board member from taking personal advantage of a beneficial opportunity available to the nonprofit which the director became aware of in connection with his or her board service, unless approved by the board. Similarly, the duty of loyalty prohibits a board member from benefiting an entity with which he or she is affiliated in taking advantage of such an opportunity.

For example, if a director of an art museum board becomes aware through his or her role on the board that a private collector is preparing to sell his or her art collection, including several items that would be of interest to the museum, the director would be violating the duty of loyalty by contacting the seller and buying such items himself or herself. In such a circumstance, the duty of loyalty would mandate that the director assure that the offer was first made available to the museum. Only if the museum rejected the opportunity could the director take advantage of it.

On the other hand, if the director is an art dealer whom the collector approaches directly about buying his or her collection, the director could purchase the items without violating his or her duty of loyalty, even if he or she knew that the museum also would be interested. Such action would be appropriate because the opportunity was presented to the board member in a capacity unrelated to his or her board membership. Nonetheless, to avoid the possible appearance of impropriety, the director may want to disclose the opportunity and his or her intention to purchase the item or items to the board, and perhaps even arrange for the collector to offer the museum an opportunity to purchase certain items from his or her collection. The Model Nonprofit Corporation Act (3rd ed.) provides a process for handling business opportunity situations (Section 8.70).

Another aspect of the duty of loyalty is the obligation of board members at all times to retain the confidentiality of the nonprofit's information and board deliberations, unless such information becomes publicly known through no fault of the board member, or is otherwise a matter of public record. Disclosure of nonpublic information may adversely affect the nonprofit organization's competitive advantage or reputation in the community. The appropriate action for any director who is uncertain about whether the entity has disclosed particular information, or whether the information is otherwise public, is to refer questions regarding that information to the Board Chair, the Executive Officer, or other management executives of the nonprofit.

Some commentators and courts suggest that directors of nonprofits have an additional duty described as the duty of obedience: a duty to be faithful to and foster the nonprofit's mission and to avoid actions inconsistent with the purpose of the organization. Others take the position that there is no such separate duty and that a director's obligations to be faithful to and to foster and to take action consistent with the nonprofit's mission are simply aspects of the duty of loyalty. In either case, adherence to or support of the organization's mission is a fundamental expectation for nonprofit directors.

Conflict of Interest Policies. One way to help ensure that the duty of loyalty is adhered to is for the board to adopt and enforce a conflict of interest policy that defines what is expected of board members and provides procedures to ensure that the conflict of interest policy is followed. A conflict of interest policy defines when a conflict exists and specifies what procedures are to be followed in the event of a conflict involving a board or committee member. Such policies have long been encouraged by legal and governance experts. Additionally, most exempt organizations must file a Form 990-Return of Organizations Exempt from Federal Income Taxation annually with the Internal Revenue Service (IRS). This IRS form requires nonprofits to state whether or not they have a conflicts policy and whether such policy is followed. Organizations that do not have or do not routinely enforce a conflict of interest policy may be subject to additional scrutiny by regulators, donors, or beneficiaries, especially if it appears that the potential for conflicts of interest exists within the board. Additionally, the IRS has for some time required a conflict of interest policy for new applicants seeking tax-exempt status.

Appendix 2 has a copy of the IRS sample conflict of interest policy and a sample bylaw provision related to conflict of interests.

The Practical Advice Section of this Chapter has suggestions on actions that Board Chairs and Executive Officers can take to help board members understand and meet their duties of care and loyalty. See pages 26–27.

Basic Legal Rights of Directors

Director Rights. Directors have rights as well as duties. These include the right of access to relevant information about the organization that board members need in order to perform their duties. Access to information means access to the nonprofit's books and records and to key members of management and outside advisors. Board members have the right to all relevant information regarding a decision they are asked to make, including the right to a full discussion of the matter at a board or committee meeting. Access to information also includes access in an appropriate form. For example, if the board is provided with a long report or very detailed data, it is within the board's prerogative to ask for summaries of key information contained in such reports or data and to be given adequate time to review material.

While board members have the right to request information, requests for information from individual board members outside of board or committee meetings can raise a number of issues for board leadership and Executive Officers. For example, unless certain directors have been delegated specific individual responsibilities, all of the members of the board or a committee have a right to the same level of information. In addition, director requests for information may cause management to be unduly absorbed by information gathering or compilation in response to the request, at the expense of time needed to attend to operational matters. The potentially burdensome nature of these requests can be lessened by channeling these requests for information to designated members of management.

Board members have the right to dissent from a decision made by a majority of the board. A dissenting board member may choose to have his or her dissent recorded in the minutes of the meeting at which the decision was taken, and many nonprofits identify dissenters in minutes as a standard practice. Board members also have the right and the duty to approve minutes of prior meetings and to have access to minutes of meetings of committees and the full board. Exercise of these rights helps ensure that all important matters are accurately described and recorded.

Business Judgment Rule. Actions of boards are sometimes subject to legal challenge, most typically after something has gone terribly wrong. However, boards and board members are not required to be infallible. Their decision-making may be protected by what is known as the business judgment rule. The business judgment rule presumes that the board's judgment in reaching a particular decision was correct and, therefore, not subject to challenge by others, except in the event of outrageous conduct. This means that if a board member and the board have acted in accordance with their duties of care and loyalty and if their actions appear to have been rational at the time taken, their actions will be permitted to stand and no liability will attach to the board, the nonprofit, or the individual board member. The business judgment rule does not add to the duties of board members but reinforces the importance of acting in accordance with the duties of care and loyalty.

In the case of a business corporation, the business judgment rule is generally raised in litigation brought by or on behalf of shareholders. In the case of a nonprofit, where there are no shareholders but what is at stake is the public interest, there is a paucity of case law. However, there are courts that have applied the business judgment rule to nonprofit board actions, and it is generally believed that the business judgment rule would be applied in cases involving nonprofits to protect those boards that have acted in accordance with their duties of care and loyalty.

Making a successful business judgment defense to a challenged board action (such as a merger, termination of the Executive Officer or other significant decision) must often be done long after the fact. Proving that the board's action was undertaken in a manner consistent with its duties of care and loyalty will be easier if accurate meeting minutes are written and approved within a reasonable time after the meeting approving such action.

There are potentially other liability protections for directors, such as statutory liability shields discussed below.

The Practical Advice Section of this Chapter has advice on actions to help boards obtain the benefits of the business judgment rule discussed in the next section, including suggested practices for minute writing. See pages 26-27.

Liability of Directors

Although a board acts collectively, the duties of care and loyalty are individual duties of board members. If nonprofit board members fail to carry out these duties, it is possible that they may be liable for that failure if harm to the organization results. Similarly, if the board as a whole fails to exercise its duties in an appropriate manner (for example, if it fails to exercise ordinary diligence in its operations), not only may the organization suffer, but in some cases directors may be subject to liability. Legal action to enforce these duties or claiming that harm to the organization resulted from a breach of such duties by one or more board members (such as a claim of taking a corporate opportunity, failure to disclose a conflict of interest, or failure to assure that the organization's funds were invested in an appropriate manner) may be undertaken by or on behalf of the organization based on enforcement powers provided under state law and the organization's articles, bylaws, or other governing documents. In most states, the attorney general has power to challenge boards or board members for breach of fiduciary duty.

Depending on the circumstances and applicable state law, director actions may also be challenged by other board members, members of the organization, and, in limited cases, donors, beneficiaries, or other stakeholders. In some instances, a director's actions also may be challenged by third parties who allege that they suffered harm due to some action taken by the organization that was or should have been overseen by the board. Federal regulators, including the IRS, also may bring action against board members if violations of law are alleged, such as an organization's failure to pay payroll taxes or receipt of an undue or prohibited financial benefit by a board member, officer, or other person.

Directors of nonprofits may not always be aware of the potential personal liability they face by serving on a board. Many focus more on the honor of being asked to serve or on their own desires to participate in the organization's mission. However, it is a mistake to think that board members of a nonprofit cannot be sued for their actions or inactions. Informing directors of this potential liability in the orientation materials for new directors, as well as through periodic reminders to all board members, can help directors better understand the significance of their service from a legal standpoint.

Protection Against Liability for Directors

State and Federal Law.   State and federal laws may provide some protection against liability for directors of certain nonprofit corporations. Although state laws differ, several provide immunity from lawsuits based on allegations of breach of the duty of care (but not breach of the duty of loyalty) for board members of nonprofit corporations that are tax-exempt under Section 501(c)(3) of the IRC. In some states, the immunity is provided only if the board member received no compensation for serving on the board other than reimbursement of actual expenses. In other states, board members may receive a fairly low level of compensation and still qualify for liability protection. Such liability protection statutes typically exclude from protection director conduct involving gross negligence or intentional misconduct.

The Model Nonprofit Corporation Act (3rd ed.) (MNCA) eliminates a director's liability to a charitable nonprofit corporation and its members for money damages for actions taken or not taken as a director with certain exceptions. In addition, the MNCA permits noncharitable nonprofit corporations to eliminate or limit a director's liability to the corporation or its members for money damages for actions taken or not taken as a director, with the same exceptions, even if the board member receives compensation for board service.

Under the federal Volunteer Protection Act, a board member and other volunteers for a 501(c)(3) nonprofit organization who receive no cash compensation or noncash compensation of no more than $500 per year may have a defense against any lawsuit seeking to hold them personally liable for damages resulting from actions taken in connection with his or her service to the 501(c)(3) organization. This Act still permits lawsuits to be brought against a volunteer board member by the organization itself and does not immunize an uncompensated board member against liability for crimes of violence, hate crimes, acts related to sexual offense convictions, civil rights violations, and acts done under the influence of drugs or alcohol.

Indemnification and Insurance. Because state and federal immunity laws are not absolute, and because a board member who is sued may still need to hire counsel and pay legal fees to assert a defense, the availability of indemnification and insurance are important issues for directors and individuals considering service on a nonprofit board.

Indemnification. State laws allow nonprofits to indemnify (protect against loss) individual board members against liability, with certain limitations (e.g., certain intentional acts may not be covered). In some situations, state law may actually require indemnification; in other situations, indemnification is permissive and in others indemnification may be prohibited. Indemnification means that the nonprofit's resources will be available, with certain limitations, for use in paying board members' legal costs, judgments, and settlements if board members are sued for breach of their duties to the nonprofit. Indemnification provisions are typically found in a nonprofit's bylaws (although they may be contained in the articles) and may provide for indemnification up to the maximum permitted by state law. Indemnification generally is available whether or not board members are compensated for their service on the board. In some cases, board members may also enter into separate indemnification agreements with the organization, although this is relatively rare in the nonprofit sphere. It is important to understand that indemnification is only helpful to the extent the organization has the financial resources to be able to fully indemnify individuals covered by its indemnification obligations.

A nonprofit's obligation to indemnify or to advance legal expenses may require board approval, and may be subject to the director or officer agreeing to repay any legal expenses if he or she is found not to have satisfied the relevant standards or duties of care.

Insurance. Most nonprofit organizations of significant size purchase directors and officers (D&O) insurance to cover both possible liability and the cost of defending against a lawsuit. D&O insurance can be important even in states that provide immunity from liability because of the risk of incurring up-front legal fees during litigation. In addition, D&O insurance may provide coverage for directors and officers that is broader than indemnification allowed under state law. Another benefit is that insurance shifts the liability for paying board members' legal costs, judgments, and settlements from the nonprofit to the insurer, so that the availability of protection from legal costs is not dependent on the availability of the nonprofit's resources. However, insurance may be expensive, especially for a small or new nonprofit, and it must be purchased and maintained in advance of any incident that might create liability.

When commercial D&O insurance is not available at a reasonable cost, an alternative may be for the nonprofit to maintain a self-insurance fund to cover its indemnification and insurance obligations. However, self-insuring is a complex process that may not be feasible for many nonprofits and does not result in shifting risk and cost from the nonprofit unless the assets of the self-insurance fund are legally segregated. In either case, the cost of insurance is a factor for the board to consider in determining what protections are prudent and necessary.

Periodic Review and Communication with the Board on Indemnification, Insurance Coverage, and State Law Protections. It typically falls to the Executive Officer and other management personnel to remain current on D&O insurance coverage options and costs and to work with counsel to make sure that the indemnification offered by the nonprofit remains appropriate under state law, court decisions, and regulatory requirements. Regular reviews are important as insurance companies may alter the scope or cost of coverage, and insurance that was prudent and fiscally responsible in one year may not be so in the next. Modification and updating of indemnification provisions or insurance coverage become difficult, if not impossible, once a problem calling for indemnification or insurance actually arises.

The Executive Officer also typically has the responsibility of keeping the board informed about insurance and indemnification as well as the statutory liability protections available to board members, usually through regular presentations to the board or an appropriate committee of the board.

Board members and prospective board members usually want the protections afforded by both indemnification and insurance, and the lack of such protections may discourage some individuals from serving on a nonprofit board.

The Practical Advice Section of this Chapter has suggestions Executive Officers and Board Chairs might use to help board members understand indemnification and insurance issues. See pages 27–28.

Leadership Roles

Role of the Board Chair

Position Structure. The nonprofit Board Chair usually is elected to the position by fellow directors. Some organizations place limits on the number of years an individual may serve as Chair. Because the role is often a volunteer position, and/or because of term limits, it is not unusual for there to be frequent turnover in the role. Organizations without term limits sometimes find it difficult to dislodge a founder or other long-term board member or a major donor from the Chair position. While term limits for the Board Chair and committee chairs, as well as board members generally, are often seen as a good governance practice to assure that fresh perspectives are brought to the work of the board, conversely, institutional knowledge and experience, which often accompany longer term service, can be critically important to effective functioning of the entire board.

Frequent turnover in the position of Board Chair, as a result of term limits or otherwise, may have the subtle effect, over time, of increasing the power of the Executive Officer, resulting in his or her effective exercise of greater influence over the board than the Board Chair. While such a situation may not clearly result in ineffective oversight of the organization, boards and Board Chairs need to be sensitive to the practical reality that term limits may have on their exercise of power and their relationship to the Executive Officer.

While in many public companies the Chief Executive Officer also serves as Board Chair, the roles of CEO and Board Chair are usually separate in nonprofit entities, with the Executive Officer typically serving as CEO. This separation makes a close working relationship between the nonprofit Board Chair and the Executive Officer key to effective governance.

In some organizations, however, the various board leadership responsibilities are divided between a Board Chair and a President of the Board. This division of responsibility can make it easier to find individuals willing to assume leadership positions, particularly if one position focuses mainly on areas in which an individual has specific expertise. However, division of responsibility also adds an additional level of complexity to the board structure and board member relationships, as well as to management of the board's relationship with the Executive Officer. To avoid confusion, if there is a separate Board Chair and President of the Board, it is important to clearly delineate their respective duties and authority in the organization's bylaws or other governing document.

Main responsibilities. An organization's bylaws typically provide that the role of the Board Chair is to preside at meetings of the board. Often that is the only description of the Chair's responsibilities. Nonetheless, the role of the Board Chair of a nonprofit is usually multifaceted, going well beyond the simple wielding of the gavel. In effect, the principal role of the Board Chair of a nonprofit is to provide board leadership and to work closely with the Executive Officer to help assure that the organization achieves its mission. Common aspects of this leadership role generally include the following:

- *Presiding Officer.* As the title implies, an important aspect of the Board Chair's role is to preside at board meetings. This presiding officer role includes working with the Executive Officer to set agendas and to determine the types of information to be furnished to directors and the matters to be considered by the board.

- *Oversight of Board and Committees.* As leader of the governance oversight body of the nonprofit, the Board Chair is also principally responsible for the smooth functioning of the board and its committees and for making sure that the board has appropriate and sufficient resources to perform its legal and functional responsibilities. This leadership role also generally includes active participation, if not direct responsibility, for nominating or appointing board members to particular committees and monitoring committee and committee chair performance. As an officer of the organization and leader of the board, monitoring board and committee performance usually includes leadership and active participation in board and director evaluations. Strong Board Chair leadership in this role can be extremely important in the long-term building of a strong governance oversight body and in facilitating overall effective governance of the organization.

- *Liaison with Management.* Another important role of the Board Chair is to serve as the board's liaison or representative with organization management between meetings. This function generally includes working with the Executive Officer in determining what information is to be provided to board and committee members both in connection with and apart from meetings. It also includes providing counsel and direction to the Executive Officer between meetings as well as serving as a sounding board for him or her on issues related to the organization's management.

- *Evaluation of Executive Officer.* The Board Chair's role in governance leadership and as liaison with management also means that the Board Chair has a significant role in the major board governance function of evaluating and providing feedback on the performance of the Executive Officer.

- *Organization Representative.* In some organizations, the Board Chair may be the public face of the organization in its community and a major advocate on behalf of the organization with a variety of constituents.

- *Fund-Raising.* For organizations that raise charitable donations from the public, active personal participation in fund-raising activities is a critical role of the Board Chair. In such organizations, the Board Chair also may be expected to make a personal donation at a leadership level. The particular importance of the Board Chair in fund-raising activities is both to set a good example and to encourage and, if necessary, enforce, the participation of other board members to the extent of their abilities and commitments. While the nonprofit staff is generally responsible for many development activities and certain specific activities may be delegated to a development committee of the board and its chair, the Board Chair is generally responsible for ensuring that all board members are satisfying their personal fund-raising commitments and any required contributions to the organization.

While aspects of the responsibility for building effective board governance, evaluating the Executive Officer, and representing or advocating for the organization with the general public can be delegated to board committees or individual board members, success in the Board Chair role typically requires strong leadership and active participation by the Chair as well as close cooperation between the Chair and the board and the Executive Officer. A weakness of leadership in the Board Chair position can harm the entity's ability to achieve its mission.

The Practical Advice Section of this Chapter lists a number of considerations related to selection of a Board Chair and for prospective Board Chairs to ask themselves prior to agreeing to serve (see pages 29–31), as well as suggestions for building the relationship between the Board Chair and the Executive Officer (see page 31).

Role of the Executive Officer

Position Structure. If the nonprofit has employees, the Executive Officer will generally be a full-time staff member hired after a board-conducted search process. The Executive Officer may be specifically appointed by the board or in a manner specified in the nonprofit's bylaws and may or may not also be a board member. As an employee, the Executive Officer is typically compensated for his or her work, and may either be under contract for a specified period or serve at the pleasure of the board.

Main Responsibilities. The Executive Officer is the senior management officer of the nonprofit organization and, as such, the person primarily responsible for day-to-day operations and for keeping the board advised of the organization's performance, key activities, and initiatives. The Executive Officer is also responsible for implementing the directives and policies adopted by the board, the members, or another policy-making body (such as a House of Delegates), providing leadership to the staff and serving as primary liaison between the staff and the board. Common aspects of the Executive Officer's leadership role include:

- *Leading the Organization and Communicating with the Board.* The Executive Officer manages the operations of the nonprofit on a daily basis. His or her knowledge of the substantive work of the organization and the environment in which the organization operates usually makes him or her the primary person on whom the board relies for insight into issues that may suggest needed refinements or changes to the organization's operations, its mission, or its strategy. This is a critically important role which requires that the Executive Officer directly, or through the Board Chair, communicate with the board in a timely and complete manner on issues and matters that may assist the board in its governance and oversight roles. Such communication includes furnishing board members with information regarding strategic, financial, and other issues that could affect the future and mission of the organization. Regular communications between board meetings are particularly important if the board meets relatively infrequently (e.g., quarterly).

- *Relationship with the Chair.* The Executive Officer works closely with the Board Chair between meetings of the board, appraising the Chair of developments, working with the Chair on matters requiring board or Board Chair attention or involvement, and often using the Board Chair as a sounding board for ideas, projects, or problems. Developing a relationship of trust and mutual respect with the Board Chair can be critical to an Executive Officer's success and to the success of the organization. This process can often be difficult when Board Chairs serve relatively short terms which limit the time available to develop such a relationship and also require the Executive Officer to build an entirely new relationship with some frequency. Frequent turnover may also deprive the Executive Officer of the feedback, questioning, and support that may come from a Board Chair with whom a longer relationship is possible, making it even more important for the Executive Officer to quickly build a strong working relationship with a new Chair.

- *Balancing Goals and Issues.* Although the board is responsible for setting priorities and goals and the Executive Officer reports to the board, a Board Chair may take office with a particular agenda or goals in mind. In such a case, the Executive Officer must engage in a delicate balancing act: being generally responsive to the Chair's aspirations, while continuing to make sure that the board is also addressing other pressing organizational issues and previously established priorities.

Whether or not an incoming Board Chair has a particular personal agenda, building a constructive relationship between the Board Chair and Executive Officer requires maturity and willingness to confront issues directly but with both tact and honesty.

- *Relationship with the Board.* Establishing solid working relationships with other board members in addition to the Chair is important to the effectiveness of an Executive Officer, since mutual trust helps minimize misunderstandings. These working relationships also help provide directors and the Executive Officer the opportunity to better understand each other's views, backgrounds, experience, and preferences, which can be of great assistance in planning and decision-making. Because the quality of the Executive Officer's relationship with the board is so important to the effective functioning of both the Executive Officer and the board, it often is a principal focus in both performance evaluations of the Executive Officer and board self-evaluations.

- *Relationship with Members.* In nonprofits with members, the Executive Officer typically oversees the interaction between the nonprofit's staff and the members. The Executive Officer often is responsible for providing services to members, working with the officers to send out notices of meetings of members, and otherwise maintaining a good relationship between the members and the nonprofit.

- *Shaping Governance and Building an Effective Board.* While the board and the Board Chair are primarily responsible for governance and oversight of a nonprofit's operations and mission, the role of the Executive Officer is also critical in helping to assure effective board governance. Lack of a shared understanding between the board and the Executive Officer on board governance issues can be a source of annoyance and friction, and perhaps even a source of organizational dysfunction. As the individual most responsible for the effective day-to-day operation of the nonprofit, and the primary intermediary between the staff and the board, the Executive Officer is key to making sure that frictions do not impair the work of the nonprofit and that everyone involved is contributing to the advancement of the nonprofit's mission. A board that is not functioning effectively not only interferes with the nonprofit's ability to achieve its mission, but also denies the organization the leadership benefits that an effective board provides.

The Practical Advice Section of this Chapter has further suggestions for how Executive Officers might participate in helping to shape board governance (see pages 31–34), and for building a relationship with the Board Chair (see pages 34–35).

Liability of Executive Officers and Other Officers or Management Leaders

Executive Officers may be subject to personal liability for breach of fiduciary duty that allegedly harmed the organization (such as a conflict of interest) or for harm to a third party caused, for example, by negligent supervision. Other officers or management leaders of a nonprofit may be similarly subject to a lawsuit on behalf of the organization or by third parties, depending on the degree to which such individuals are directly involved in operations. Uncompensated volunteer officers, such as board members who serve as officers but whose function is primarily one of oversight (such as a board member serving as Treasurer), may have a different (lesser) level of exposure compared to a management executive holding the title of Treasurer and also serving as the full-time, paid Chief Financial Officer. Depending on the nature of the claim, this lesser level of exposure results from the more favorable treatment accorded uncompensated or minimally compensated volunteers for nonprofit corporations under the federal Volunteer Protection Act and some similar state laws.

Protections Against Liability for Executive Officers and Other Officers or Management Leaders

Executive Officers and other compensated officers and management leaders are generally protected from liability arising in connection with good faith performance of their management duties under the organization's indemnification provisions in its bylaws, as well as by any D&O insurance policy maintained by the organization. However, such indemnification or insurance coverage typically does not cover, or will require repayment of amounts paid on behalf of, the executive if it is determined that he or she personally engaged in criminal or other material and intentional misconduct. (For example, an executive may be covered by the organization's D&O policy for an employment discrimination claim, but not for a proven claim of sexual harassment.) State indemnification statutes limit a nonprofit's ability to provide indemnification to situations in which the officer met certain standards of care.

Practical Advice on Governance Basics

Practical Realities

There are a number of practical considerations to take into account in shaping the governance practices of a nonprofit:

- Governance practices of an entity reflect its origins and traditions, as well as decisions and philosophy about the allocation of responsibility and influence for decisions affecting the organization and its operations.

- Any significant change in an organization's governance structure can be difficult and may cause internal disruption.

- Changes to governance structures and practices may have political or social implications, since such changes (such as imposition of term limits, changes in delegated authority, revisions to committee structures, or modifications to board meetings or materials) may affect individual board members or members of management who may view such changes as a personal affront or as a negative statement on past practices.

- Good governance is not something static that can be achieved through bylaw provisions and policies that are put in place and then forgotten. Achieving and maintaining good governance requires continued attention and refinement.

- Good governance does not necessarily require immediate major changes to board operations or adoption of totally different policies and procedures. While sometimes a nonprofit will determine that significant changes in governance structures are required within a short period, more often good governance structures and practices evolve over time through regular reviews of board effectiveness. Such reviews typically result in incremental changes and, as important, help build openness and support among board and staff for a regular, transparent process for adoption of revised or new practices.

- One size does not fit all. Certain governance structures and practices may be quite effective in some organizations and less so in others, but despite this fact, some choices may be viewed more favorably than others by various constituents of an organization or by certain governance experts.

State nonprofit laws typically require that nonprofit corporations have a board with overall responsibility for the organization and have certain specified officer positions (the titles of which may vary), although neither board nor officer duties are typically specified in other than the broadest terms. Also, for nonprofits with members, state nonprofit laws typically reserve certain powers to the members of the nonprofit.

Recently, some states have mandated specific governance practices. California, for example, requires nonprofits with income over $2 million to have an audit committee and requires board or committee approval of certain management salaries. However, relatively few governance practices are mandated by law, which leaves boards, Board Chairs, and Executive Officers with a great deal of flexibility to suggest structures and shape practices that are likely to work most effectively for the organization. The following points may be useful to keep in mind when reviewing an organization's governance structure and practices:

- There is no universally agreed upon set of "best practices" for board governance, but there are many governance trends and suggestions that are useful to consider, many of which are widely recommended by commentators and regulators and have been adopted by numerous for-profit and nonprofit boards as well.

- Organizations that ignore governance trends may be viewed, fairly or unfairly, as less effective, out-of-step, and as taking legal and operational risks, making it harder to attract needed board members, management, donors, or other funders. Additionally, these organizations may attract unwanted and distracting scrutiny from regulators or the press which may draw unflattering parallels with nonprofit organizations that have experienced high-profile scandals.

- Some governance practices and trends have, particularly recently, been included in various state and federal laws or inserted in regulatory applications for nonprofit status or highlighted for discussion in annual report or informational returns such as the IRS Form 990.

- A list of governance issues that many organizations and commentators consider important to consider is contained in Chapter 3. In addition to the suggestions contained in this text, there are a number of other sources of information that can be helpful to boards, Executive Officers, and Board Chairs seeking to improve the governance of their organization.

Appendix 3 has a partial list of additional sources of information about evolving governance practices and standards for nonprofits.

Beginning Discussions About Governance

There are many ways to start a review of an organization's governance structures and practices: the Executive Officer and Board Chair might review and discuss governance issues together; a committee of the board might be charged with comparing the organization's practices to governance trends; the board might conduct a self-evaluation, or use a consultant to conduct a board effectiveness review.

Perhaps the easiest way to begin discussions about governance issues and how well a particular nonprofit is governed is for the Executive Officer and the Board Chair to consider and discuss the types of questions and issues listed below. The critical points of such conversations are to raise the issues, identify and discuss any differences of opinion between how the Board Chair and the Executive Officer may view governance matters, and determine whether changes in governance are needed or may be helpful. The Board Chair and the Executive Officer can then discuss how best to bring about any such changes, including how and when to engage board members or a board committee in the process. However, because of the fundamental importance of governance matters to board performance, it is important for the board or a board committee to become involved as soon as practical.

There are a variety of topics and questions to consider in getting started.

- Do the amount of time and effort spent on board, and in particular governance, matters by the Chair and the Executive Officer move the mission of the nonprofit forward?
- How much of the board's time is devoted to strategic matters and major decision-making, oversight/advising, and leadership? Is the relative amount of time spent on each of these activities appropriate to the organization's needs and do these efforts move the organization's mission forward?
- What role does the board play in the nonprofit organization: Boss? Active/Passive Consultant? Cheerleader and Fund-raiser? Partner? Leader? A combination of all of the above? Might changing the mix or the emphasis on these different roles make the board more valuable to the nonprofit and assist in achieving the organization's mission?
- In a nonprofit with members, what role do the members play? How do members view the actions of the board or other policy-making body (such as a house of delegates)? How do the members interface with the board? With the Executive Officer? With the rest of the staff?
- Are the amount of time and degree of effort spent by board members and by staff on board matters, including work in committees, sufficient to provide effective oversight and direction? Do they provide value and aid in achieving the mission?
- Does the board understand and appreciate the nonprofit's mission and accomplishments?

- Does the staff understand and value the board's oversight and governance?
- How would other board and staff members respond to the above questions?
- Is there a difference between how the board currently operates and how boards of other similarly situated nonprofit organizations appear to operate, or between how the board operates and the societal/constituent expectations of how the board should operate?
- Have board members, or members of the nonprofit if there are members, suggested that the governance process and procedures are lacking in some significant way or recommended other than minor changes?
- Does the board have appropriate and effective committees?
- Does the board have a committee charged with oversight of the board's governance practices, and if so, is it functioning effectively? If such a committee does not exist, would one be helpful to the organization? If there is such a committee, but it isn't functioning well, what changes in its function or membership might help make it more effective?
- Do board members understand their legal responsibilities and liabilities as well as current governance trends for nonprofits? Is there an effective initial and continuing education program for board members in governance matters?

Basic Practices That Can Help Directors Understand and Meet Their Duties of Care and Loyalty and Help Provide Protection of the Business Judgment Rule

The Executive Officer and Board Chair can help directors satisfy their legal responsibilities, reduce the possibility of challenge to board decisions, and improve the board's defense of its decision-making process, if challenged, by actions such as the following:

- Actively encouraging all directors to attend board meetings and meetings of the committees on which they serve;
- Providing presentations that help educate the board on the scope of operations and the issues and challenges that the organization faces;
- Scheduling mission-critical matters for discussion at board or committee meetings or at board retreats;
- Providing the board and its committees with information that is relevant, accurate, succinct, clear, easy to understand, and free of technical jargon;
- Providing the board and its committees on a regular basis with information and background material well in advance of meetings to allow time for review;

- Prioritizing agenda items so there is sufficient time for major issues to be adequately discussed;
- Allowing adequate time at board and committee meetings for members to ask questions and discuss issues;
- Allowing time for executive sessions of the board on a regular basis;
- Creating an atmosphere at board meetings that welcomes questions and does not shrink from challenges, without encouraging irrelevant digressions;
- Enforcing a board-adopted conflict of interest policy, including requiring board members to leave the room during discussions of matters in which they have a conflict;
- Providing formal written resolutions as well as less formal descriptions of actions to be approved to help ensure that board and committee members fully understand the action they are being asked to take;
- Ensuring that accurate minutes of all meetings are maintained and taking the time to read each set of minutes before they are sent out to board members;
- Distributing minutes promptly to board and committee members, including those not present at the meeting;
- Distributing committee minutes, or a summary of committee actions, to the full board as soon as practicable;
- Ensuring that minutes are filed and accessible for future reference and in the event of litigation or a regulatory investigation;
- Creating a document describing general expectations for board members (such as regular attendance at board meetings, adequate preparation for meetings, constructive participation in board discussions, disclosure of conflicts of interest, etc.) which is approved by the board, and periodically redistributed to each board member and discussed at board meetings;
- Including discussion of board member duties and rights and the potential for liability in board member orientation meetings and materials, and reviewing such matters periodically at board and committee meetings or retreats or special educational sessions;
- Making board members aware of some of the publications, many of them free, that cover such matters as board member liability and other issues to help board members understand their roles; and
- Encouraging board member attendance at director training programs offered by outside groups.

Indemnification and Insurance to Protect Directors

Make It Easy to Understand. Once directors understand that there is the potential for personal liability for their actions or failure to act, they typically want assurance that indemnification and insurance are available to help protect them.

- Orientation meetings and materials can be used to inform board members of the protection offered by the organization's indemnification and insurance arrangements.
- Brief, plain English summaries of indemnification, insurance coverage, and legal protections against liability can be helpful to board members, as these issues can be difficult to understand as presented in organizational, legal, or insurance documents. Legal counsel and insurance agents are often willing to assist in reviewing such summaries for accuracy.

Particular Issues. In providing information on indemnification and insurance, it may be helpful to highlight the following issues:

- Under what circumstances is the nonprofit required to indemnify a director, officer, employee, volunteer, or member?
- Under what circumstances may the nonprofit choose whether or not to indemnify a director, officer, employee, volunteer, or member?
- Under what circumstances is the nonprofit required to advance certain litigation expenses to a director or to others?
- Under what circumstances may the nonprofit choose to advance certain litigation expenses to a director or to others?
- What findings and actions are required for the board to indemnify or advance expenses?
- Under what circumstances might a board member or another person be required to reimburse the nonprofit for expenses advanced by the nonprofit?
- Which laws and legal documents specify the organization's indemnification obligations: state nonprofit corporation act, the organization's own articles/charter, its bylaws, individual contracts, or a combination of these?
- How frequently does legal counsel review the nonprofit's indemnification arrangements?
- What is the process for assuring that indemnification provisions remain current?
- Has the organization purchased insurance to cover matters that are or cannot be covered by indemnification?
- Does the insurance coverage also extend to spouses or others who might be sued, including the estate of the board member?
- Are employment practices covered? Are there specific processes that need to be followed to obtain this coverage?
- Is service on affiliated boards covered?

- Has the board or a board committee reviewed the organization's D&O coverage limits, deductibles, co-insurance requirements, and premiums and determined that the insurance coverage obtained covers necessary risks and was and remains at a cost that is competitive and that the non-profit can afford?
- Is the insurer well-rated and is the rating reviewed periodically? (From time to time, especially in times of national or global economic distress, solvency of insurers can become a significant issue.)
- What information is available on the insurer's record of payment under similar policies and have similar nonprofit organizations been satisfied with the insurer's handling of claims made? (Often insurance brokers and litigation attorneys who have defended nonprofit organizations are good sources of information on an insurer's reputation and the experience of similar organizations when a claim was made.)
- Has the organization requested bids from other insurers to evaluate whether the current carrier's coverage is the best option?
- If the organization does not have D&O liability insurance, does the organization have sufficient financial resources to satisfy potential indemnification claims or obligations?

Role of the Board Chair

Leadership Considerations. Leadership by the Board Chair is critical to effective governance. It is important for the board and the person holding, or being considered for, the position of Chair to weigh carefully both the current needs of the organization and the skills of the Chair to make sure they are compatible. The Board Chair also needs to understand and be responsive to the views and expectations of other board members and to work with them to enhance their effectiveness. The following points may be helpful to consider in selecting a Board Chair:

- Not everyone is suited to be a Board Chair and even someone with strong leadership and interpersonal skills may not be the right person for the job at a particular time.
- Weaknesses in certain skills of the Board Chair can be compensated for, at least in part, by appointing other officers with a mix of the requisite skills.
- Creating a job description for the Board Chair can be helpful in assuring compatibility between organizational needs and individual skills, although this task is not easy and typically requires a careful review of how the board is currently functioning as well as a review of organizational leadership priorities.
- Although a board committee charged with governance matters or the nominating committee might be a logical place for initial development of

a written job description for the Chair, input from the Executive Officer and former Chairs is also valuable.

- Because organizational and board leadership needs may change, a written job description for the Board Chair requires regular review to determine if modifications or changes in emphasis are needed.

Appendix 4 has two sample Board Chair job descriptions.

Factors for Board Chairs and Prospective Board Chairs to Consider. Because the role of Board Chair varies greatly among organizations, it is particularly important that the Chair or someone considering a Chair position consider a number of factors before agreeing to become or to continue as Chair. Here are some practical questions that may be helpful to consider, regardless of the size or type of organization:

- *Importance.* Is your leadership of this organization something personally or professionally important to you, and if so, why? Are your reasons for considering the position consistent with the organization's aims and mission?

- *Time.* How much time are you willing and realistically able to devote to the organization during the anticipated term? Is the time you have available consistent with the organization's expectations and needs?

- *Skills Needed.* What skills does the organization need from its Board Chair?
  - Does it need a public face/advocate in the community, a fund-raiser, a governance expert, someone to reinvent the board, a financial expert, or a turn-around expert?
  - Are your skills and what you want to accomplish as Board Chair a good match for the organization's current needs?

- *Scope of Job.* Is it feasible for the various duties of the Chair to be divided between a Chair and another officer, or might some duties be formally delegated to one or more Vice Chairs or Vice Presidents? Is delegation or division of labor consistent with your leadership style and with the nature and tradition of the organization?

- *Financial Commitment.* If the organization raises funds, are you prepared to make a personal financial donation at a leadership level, and will the level of your donation be considered adequate by the organization for its Board Chair?

- *Type of Board.* Is the board functioning as an operating board or a governance board, and is its form of operation consistent with your view of the governance leadership role needed by the organization and with your own governance views?

- *Needs of the Organization.* What does the organization need most from its board and its board leadership at this time?
  - Is the board structured to provide for the organization's current needs?
  - If you believe there is a gap between what the organization needs and what it has, are you willing to assume the responsibility of leading a restructuring of the board, its membership, or its operations?

- *Board Composition.* What is the composition of the board?
  - Are the board members independent of management?
  - Is the board as a whole and are individual board members functioning effectively?
  - If there are weaknesses in board composition, are you willing to ask people to resign? Will your influence be helpful in attracting new board members?

- *Support from Board Members.* Are there individuals on the board on whom you can rely to support your leadership efforts or, conversely, are there individuals on the board who might undermine or resist your leadership?

- *Support from Members of the Nonprofit.* If the nonprofit has members, are there individual members, or groups of members, on whom you can rely to support your leadership efforts or, conversely, are there individual members or groups of members who might undermine or resist your leadership?

- *Relationship with the Executive Officer.* Are you comfortable with the Executive Officer's leadership? Do you have a good working relationship with the Executive Officer or do you perceive that there may be impediments to your being able to work together well and develop trust?

- *Relationship with Affiliates.* Do you understand the relationship between the nonprofit and any affiliated or fund-raising organizations that support your programs or operations? Are you comfortable with the leadership of such affiliated organizations or are there impediments to your being able to work together with their leadership?

- *Understanding Operations.* Do you understand the nonprofit's operations and financial status sufficiently to be able to assume a board leadership role with respect to operations and governance?

- *Tolerance for Criticism.* Do you feel you are able to take constructive criticism from fellow board members and the Executive Officer? Are you willing to modify your leadership to address criticisms?

- *Administrative Support.* Do you feel that you will require administrative support from the organization and, if so, is it available? If you are required to provide your own administrative support, do you have the resources to do so?

Role of the Executive Officer

Helping to Shape Board Governance. Many Executive Officers mistakenly view board governance matters as something of concern only to the board. Whether or not the Executive Officer is a board member, effective board functioning is a matter that can affect the Executive Officer's ability to manage the organization. The Executive Officer, as the senior organizational executive, is well-positioned to identify strengths and weaknesses in board operations. There are a number of ways in which the Executive Officer can assist in shaping and improving board governance:

- *Discussions with the Board Leadership.* One important way in which the Executive Officer can help shape board governance is simply by being frank with board leadership if he or she believes that the current board:
  - Does not appear to add value or provide adequate leadership;
  - Does not seem to understand the organization or its mission;
  - Is not uniformly interested in or supportive of the work of the organization;
  - Micromanages or requires an inordinate amount of staff time to respond to board requests for information or assistance; or
  - Spends too much time on minutiae and too little time on strategic matters.

These types of issues all indicate a need for a review of board effectiveness and usually signal that the board is not as effective as it might be or that the relationship between the board and the Executive Officer has deteriorated or needs attention. Whether in reality or just perception, if there appears to be disagreement between the Executive Officer and the board on these sorts of issues, it is important to have the differences brought out so that steps can be taken to work out any problems and better align perceptions and reality.

Sometimes the conduct of individual board members affects the functioning of the board negatively, or creates significant problems for management. The Executive Officer can also help shape board governance by pointing out such problems and working with board leadership to address them.

- *Staying in Touch with Industry Trends.* Since the Executive Officer is frequently a member of one or more associations of similar organizations, he or she can provide information to the Chair and other board leadership on how similar organizations are addressing governance issues and can report on recommendations on governance from associations to which the organization belongs.

- *Working with a Corporate Secretary or Board Liaison.* Another way in which an Executive Officer may affect board governance is by working with the Corporate Ssecretary or a board assistant or liaison who assumes these functions. A competent Corporate Secretary or board assistant can be very helpful to the effective functioning of the board. He or she is often the main point of contact between the organization and its board members.

A Corporate Secretary or board assistant typically performs a number of important clerical and administrative duties, including:

- Maintaining and updating important and useful personal information about directors (e.g., contact information, date elected to the board, date term ends, number of terms on the board, past and present committee memberships, expertise, current employment, personal attributes related to board service criteria or needs, biographical information, and similar information);
- Helping to schedule meetings;
- Drafting meeting notices, sending them when approved, and tracking responses and actual attendance;
- Creating first drafts of agendas and finalizing them based on input from the Chair and Executive Officer;
- Collecting materials to be sent to directors in advance of meetings;
- Distributing meeting packages;
- Making arrangements for meeting locations and rooms and seeing that the arrangements are carried out;
- Collecting materials following the meeting to assure appropriate disposal;
- Taking minutes at meetings and creating a first draft for the Board Chair and others such as the Executive Officer, and perhaps other key directors or officers, to review;
- Maintaining the minute book, meeting files, and other board records;
- Providing other administrative assistance to the Board Chair; and
- Handling routine inquiries and requests from board members.

Diplomacy, attention to detail, good organizational and follow-up skills, and the ability to keep confidences are among the most important attributes of any individual assigned to this role.

In many nonprofits, the board assistant or liaison is the administrative assistant to the Executive Officer. Larger nonprofits may have a more senior person serving as the functional equivalent of a Corporate Secretary in the for-profit arena. Such an individual would typically occupy a senior position in management and would:

- Oversee the administrative tasks listed above;
- Serve as the principal focal point for communication between and among board members and senior management and many of the organization's other constituencies;
- Advise the Executive Officer and the board on governance trends;
- Assist the Executive Officer and Board Chair in developing substantive agendas;

- Help develop and review materials to be sent to the board;
- Assist the Executive Officer and Board Chair in the administration of critical matters related to governance, the board, and, in some cases, senior management; and
- Serve as a sounding board and confidant to the Executive Officer and Board Chair on governance and other matters related to the effective functioning of the board.

- ***Interacting with the Board and Relationship Building.*** Another way in which the Executive Officer assists with governance matters is through his or her interaction with board members. These interactions provide the Executive Officer an opportunity to understand individual board members' points of view, backgrounds, values, and concerns, and give board members an opportunity to understand the Executive Officer's vision and aspirations for the organization, his or her management style, and the problems or issues the Executive Officer faces in day-to-day management. This knowledge not only helps build the level of understanding between the board and the Executive Officer but may also create a level of trust which can be critical to board effectiveness.

   Relationship building between the Executive Officer and board members usually involves personal outreach on the part of the Executive Officer, finding opportunities for one-on-one or small group interaction with board members outside of regularly scheduled meetings. A level of comfort in these relationships does not happen overnight or only through board or committee meetings but takes continuous effort. The value of the effort is likely to be most evident when organizations face difficult decisions or problems. When individuals have spent the time on building relationships, important discussions are likely to be more productive.

   The Executive Officer can also work with the Board Chair and other management or board leadership to promote relationship building among board members. This may occur through formal and informal opportunities for groups of board members to spend time together, such as lunches, post-board meeting receptions or meals, board retreats, and board and management holiday gatherings.

Relationship Building Between the Board Chair and the Executive Officer

Building solid relationships between the Executive Officer and Board Chair often takes serious effort. Here are a few suggestions that may help:

Understand the Importance of Past History. Expectations are shaped by past history and traditions. When a new Board Chair or Executive Officer takes office, each will have expectations based on how each sees his or her role and the role of the other, how such roles have been conducted in the past, and how each perceives such roles might need to change. Often such expectations are left unstated and their basis unexplored, particularly if the organization's founder is still involved in leadership. Acknowledging the potential importance of past history in creating expectations may help avoid misunderstandings and discomfort in building the Executive Officer-Board Chair relationship.

Build Mutual Understanding and Agree on the Roles. Establishing sound relationships can be greatly facilitated by mutual understanding and agreement as to the role the Board Chair and the Executive Officer are each to play in the organization and by agreement on the form and frequency of regular communication each expects from the other.

- *Job Descriptions.* Creating written job descriptions for both the Board Chair and the Executive Officer, if not already established, may be a good starting point.

- *Diary.* Maintaining a list of activities actually handled by the Board Chair may provide a useful picture of the actual Board Chair role, clarifying not only where the Board Chair is actually spending time, but also suggesting areas for which greater or lesser attention is needed.
  - Such a list can be maintained by either the Board Chair, the Executive Officer, or both. The Executive Officer might provide a log for the Board Chair which lists categories of typical activities, such as planning for board meetings, attendance at meetings, fund-raising, consultation with the Executive Officer, consultation with other board members, and review of information, and provides space for time expended.
  - Such a list can be given to subsequent Chairs and Executive Officers to help them understand past practices, or to help the board develop a written job description for the Chair, if none exists. The board or the Board Chair might also use such a list to consider reallocation of time spent in specific activities.

- *Goals and Priorities.* Creating a list of goals or priorities for both the Executive Officer and the Board Chair for the upcoming board year can also be helpful.
  - Priorities can be developed independently and then agreed upon after mutual discussion, or developed jointly by the Executive Officer and the Board Chair.
  - Recognizing and agreeing on areas of mutual interest or responsibility in which both the Board Chair and the Executive Officer would like to have input or some discussion before a decision is made can be helpful. While such agreement can be made in advance, often issues will surface that were not envisioned. Nonetheless, understanding each other's interests and priorities may help minimize problems in these situations.

- *Form of Communication.* Establishing agreement on frequency and preferred forms of communication (monthly, weekly, daily, in person, by e-mail, or by phone) can also be important to creating a sound working relationship between the Board Chair and the Executive Officer. Those who rely on e-mail may be surprised to find that others rarely use it. Those who dislike long voice mail messages may not listen to a long message.

Be Colleagues, Not Necessarily Friends. The Executive Officer and Board Chair need not be close friends, but their relationship will be more effective for the organization if they seek opportunities to build camaraderie and understanding.

- Too close a relationship between the Board Chair and the Executive Officer might, at some point, interfere with the ability of each to act in the best interests of the organization.
- Events and other opportunities outside of board-related events, such as social lunches or dinners, attendance at social events, traveling together to out-of-town meetings, and the like can assist in developing understanding and building trust that might otherwise take longer to create.

Give Constructive Feedback. Providing constructive feedback is critically important to building relationships of trust. Both Executive Officers and Board Chairs can profit by reviewing recommendations from human resources experts and others on how best to provide feedback. Such experts generally recommend a feedback process that:

- Provides recognition and praise for accomplishments;
- Gives specific information about what has worked well;
- Clearly indicates when the conversation is moving from discussing accomplishments to areas in which performance was different than expected, rather than switching the conversation abruptly or moving back and forth between discussions of strengths and weaknesses;
- Provides specific suggestions for improvement;
- Focuses on current and relevant issues, not old grievances;
- Is respectful to the individual being evaluated, even when there is disappointment in performance, and avoids personal attacks (for example, consider "I was disappointed" rather than "You disappointed me" or, "It's important for the organization that you do X…." rather than "You can't do Y");
- Takes word choices seriously and recognizes that neutral words can often be used in place of words with a more negative connotation yet achieve the same result (for example, consider "areas for focus" rather than "areas for improvement");
- Focuses on issues that are capable of improvement and avoids matters over which the individual has no control;

- Allows participants to engage in a conversation, rather than separate monologues, and encourages participants to listen to what the other individual has to say;
- Allows for comments and suggestions to be revised if it becomes clear that certain facts or assumptions were incorrect or misunderstood;
- Encourages the evaluator to take responsibility for assisting with needed changes, asking, for example, "What can I do to help you accomplish X"; and
- Ends by focusing again on accomplishments and strengths, as well as on next steps for addressing areas that need attention.

Alternative Methods of Surfacing Issues

Some Executive Officers and Board Chairs may find it personally difficult to criticize or confront issues with each other despite efforts to create an open atmosphere or to build trust. In such cases, board effectiveness studies and board member evaluations, which are discussed later in this publication, may provide ways to raise issues that might otherwise be left unstated and negatively affect the ability of the Board Chair and Executive Officer to work together effectively.

Chapter 2: Dealing with Substantive Issues

Dealing with Substantive Issues

Developing the Knowledge Base

Understanding the Organization. Understanding the mission of the organization and the environment in which it operates is crucial to a board's effective exercise of its responsibilities. While board members of a nonprofit are not responsible for the day-to-day operations of the organization, they need to understand how management and the organization function. Directors obtain this understanding by making reasonable inquiry into operational matters. Such inquiry involves, among other things, participation in discussions and raising questions at board and committee meetings; review and discussion of presentations and materials prepared by management, fellow board members, and outside consultants; attendance at events and programs sponsored by the nonprofit; and interaction with various constituents. But it is at board and committee meetings that the majority of the board's work of building its understanding of the organization takes place. The exchange of information, discussion, and questioning at these meetings on issues such as organizational strategy and performance, operations, competition, and risks help assure that adoption of policies, strategic decisions, delegation of authority, and risk management are based on a thorough understanding of the organization.

Interference versus Legitimate Inquiry. Executive Officers occasionally find the level of detail requested by board members or the intensity of the board's questioning or interest in particular areas intrusive. Board members need to understand that some inquiries may be too burdensome on an Executive Officer's and other staff's time, energy, and focus on normal operations. Management needs to understand that boards require substantial information to carry out their governance role effectively.

Distinguishing between time-consuming interference and legitimate inquiry can be difficult for both the board and management. Since the early 2000s, there has been increasing legal, regulatory, and public pressure on for-profit boards regarding their oversight of management and operations. Such pressure affects the nonprofit sphere as well. For example, most of the provisions of the Sarbanes-Oxley Act (which was adopted to address perceived shortcomings in governance by public company corporate boards) apply only to for-profit, publicly traded companies. Nonetheless, many of the assumptions about good governance practices reflected in the Sarbanes-Oxley Act—such as provisions in the Act related to the function and composition of audit committees—now also are regarded as good governance practices for nonprofit organizations. The Internal Revenue Service (IRS), in the current version of the Form 990 informational return filed by most tax-exempt organizations, explicitly assumes that certain governance structures and processes tend to result in good governance.

The general increased public and governmental attention to governance practices may result in additional levels of inquiry by boards into many issues that once may have seemed to be the sole purview of management. Such heightened levels of inquiry may cause some Executive Officers to feel the need for more frequent discussions with the Board Chair or other board or management leaders on whether such inquiries are appropriate or an attempt to micromanage in particular circumstances. However, rather than attempting to define specific areas of board or management responsibility or what might constitute micromanagement, it may be more useful for Executive Officers and Board Chairs to acknowledge that many day-to-day issues may have governance implications requiring board understanding and attention, and to focus on how the board's understanding of the organization and its issues can be satisfied without overburdening management or interfering in management functions.

The Practical Advice Section of the Chapter has suggestions on how Board Chairs and Executive Officers may help develop the board's knowledge base. See pages 84–85.

Tackling the Issues

Balancing the Present, Past, and Future. Board and committee meetings typically focus on issues that may be categorized as evaluative of the organization's past performance, relevant to its current operations, or integral to its future. A critical role for the Executive Officer and the Board Chair is to assure that the board addresses all these areas and does not focus on one to the exclusion of the others, ignoring the future, for example, by devoting the bulk of the board's attention to past performance.

Scope of Agendas. Over time, nonprofit board agendas typically cover the following issues:

- Accomplishment or redefinition of the mission;
- Strategic planning and goal setting;
- Evaluating, and/or hiring or firing the Executive Officer;
- Financial performance, including fund-raising and funding issues, and budgets;
- Review of audits, if any;
- Organizational achievements or setbacks in accomplishing the mission; and
- Risks inherent in the organization's operations and industry.

The specific issues to be addressed within these broad categories vary from organization to organization.

Mission

Development of the Mission. A primary role of a nonprofit board is to assist the organization in achieving success in its mission. Initial development of a nonprofit's mission is usually done by the organization's founders, who start with a vision and then consider the organizational and operational structure needed to achieve the mission. Implementing the mission requires assessment of the organization's activities, the applicability of particular laws and regulations, the market for the programs proposed, and the feasibility of achieving necessary funding levels. The founders may also decide to canvass potential donors, intended beneficiaries, and other organizations engaged in similar activities to assist in confirming whether achievement of the proposed mission is viable. Once initial assessments are complete, the founders then initiate the necessary steps to establish the nonprofit, obtain tax-exempt status, if available, and find initial board members who support the organization's mission. When the organization has sufficient funding, the initial board members will hire the Executive Officer, who may or may not be the founder, and work with him or her to begin the process of building an organization capable of executing the mission.

Ongoing Review of the Mission. Once the mission is established and the nonprofit is operational, an important and ongoing responsibility of its board is to review the organization's mission periodically and determine whether the mission is still viable and is being achieved. Review of an organization's mission is not necessarily the same thing as review of its mission statement, although the two are connected. The mission is the nonprofit's reason for being, its purpose. Its mission statement is its articulation of that reason for being. The purposes of the nonprofit are set forth in its articles of incorporation. The organization's mission is derived from its purposes and must be consistent with the purposes of the nonprofit.

Board review of a nonprofit's mission requires evaluating how well the nonprofit is fulfilling its mission, including analysis and discussion of the mission's viability, whether the mission might be accomplished better by combining with other organizations or by changes in programs or services, and whether circumstances suggest a need for major or minor modification to the mission itself or to the process of implementation. Scheduled and thorough reviews are advisable every three to five years, but particular circumstances may suggest the benefit of a review at an earlier time. Mission reviews are not necessarily conducted on a stand-alone basis, but are often conducted as part of an organization's strategic planning process.

Appendix 5 has a number of nonprofit organization mission statements taken from Form 990 filings available on the guidestar.org website.

The Practical Advice Section of this Chapter has further suggestions to help make sure the board understands and supports the organization's mission. See pages 85–87.

Strategic Planning

Overview. Strategic planning is the process by which an organization establishes, in broad but specific terms, the goals it wants to achieve in support of the mission over a specific period of time. A strategic plan is the result of a focused review process. The plan describes the organization's goals for the future and outlines how it intends to achieve those goals. There is no specific template for the form of a strategic plan. Each is unique to the particular organization. Approval of a strategic plan is generally agreed to be a board responsibility, but the Executive Officer, who will ultimately be charged with implementing the plan, typically plays a major role in developing the ideas to be considered in the planning process as well as in providing materials and other assistance needed for envisioning the organization's future and creating the strategic plan.

The Process. There are many ways to conduct strategic planning. It may be staff-initiated, with the staff assembling, assessing, and using the information it has gathered to help develop a plan for board approval. It may be board-generated and conducted, with the board perhaps using outside consultants or constituencies as well as the staff for input and then preparing and circulating a proposed plan for final consideration and approval. Another alternative is for the nonprofit to retain an outside consultant to do some or all of the actual work or, perhaps, just provide suggestions as to the process and the specific tasks to be done by board or staff. A consultant may also be valuable in leading a planning session at which some or all of the ideas presented are discussed and considered.

Regardless of the specific process chosen, strategic planning typically includes:

- Affirmation or modification of the mission;
- Analysis of the organization's financial capacity and current operations, including issues that affect delivery of programs or the viability of the organization;
- Analysis of the external environment—economics, competition, demographics, government regulation—as it affects the organization's mission now and in the future; and
- Articulation of goals to be achieved during a specified period, including allocation of resources and criteria for determining success.

Outside consultants may be useful in strategic planning efforts because the process of developing a plan can be difficult and time-consuming, particularly for organizations that have never engaged in the process before and for organizations with limited staff resources. Strategic planning generally requires substantial staff work and may reduce the time available for operational responsibilities, potentially increasing organizational stress. However, the process can also be quite valuable to staff. It provides the opportunity for disciplined self-analysis, not only with respect to how the organization currently operates, but also with respect to its capability to address issues and achieve goals necessary for continued viability and success. The insights obtained through developing a strategic plan and monitoring its progress help the board evaluate organizational strength and capacity and the strength of the management team charged with leading the organization.

Planning for a strategic review usually requires

- Determining who will participate in the review and to what extent: the Executive Officer and staff, board representatives, outside consultants, other facilitators, representatives of other constituencies, including donors, beneficiaries, or community representatives;

- Determining the scope of the planning process;
- Determining the time frame for plan development;
- Determining and obtaining, if necessary, funding for the process;
- Assembling and disseminating relevant operational data;
- Deciding on a location and times for meetings (on-site or off-site, during regular work hours or during evenings or weekends); and
- Communicating relevant information about the process with all participants and constituencies before, during, and after the process.

Planning responsibilities are often shared jointly by the Executive Officer and the Board Chair or other board or officers charged with leading the planning process on behalf of the board. While deciding on the appropriate framework for the process is ultimately a board responsibility, the Executive Officer or other board or management leaders typically play a major role in making sure the board has the necessary information to make an effective decision on the framework to be adopted. They may propose one or more strategic plan structures and often assist in identifying, screening, and negotiating with possible consultants and facilitators.

Implementing and Monitoring the Plan. Once adopted, management's role is to implement the plan and to report progress on implementation to the board. The board's role is to provide ongoing monitoring of progress. Typically the Executive Officer and the board, or a board committee, work together to determine how achievement of plan goals may best be measured and reported to the board. Monitoring progress against measurable objectives and timelines helps ensure that the plan is pursued actively and effectively. It also may alert the board to needed modifications to the implementation process or to the plan itself, or to the need for an entirely new strategic planning process. Regular review of the plan is a critical board function and essential to effective governance.

Time Frame for the Plan. Although strategic plans are meant to cover multiple years, there is no specific period that strategic plans are typically designed to cover, or by which a new strategic planning process ought to be undertaken. Sometimes, circumstances will make a three-year strategic plan out-of-date in a year or two. As the board oversees the plan's implementation, it may make revisions to address unexpected developments.

The Practical Advice Section of this Chapter has further suggestions on conducting Strategic Planning. See pages 87–89.

Financial Performance

Review of Key Financial Documents. A key function of the board of any corporation, including a nonprofit, is to oversee the entity's financial results, the status of its financial resources, and its prospects with respect to future financial performance. For a director of a nonprofit, this responsibility usually includes periodic review, analysis, and discussion of the nonprofit's financial statements, forecasts, tax returns (Form 990 and state-mandated reports), and other annual reports and audits, as well as approval of its budgets and oversight of its system of financial and accounting controls.

IRS Form 990 and Annual Reports

Public Reporting. Nonprofits are not required to publish annual reports of the sort that public for-profit companies file. The Form 990 required by the IRS is the basic public filing for most nonprofits (churches and certain other religious organizations are exempt from this filing and private foundations file a Form 990PF). The Form 990 requires detailed information on the governance practices and mission accomplishments of the organization in addition to financial information from all but the smallest nonprofits.

See Appendix 6 for Part III of Form 990, which requests information on program accomplishments, and for Part VI of Form 990, which requests detailed information about governance practices and polices the IRS has determined promote good governance for nonprofit organizations.

The information required to be disclosed on the Form 990 is being increasingly relied upon by the IRS, members of the public, funders, and others to evaluate a nonprofit's program accomplishments, significant aspects of its operations, and its governance structure.

Many charitable organizations, especially the larger charities, publish an annual report in addition to their Form 990 to highlight program accomplishments and to provide the organization's financial status information in a convenient form. This type of annual report generally serves more as a marketing tool than as a financial report.

Board Review of Form 990. The Form 990 specifically asks if the Form was provided to the organization's board prior to filing and requires a description of the process used by the organization for review of the form. As a result, management now needs to be prepared to provide information and respond to board questions on the information included in the Form 990 and to adjust scheduling to allow not only for gathering information and completing the form, but also for board review and possible revisions to the form prior to filing.

Financial Statements, Financial Accounting

Purpose. As in the for-profit arena, nonprofit financial statements set forth the organization's financial position as of a particular date and show changes in financial position over a particular period of time. The information is useful for understanding nonprofit revenues and expenses, the value of its assets and extent of its liabilities, and how the organization has actually performed from a financial standpoint. However, a nonprofit organization's financial statements may not be in the same format as the financial statements of for-profit organizations. Many nonprofits use fund accounting, which requires that the organization's revenues and expenses be broken down by its various programs or types of programs.

Understanding Key Financial Issues and Metrics. For board members to effectively exercise the duty of care and loyalty, it is essential that they have a working knowledge of the manner in which the organization's financial statements are presented. Developing this knowledge, even for board members who have a financial background, may require a significant introduction to fund accounting and other aspects of how the organization's statements present financial information. While new board member orientations may include information on the organization's financial accounting practices and on how to understand its financial statements, ongoing reminders and information may be required to assist the board in this area.

To aid board member comprehension of nonprofit accounting and financial statements, many nonprofits develop a system of line-item explanatory notes on the financial statements given to board members, or provide additional summary highlights of important issues. Additionally, the organization's Executive Officer, Chief Financial Officer, or outside accountant typically present the financial statements to the board and, through such presentations, assist board members in learning how to read and understand key financial documents and to focus on important performance indicators. Such assistance enhances the effectiveness of individual board member review and understanding of financial performance.

While a general understanding of how to read the organization's financial statements is important for all board members, depending on the size of the nonprofit and the complexity of its financial statements, it may be appropriate to have a separate finance committee and/or audit committee charged with reviewing financial statements. Such a committee can provide a detailed review of the organization's financial statements and accounting practices as well as any information received from outside auditors or accountants. Committee members with financial expertise may be able to offer specific recommendations or suggestions on technical financial reporting, accounting, or internal control issues and may play a role in helping to explain and report key issues to the full board. The governance trend is to create such committees and to ensure that board members with financial expertise are appointed to them.

The Practical Advice Section of this Chapter has further suggestions of ways to assist board members in understanding financial issues.

Budgets

Staff Initiated, Board Approved. A nonprofit's annual budget is typically created by the organization's staff and presented to the board for approval prior to the start of each fiscal year. A board committee, such as a finance committee or executive committee, may be involved in reviewing and commenting on the budget as it is being developed, and may formally recommend adoption to the full board. In many organizations, approval of the budget serves as the broad basis of authority for management actions and expenditures throughout the year so long as the funds spent are within the budget and actions taken were contemplated in the budget.

Comparing Performance to Budget and to Forecasts. Most boards conduct regular reviews of the nonprofit's financial performance results compared to budget and require that staff explain differences. Most boards also ask management to forecast future performance in comparison to budget so that the board understands how assumptions and estimates used in creating the budget compare to expected performance. Significant variations from budget may indicate problems with management's ability to anticipate revenues or to control expenses or reflect major changes in the external environment in which the organization operates. The information obtained from explanations of budget deviations and from forecasts helps the board and management determine whether action is required to cut expenses or adjust programs in order to achieve acceptable overall financial performance for the year.

Audits

Types of Audits. Audits are detailed reports on particular issues, usually conducted by independent experts. Audits are generally thought of as covering financial reporting and accounting practices, but audits may be conducted in any area if an organization has concerns or wants independent assurance about how a particular program or area is functioning.

Review by the Board. Boards generally need to review and understand the results of financial audit reports or investigations. Such reviews are often conducted under the oversight of a committee of the board, such as the finance, audit, or compliance committee, which then reports the results of the audit in committee minutes or reports to the board. Executive Officers, Board Chairs, and other board and management leaders often review and discuss any surprising or negative results of an audit in advance of any board or committee presentation, so that appropriate explanation is prepared and given to the board or committee, and the organization can begin the process of addressing such matters. Presentations to the board or a board committee by outside auditors may include executive sessions in which management is asked to leave the room so that board members can ask questions of the auditors or other experts about management's handling of the audit and response or reaction to issues cited in the audit.

Value of Audits. There is no general legal requirement for nonprofits to conduct a financial audit, or any other sort of audit, although some state laws may require audits for certain types or sizes of organizations and some funders may also impose such requirements. Many small organizations do not conduct such audits, or feel they cannot afford the cost. However, financial audits (or the less stringent financial review) by an outside audit or accounting firm can be useful in helping assure the board that the organization's financial accounting process and procedures have integrity. Governance trends encourage financial audits and the creation of separate audit committees to review both audits and other compliance efforts.

Investment Management

Definition. Investment management is the process of managing funds and other assets to improve their effective utilization. All nonprofits have some investment management needs, even if it is simply cash management of short-term funds used in day-to-day operations. Short-term cash management is usually a matter discussed within a finance committee or at the board level in connection with review of periodic financial statements. Management of longer-term investments often requires establishing a special board committee and adopting an investment policy or policies by the full board. Long-term investing, especially of substantial sums, typically requires use of outside money managers.

UPMIFA. The Uniform Management of Institutional Funds Act (UMIFA) was promulgated in the early 1970s and was adopted in many states, helping to set standards related to nonprofit management of investment assets. Under UMIFA, most organizations established policies that restricted their ability to use the principal of these investment funds. UMIFA has now been updated and amended by the Uniform Prudent Management of Institutional Funds Act (UPMIFA), reflecting not only modern investment techniques, but also changing standards of prudence.

UPMIFA provides that each person responsible for managing and investing an investment fund shall manage and invest the fund in good faith and with the care an ordinarily prudent person in a like position would exercise under similar circumstances. UPMIFA further provides that, except as otherwise provided in a gift instrument, in managing and making investment decisions for an investment fund, the following factors, if relevant, must be taken into account:

- General economic conditions;
- The possible effect of inflation or deflation;

- The expected tax consequences, if any, of investment decisions or strategies;
- The role that each investment or course of action plays within the overall investment portfolios of the investment fund;
- The expected total return from income and appreciation;
- Other resources of the organization;
- The needs of the organization and fund to make distributions and to preserve capital; and
- The asset's special relationship or value, if any, to the charitable purposes of the organization.

UPMIFA also significantly increases an organization's legal flexibility for spending endowments and other investment assets and also raises important and potentially difficult issues for boards to consider in determining how to protect or use the principal of such investments, particularly in challenging economic times when investments may not grow significantly or may actually decline in value. Because use of principal or borrowing from endowments or other long-term asset investments may affect donor trust in the organization, changes in policy to permit such uses will likely require consideration at the board level, even if the changes have been thoroughly considered and recommended by one or more board committees and/or management.

UPMIFA specifically provides that subject to the intent of a donor, an organization may appropriate for expenditure or accumulate such portion of an endowment fund as the organization determines is prudent for the uses, benefits, purposes, and duration for which the endowment fund is established. In making a determination to spend or accumulate endowment funds, an organization must act in good faith, with the care an ordinarily prudent person in a like position would exercise under similar circumstances, and must consider, if relevant, the following factors:

- Duration and preservation of the endowment fund;
- Purposes of the organization and of the endowment fund;
- General economic conditions;
- The possible effect of inflation or deflation;
- The expected total return from income and appreciation;
- Other resources of the organization; and
- The investment policy of the organization.

UPMIFA has been adopted in most states.

Taxes and Tax-Exempt Status

Tax-Exempt Status. Many types of nonprofits enjoy tax-exempt status. This tax-exempt status is derived under the Internal Revenue Code (IRC) and ordinarily granted by the IRS. Section 501(c)(3) organizations are the entities most commonly thought of as being tax-exempt. However, many other nonprofits are tax-exempt for at least some purposes, including:

- Civic leagues and other broad social welfare organizations—IRC Section 501(c)(4);
- Labor, agricultural, or horticultural organizations—IRC Section 501(c) (5);
- Business leagues, chambers of commerce, real estate boards, trade associations, and boards of trade—IRC Section 501(c)(6);
- Social clubs—IRC Section 501(c)(7);
- Fraternal beneficiary societies—IRC Section 501(c)(8); and
- Other organizations that serve the welfare or convenience of a wide class of individuals or organizations and do not provide personal enrichment of individuals running the organization, such as employees, officers, board members, or major donors—other subsections of IRC Section 501(c) and certain other sections of the IRC.

Because receiving and maintaining tax-exempt status is of major importance to nonprofit organizations, boards usually want to be assured that the organization has made the proper filings to receive the exemption to which it is entitled and is operating within the requirements of the law that bestowed such status. Most nonprofits (other than churches, synagogues, and mosques) must file an annual information return or Form 990 (or, in the case of very small organizations, a postcard or Form 990N). In addition to questions in the Form 990 asking about the organization's process for review of the Form 990, certain questions require detailed information on how the organization's activities further its tax-exempt purposes. These questions make it important for both boards and management to focus on these issues, and may lead boards to more detailed discussion with the Executive Officer or legal counsel regarding the relationship between the organization's tax-exempt status and its activities. Because of the trend toward pre-filing board review of the Form 990 and the fact that preparation of the Form may raise questions that require consultation with outside tax counsel or the organization's auditors, Executive Officers and Chief Financial Officers need to make sure the process of preparing the annual Form 990 is begun well in advance of the filing deadline.

The rules and regulations for tax-exempt status are complex and their application to specific types of exempt organizations varies. For example, while the focus of this publication is on nonprofit organizations that operate and receive public support, tax-exempt organizations whose financial support is derived from a single source or small number of sources (such as funds provided by the larges of a family) generally are referred to as private foundations under the IRC and are subject to specific rules and regulations. Complying with these rules and regulations usually involves the need for advice from legal and accounting experts.

Some Income May Be Taxable. Tax-exempt organizations are subject to tax on income generated by their regular involvement in a trade or business unrelated to their tax- exempt purpose. Examples of unrelated business income might include income from sales of unrelated items by museums, pet-grooming services by a society for the prevention of cruelty to animals, or the sale of excess computer time to the general public.

The IRS has a three-part test to aid in determining whether an activity generates unrelated business taxable income: first whether the activity constitutes a trade or business; second, whether the activity is regularly carried on; and third, whether the activity is substantially related to the organization's exempt purpose. Making such determinations usually involves advice of outside tax advisors or legal counsel and boards may periodically want further advice from legal and accounting experts with regard to the organization's unrelated business activities, as the rules and regulations are complex and their application to the organization may change as the organization's unrelated business activities change. Often a finance or compliance committee will be delegated authority to oversee an organization's unrelated business income activities and compliance efforts.

Fund-raising for Charitable Organizations[1]

Fund-raising Oversight. Because fund-raising is integral to the survival of many Section 501(c)(3) organizations, oversight of a charitable organization's capacity to attract funding and manage donations and donors is an important board function that is woven into many other areas of board oversight for such organizations, including:

- *Mission Development:* Is the mission clear and will it attract support from donors and be differentiated from that of similar organizations?

- *Financial Budgeting:* Are projections of contributions realistic? Is the organization overly reliant on certain types of donations or certain funders? Does the organization have financial reserves or other means to weather a decrease in financial contributions due to economic downturns, loss of significant donors, or other events having an adverse effect on donations?

- *Financial Reporting and Management:* Are contributions properly accounted for? Are donor designations monitored and complied with? Is the organization in compliance with the special accounting and reporting requirements typically associated with government funding?

---

1. Not all nonprofits engage in fund-raising to support operations. For example, some foundations are set up to manage and distribute previously donated funds from one or more specific donors who created the foundation for a specific purpose, set up the terms or process for distribution, and do not expect or permit the foundation to raise funds from others.

- *Legal Compliance:* Are solicitations in compliance with do-not-call and anti-spam regulations? Do any of the solicitation materials include language that creates a restricted gift or endowment? Are reporting and registration requirements being followed in all states and localities in which the organization is involved in active fund-raising? Are donors sent acknowledgements in accordance with IRS requirements?

Appendix 7 has a summary of state charitable solicitation registration requirements and forms.

- *Policy Development:* Is there a board-approved gifts policy to help provide guidance to staff and help avoid potentially negative publicity or organizational disruption from receipt of a potentially controversial gift or one that require an inordinate amount of time and money to manage? Is there a board-approved gifts policy that addresses the acceptance of restricted gifts? Does the organization have an investment policy guiding asset allocation for invested funds and the percentage of earnings that can be drawn for use in the operating budget?

- *Investment Management:* Who actually oversees management of investments and what has the performance been? Is better management of assets achieved by a single investment manager or by distribution among more than one?

- *Human Resources:* Are fund-raising efforts adequately staffed and internally coordinated, and does the entire organization understand the importance to operations of fund-raising and relationships with donors?

- *Reputation Management:* Does the organization have a reputation for careful management of resources, efficient execution of its mission, and attentiveness to donors?

- *Board Participation:* For charitable nonprofits that expect their board members to donate or actively solicit donations at a certain level, are expectations clearly communicated and being fulfilled? Is it clear that even directors who are significant donors also have fiduciary duties of care and loyalty equivalent to other board members? If board members are not meeting their donation or solicitation expectations, what is the reason and what, if any, corrective action needs to be taken?

Treat as Integral to Operations. For nonprofits that engage in significant levels of fund-raising to support their operations, fund-raising and donor relationships are a significant part of the organization's operations. Treating them equally with the organization's other activities in reports to the board and in discussions at board and committee meetings can be an effective way to ensure that directors understand the importance to the organization of fund-raising and donor cultivation, the importance of board oversight of these activities, and the importance of individual board member participation in fund-raising and donor cultivation.

Issues Differ with Different Forms of Fund-raising. A board's effectiveness in fund-raising and in oversight of fund-raising activities requires an understanding of the various types of fund-raising and the governance implications of each. There are legal and accounting issues related to fund-raising which board members need to understand, including the fact that donations to endowments and capital campaigns and foundation grants may or may not be restricted by donor designation or otherwise. Any donor restrictions may require the recipient organization to account for and monitor compliance with the designation or restriction accurately and to ensure that these funds are not available for general use. Ensuring that the nonprofit's systems honor donor designations is crucial not only from a legal and accounting standpoint but also to retain donor trust and confidence.

Sometimes compliance with a designation or restriction becomes impossible, for example if a program is discontinued. The board needs to be confident that systems are in place to redirect the use of such funds, either with the donor's specific consent or by having a well-defined and disclosed policy allowing the organization to make such a change without donor consent under specified circumstances, or by obtaining a court order allowing funds to be used for purposes other than the original designation.

Management of fund-raising and donations can raise ethical concerns. For example, if the chain of ownership of a donated item (such as a piece of art or an artifact) is in question, under what circumstances should an organization agree to accept it? Are a donor's restrictions on a gift feasible for the organization and appropriate given its mission? Do the restrictions set by the donor impose a burden on the organization that outweighs the gift's apparent value? A well-thought-out gift acquisition policy adopted by the board can provide guidance to staff and protection for the organization.

The Practical Advice Section of this Chapter has additional background information and suggestions to assist in creating successful fund-raising boards and organizations. See pages 92–98.

Costs of Fund-raising. The board and management will also want to monitor the nonprofit's cost of fund-raising. While there are always costs associated with raising money, it is important to know how much of each dollar raised goes not for substantive programming but to cover the administrative costs of fund-raising. Excessive costs are an increasing concern among donors and regulators. There are organizations that monitor fund-raising costs, rate organizations on their efficiency in fund-raising, and publish their findings on the Internet and in publications easily accessible to donors.

Appendix 8 has a partial list of organizations that evaluate nonprofits on fund-raising efficiency and other criteria.

Hiring, Evaluating, and Terminating the Executive Officer

Critical Oversight Function. One of the most important roles of a nonprofit board is oversight of the Executive Officer: specifically the hiring, evaluation and, if necessary, replacement of the individual in this position. This board oversight role is key to how the board affects the nonprofit's ability to achieve its mission because the Executive Officer is responsible for the day-to-day operation of the organization and achievement of its mission in accordance with its strategic plan and other board directives and policies. He or she has the principal responsibility for organizational effectiveness in executing the mission. Because the Executive Officer reports directly to the board, or indirectly to the board through a board committee or the Board Chair, the board is responsible for evaluating the Executive Officer's successes and failures in carrying out these responsibilities.

Hiring the Executive Officer

Establishing Hiring Parameters. When a new Executive Officer is to be hired, the board is responsible for establishing the overall parameters for the position and the search, such as:

- What education and experience levels, skill sets, leadership, and management qualities are desired in the new Executive Officer?
- Will the new Executive Officer be expected to continue operations more or less as in the past or lead the organization in a new direction?
- Will "inside" candidates be considered, or will a search that includes both internal and external candidates be needed?
- What salary and other benefits are appropriate and feasible?
- Will a search firm be required to assist in sourcing candidates?
- Within what time frame and geographic area is the search to be conducted?

Consideration of issues such as those listed above is a vital first step in the search process and typically requires input from the full board.

Conducting a Search. Once the basic search parameters are established, a board committee is often entrusted with the actual search, including sourcing and interviewing candidates, arranging for background checks, and discussing preliminary terms of employment, scope of responsibilities, and expectations. Often an outside search firm will be retained to source and initially screen candidates. The board search committee will typically request that several other board members interview one or more finalists for the position prior to making its final recommendation to the board. Full board approval is usually sought before a final decision and terms of employment are set.

Orientation of a New Executive Officer. Staff often plays a major role in preparing background material and other information to help orient a new Executive Officer and in answering his or her initial questions once on the job. If the previous Executive Officer is departing on amicable terms, he or she can be very helpful in compiling relevant information for the new Executive Officer and may even spend time with the new Executive Officer to review key aspects of the job. Sometimes the previous Executive Officer may be contractually obligated to render such assistance.

Orientation and support from the board in the early stages of an Executive Officer's tenure are important in smoothing the transition to new leadership. Many organizations consider it part of the Board Chair's responsibility to assist with orientation of a new Executive Officer. Depending on the issues being faced by the organization and the time available from the Board Chair to assist with orientation, the search committee or another committee of the board may be charged with meeting with the new Executive Officer from time to time during his or her first few months of employment to help in the transition and to provide a sounding board for the new Executive Officer. A new Executive Officer's ability to integrate quickly into the organization and to assume a leadership role is greatly facilitated when the Board Chair and other board members take the time to make sure the new Executive Officer clearly understands the board's expectations and has the information needed to do the job.

Performance Evaluation of the Executive Officer

Communicating on Performance. Once the Executive Officer has been hired, a regular formal written evaluation process can be a useful tool for both the board and the Executive Officer, helping to assure that the board and the Executive Officer have a mutual understanding of organizational and personal goals, performance priorities, and areas needing particular attention or improvement by the Executive Officer. This process of establishing a clear set of goals for the Executive Officer helps focus both the Executive Officer's work and the board's oversight. Regular communication about performance and periodic evaluations may help build open and healthy working relationships between the Executive Officer and the board, facilitating development of mutual trust by giving both regular opportunities to clarify expectations. In situations in which there are performance concerns, it is even more important that the Board Chair or the board regularly monitor and communicate regarding performance. If performance continues to fall short of the board's expectations and the organization's needs, termination may ultimately be required. Regular communication about performance and periodic evaluations also may help facilitate removal of the Executive Officer when performance has not met specified expectations.

Because the Board Chair usually communicates regularly with the Executive Officer and works closely with him or her on a wide variety of matters, the

Board Chair is often the board's representative in discussing issues related to the Executive Officer's employment and performance. In some organizations, these discussions, particularly those related to salary or employment contracts, may be delegated to a board committee. But, even if the discussions are delegated, it is customary for the Board Chair to interface between the board committee and the Executive Officer.

It may be beneficial to have at least one other board member (perhaps the Board Chair-elect) participate in any formal evaluation or in other less formal discussions of performance. Such participation helps with continuity and provides the opportunity for the Executive Officer to hear directly from more than one person on the board. It also provides the opportunity for more than one person on the board to hear directly from the Executive Officer on performance issues, in either case helping reduce the possibility of misunderstandings or mischaracterizations.

Developing a Review Process and a Written Evaluation. The development of an effective review and performance evaluation process may be delegated to a board committee charged with governance or human resource matters or the Board Chair and the Executive Officer may work with the board or a committee of the board to create the process. A review process typically starts with developing annual and long-term goals on which any evaluation would be based and may also include a determination of whether or to what extent the Executive Officer's compensation will be tied to accomplishing specific goals. Next, the process includes gathering input on performance from key constituencies; the establishment of a schedule for a formal review (e.g., annually or every other year); the determination of who, or which committee, will be responsible for conducting and communicating the results of the evaluation to the Executive Officer; and the procedure for follow-up or monitoring of performance issues or concerns and, as appropriate, for adjusting compensation up or down based on achievement of goals. From both a legal and human resources management standpoint, it is important that the basis for the review be well-articulated and understood by both the board and the Executive Officer.

Once the general evaluation procedure is established, the process of initiating and managing the evaluation of the Executive Officer generally falls to the Board Chair, but the process may vary among organizations. Often the process begins with the Chair sharing his or her observations on the Executive Officer's performance with the executive, governance, or human resources committee. Other board members may also be offered an opportunity to provide comments or suggestions before the evaluation is finalized. In some cases, particularly in smaller organizations, the entire board is asked for comments, either informally, or by means of a questionnaire focusing either on specific issues, or on the overall performance objectives established for the evaluation period. From time to time, it may also be useful to conduct a "360 degree evaluation" in which the Executive Officer reviews him or herself and is also reviewed by board members and staff, using a common survey form developed for this purpose (perhaps utilizing the Executive Officer's job description as a starting point for developing survey questions). This type of evaluation also may include a review to determine where there are any issues that may not have been disclosed to the board. Once information is collected, the Board Chair or some other board leader typically synthesizes it in written form, which may or may not be reviewed by members of the executive, governance, or human resources committee or other board members prior to delivery.

If a nonprofit has no formal performance evaluation process for the Executive Officer, or the existing one is not working effectively, good governance practices suggest that either the Executive Officer or the Board Chair take the initiative in moving the organization toward a formal evaluation process, since effective board oversight of the Executive Officer is such an important board function. Obtaining samples of Executive Officer goals and review forms from similar nonprofit organizations may be a helpful starting point in such a situation.

Conducting the Evaluation. The performance evaluation is typically conducted with the Executive Officer by the Board Chair, either alone or together with other senior board members. Following delivery of the results of the evaluation, the Executive Officer's reaction and any agreed action plans or goals will normally be shared in executive session with the full board or a committee, with appropriate regard for the sensitive nature of the material. Effectively conducting an evaluation can be difficult, particularly if there are significant performance issues to be discussed.

Consequences of Lack of Evaluation. Unfortunately, many nonprofits often fail to conduct effective Executive Officer performance reviews, at least as long as things appear to be progressing smoothly. There are many reasons for this failure. Board Chairs are volunteers and may not feel capable of conducting an evaluation, particularly when the position of Board Chair is a rotating one and the Executive Officer has been in place for some time and appears to be doing well. In some cases, if the Executive Officer, Board Chair, and board members maintain regular contact, the value of a formal review and feedback process may not be recognized. Some Executive Officers may discourage the process, especially if they and the board have not built relationships of trust. Occasionally, an Executive Officer may see himself or herself as an expert in his or her particular specialty and not welcome guidance from those he or she perceives to be less expert. In other cases, the Executive Officer may be the founder or have become so well-respected in the community or among the nonprofit's constituencies that the board may not want to take on the challenge of addressing performance issues if it might cause negative community or constituency reaction or the Executive Officer's departure.

From a governance perspective, failure to evaluate the Executive Officer regularly may adversely affect the board's ability to govern and to assure effective management of the organization. The process is more likely to be viewed as helpful, rather than antagonistic and confrontational, if conducted regularly and constructively. Regular Executive Officer performance reviews, like other periodic strategic and operational reviews, offer the board an opportunity to reflect broadly and to make periodic adjustments and affirmations that can strengthen the organization's ability to fulfill its mission. The performance review process also provides an opportunity for the Executive Officer to discuss his or her achievements, plans for the future, and resource or other concerns with the Board Chair or other governance representatives.

Conversely, failure to evaluate the Executive Officer may undermine the nonprofit's performance review process for other employees, and unspoken assumptions about what the board thinks or the Executive Officer understands about performance issues and expectations may not be accurate. Such misunderstandings can be frustrating and ultimately detrimental to the organization's performance. These frustrations can be minimized or eliminated by a constructive performance review process which affirms achievements, identifies and discusses problems, and holds the Executive Officer accountable for meeting specific expectations.

As organizational needs, priorities, and strategies change, leadership may also need to change, either through individual development or by change in personnel. Failure to communicate changed expectations may lead to unexpected and unhappy terminations, often resulting in litigation or creating enemies of prior supporters. Even absent such drastic results, ignoring an Executive Officer's performance issues for sustained periods usually makes any issues much more difficult to address when they become critical or can no longer be ignored. Furthermore, organizations that tolerate leadership that is less than the board expects, or less than the Executive Officer is capable of, shortchange the nonprofit's ability to deliver on its mission. The process of formal board evaluations of CEOs of for-profit companies, however imperfect, is a governance practice widely in use and favored by governance experts. As pressure builds for nonprofits to adopt various governance practices, regular performance evaluations have the added benefit of aligning nonprofit board practices with emerging governance standards, particularly if these evaluations are also used to tie the Executive Officer's compensation, at least in part, to achievement of specific performance goals as is currently the trend in the for-profit arena.

Ongoing Informal Discussions of Performance. In addition to a formal written evaluation once a year or every other year, periodic meetings between the Board Chair and the Executive Officer can be used as an effective mechanism for providing performance feedback to the Executive Officer. The key is building a relationship of trust and respect and an atmosphere in which disagreements can be aired without acrimony. This can take some work, particularly in organizations in which the Board Chair changes frequently, or if the Chair is inexperienced in providing constructive feedback.

The Practical Advice Section of this Chapter has further suggestions on establishing a successful evaluation process for the Executive Officer.

Appendix 9 has a sample Executive Officer evaluation form.

Terminating the Executive Officer

Consult with Counsel. Terminating an Executive Officer is a major step for any organization, and consultation with counsel is highly advisable in advance of such an action, regardless of the reason for termination. Failure to do so may complicate the termination process significantly and even subject the organization to legal liability for wrongful termination, discrimination, violation of contractual terms, or other issues raising the potential of legal liability.

Termination Is Rarely Easy. Sometimes the need for termination is clear, for example, if the Executive Officer is caught embezzling funds or is arrested and jailed for a major crime. More commonly, the need for termination relates to problems of leadership or competency and such problems can be more difficult for boards to address. Often such problems are not raised openly at the board level, but are the topic of quiet discussions among small groups of board members. This may be the case even in some organizations that have a performance review process, since occasionally the fundamental issue of whether this Executive Officer is the right person for the job may not be squarely addressed in the performance review process.

The act of terminating the Executive Officer is fraught with not only legal but also internal and community relations issues. The termination process may be complicated by personal issues, since some board members may be friends with the Executive Officer or have a long-term working relationship with him or her. It is never easy to deliver the message that someone has failed to do the job that was expected or does not have the skills to take the organization to the next level. For these reasons, unless there is a real crisis, some boards are reluctant to address the need to replace the Executive Officer and often ignore problems or delay taking action.

Unfortunately, problems of leadership and competency rarely, if ever, go away or work themselves out. As a result, when these problems are not addressed, board members with doubts about the leadership or competency of the Executive Officer may resign from the board, disrupting board relations or robbing the board of talent. Recruiting new board members may be difficult if it is known that there are problems with the Executive Officer. The relationship between the board and the Executive Officer may become strained and trust eroded. The organization may begin or continue to flounder and achievement of its mission may be negatively affected. In short, when a board fails to face problems with the Executive Officer, it risks failing in its leadership role.

Initiating the Process. The first step in determining whether termination of the Executive Officer is necessary is to surface and begin to address concerns about his or her leadership and competency. Initially, this can be done through a performance evaluation process that solicits input from the board as a whole or a board committee and that results in a written evaluation clearly identifying specific issues of concern or for improvement. However, if no such process exists, or if no improvements are made after issues have been raised in a performance evaluation, then the board may need to take additional steps. Those steps might include discussions in executive session to help develop board consensus on the action needed, initial consultation with counsel on documentation of issues and process, or creation of a committee or working group to further investigate allegations or concerns. Including board members or consultants who have experience with the operations of other comparable organizations on such a committee or working group can be helpful in bringing expertise and perhaps broader perspective to deliberations on board expectations and Executive Officer performance than might otherwise be the case. Other steps might include development of a corrective action plan to be given to the Executive Officer, with a specified time to address identified problems. This action is particularly important if regular performance reviews were not conducted or were lacking in specificity.

Once the decision to remove the Executive Officer is made, the board or a committee of the board will also need to consider

- Whether the Executive Officer will be offered the opportunity to resign or take early retirement;
- Whether he or she will be given, or contractually must be given, severance pay;
- Whether the Executive Officer will be asked to sign a release (releasing the organization from any claim by the Executive Officer for wrongful termination and perhaps other matters—a common condition for payment of any severance pay and benefits);
- Who will meet with the Executive Officer to deliver the board's decision to terminate his or her employment;
- Who will the board name as interim Executive Officer, unless succession plans are already in place;
- How will staff and the public be notified of the change;
- Who will be authorized to speak publicly on the termination and interim appointment and what the public message will be; and
- What degree of confidentiality will be required of those within the organization with detailed knowledge of all the facts surrounding the termination.

The Practical Advice Section of this Chapter has a number of suggestions to consider in managing a termination of the Executive Officer. See pages 101–102.

Human Resources

Human Resources and Governance. The human resources function is primarily a management function, but it can have governance implications. How staff is led and managed can mean the difference between an organization that focuses on its mission and flourishes and one that is distracted by personnel issues.

Areas of Particular Concern. Because human resources management and practices may be critical to the long-term viability of an organization and because of the plethora of laws and regulations affecting human resources practices, both the Executive Officer and the board need to be confident that the organization's human resources function is operating effectively. The Executive Officer usually gains such confidence by engaging regularly in discussions with the organization's head of human resources (if other than the Executive Officer), an employment law attorney, or a human resources consultant or manager used by the organization, on the full spectrum of human resources-related issues that apply to the nonprofit. The board is more likely to focus its attention on four critical areas: compliance with employment-related laws, compensation practices and programs (including benefits and incentive compensation), performance management and evaluations, and succession planning.

Employment law violations are among the most common bases for lawsuits brought against nonprofit organizations, particularly because legal requirements and recommended human resources practices are subject to change with some frequency. As a result, human resources management is an area that requires considerable attention by both Executive Officers and boards to protect organizations against potential liability as well as to promote employee effectiveness.

Human Resources Compliance

Employment Compliance Reviews. The governance role in human resources compliance includes adoption and review of major human resources policies designed to help the organization comply with applicable employment-related laws, and regular assessments of management's understanding of the organization's employment-related legal risks, the steps being taken to minimize the risks, and how well the organization is complying with and enforcing the policies.

Compliance Policies and Training Programs. Although not all employment-related laws apply to all nonprofit organizations, boards typically expect to approve policies, or be assured that policies have been adopted by management, addressing harassment, discrimination in hiring, promotion, or termination on the basis of age, race, gender, national origin, or other protected categories, whistle-blowers, and employee vs. independent contractor status. (As the protections awarded whistle-blowers under Sarbanes-Oxley apply to nonprofit organizations, it is important that nonprofits consider the adoption of whistle-blower processes. Form 990 specifically asks if the reporting nonprofit has adopted a written whistle-blower policy.) Beyond policy adoption, well-structured compliance and training programs and procedures help prevent problems from arising.

Reporting to the Board or Committees. Periodic oral or written overview presentations to the board or a board committee on such programs and procedures, as well as the organization's human resources structure, help provide the board with insight into how well the organization is addressing employment-related compliance risks. A process for regular reporting to a committee on specific types of human resource problems or issues as they arise may help minimize unpleasant surprises and establish credibility with the board on how such problems are being handled.

Appendix 10 has a summary of human resources and employment-related laws.

Compensation Practices and Programs

Compensation and Governance. Compensation and compensation decisions at nonprofits are based on many factors: funds available to the organization; skills required; the competitive environment; and nonmonetary employee benefits that may (or may not) make up for less than competitive monetary compensation. Compensation issues can arise with respect to both employees and independent contractors. From a governance perspective, the board may be principally concerned with compensation of the Executive Officer and any other executive officers. However, because the effectiveness and appropriateness of compensation throughout the organization may affect the organization's ability to carry out its mission, the board also needs to understand the organization's overall compensation plans and issues.

Level of Executive Officer Compensation. Concerns about the absolute level of senior executive compensation have grown in recent years for both for-profit companies and nonprofits. Negative publicity related to Executive Officer compensation at some nationally known nonprofits has not only undermined the confidence of the public in the organizations directly involved, but also has caused donors, regulators, and the public at large to question whether nonprofit organizations are setting executive pay levels appropriately. This growing level of concern with executive compensation makes it advisable for boards to establish a formal, ongoing process for understanding, reviewing, and setting the compensation of the Executive Officer and other executives. Some states, such as California, specifically require that the board or a committee of the board formally approve the compensation of those individuals serving as CEO and CFO if the nonprofit is of a certain size. There are also questions on the Form 990 which address the process to approve the compensation of the Executive Officer.

Excess Benefit Transactions with Certain Insiders—Intermediate Sanctions. For Section 501(c)(3) and 501(c)(4) organizations (other than private foundations, which have their own restrictions), payment of excessive compensation (whether salary or benefits) to an Executive Officer or other senior executives may subject the recipient, as well as any organization manager who approved the transaction, to penalty excise taxes, also known as intermediate sanctions, under IRC Section 4958. IRS regulations on intermediate sanctions are complex, but they set forth a procedure that, if followed, establishes a rebuttable presumption of reasonableness for board compensation decisions. The procedure requires that compensation decisions be approved by the board or committee (without participation of anyone with a conflict of interest) based on appropriate and objective data (as specified in IRS regulations) and that the decision be adequately and contemporaneously documented. The IRS excess benefit rules and intermediate sanctions also apply to transactions with board members or other persons having substantial influence over the organization. Questions on the Form 990 address whether an organization has followed these rebuttable presumption procedures.

Appendix 11 has a copy of the IRS Sample Rebuttable Presumption Checklist.

The Practical Advice Section of this Chapter has additional information on the process of establishing compensation for the Executive Officer. See pages 103–104.

Performance Management, Hiring, and Firing of Staff

Board Understanding of the Appraisal and Ranking Process. Effective performance management begins with regular individual performance appraisals for all staff and, depending on the size and complexity of the organization, may also include ranking of employees and positions based on overall importance to the organization and regular staffing reviews. The reviews assist in evaluating and prioritizing skill sets within the organization relative to the nonprofit's achievement of its mission.

Except for the board's own evaluation of the Executive Officer, the specific results of individual performance appraisals are less important for a board than its understanding of what the performance management process actually is and its confidence that management is conducting the process consistently. Board members may from time to time comment on the performance of particular individuals with whom they interact directly, but it is the establishment and functioning of the overall performance appraisal process that is important from a governance standpoint. Specific results of organizational staffing reviews may, however, be of significant interest to boards as they may have both immediate and long-term budgetary implications as well as implications for the organization's ability to achieve its mission.

Hiring and Terminating Staff. Hiring staff is typically a function delegated to the Executive Officer, although some boards may retain the authority to hire or approve the hiring of certain senior staff members. While boards are rarely concerned with the details of most additions to or departures from staff, board members are often interested in reviewing turnover statistics, as these statistics may highlight issues related to the organization's ability to function effectively or its vulnerability to discriminatory termination or other claims.

Terminating employees at any level may precipitate a variety of problems in any organization. Well-administered performance management programs, including documentation of performance issues in regular performance evaluations, help minimize legal problems in terminating employees. Nonetheless, termination decisions may still result in litigation or other conflicts. For this reason, many organizations centralize termination decisions and handling of terminations, whether or not they otherwise decentralize management decisions. Centralization can be particularly helpful in smaller organizations or those without a strong internal human resources function. A centralized process may involve some level of access to legal counsel or human resources consultants to help the organization avoid termination-related litigation. From a governance standpoint, the board will rarely be involved in termination decisions (other than for the Executive Officer), usually delegating to management the authority to both hire and fire staff, within certain parameters. The primary issue of concern for boards is the effective management of the termination process within the organization so that problems and the potential for litigation are minimized.

Board Review. Periodic presentations to the board or a board committee providing an overview of the performance appraisal and termination processes are an important way for the board to exercise governance oversight and assure that appropriate policies and procedures are in place and followed. Such presentations also help build the board's confidence in the Executive Officer's management skills or, conversely, may alert the board to problems with the organization's leadership in this area.

Succession Planning

Purpose and Types of Succession Planning. Succession planning may help strengthen the skills of existing staff, focus attention on organizational and individual strengths and weaknesses, and minimize organizational disruption that often accompanies replacement of the Executive Officer or other senior staff. Succession planning encompasses the process of evaluating and determining career path succession for individuals, as well as the process of anticipating and perhaps even identifying potential replacement candidates to expeditiously replace (on an interim or permanent basis) a key individual who suddenly leaves or becomes seriously ill or otherwise unavailable to the organization.

SUCCESSION PLANNING FOR STAFF

Largely a Management Function. Succession planning for staff often focuses primarily on individual career growth and is woven into an organization's performance management and evaluation process, with comments on evaluations providing an indication of an employee's future career growth potential and opportunities. This type of succession planning may also include developing and maintaining a centralized list of high potential employees with aptitude and willingness for growth who might be considered as other positions become available. Some organizations create defined individual growth plans designed to prepare specific individuals for future opportunities, although depending on the size of the organization and the nature of an employee's work, there may be relatively few paths to promotion within some organizations. The board may or may not participate in succession planning for staff other than by periodically inquiring about the existence of such a process and how it works and by encouraging the Executive Officer to help employees continue to develop skills that may benefit the organization.

SUCCESSION PLANNING FOR THE EXECUTIVE OFFICER

Joint Responsibility. Succession planning for the Executive Officer typically focuses on issues related to the departure or unavailability of the Executive Officer, whether planned or unplanned, and requires the direct involvement of the board or a board committee. However, succession planning for the Executive Officer position may be most effective if considered as a joint responsibility of the Executive Officer and the board. Without active involvement of the Executive Officer, the board may be reluctant to engage in the process absent a crisis. If the Executive Officer feels intimidated or threatened by board succession planning efforts, the board will likely miss vital information that the Executive Officer could otherwise bring to succession planning discussions.

Succession planning for a planned or unplanned departure of the Executive Officer need not be, at least initially, about identifying a specific individual to succeed the Executive Officer. It is closer to, and sometimes a part of, a strategic planning process, assessing the organization's direction, identifying the skills and experience required, and perhaps identifying individuals who may be potential candidates or organizations that might have viable candidates or assist in finding one or more such candidates.

Obstacles to Succession Planning for the Executive Officer. Long-term succession planning for the Executive Officer is often not undertaken by boards. The reasons for this include inertia when things are going well and the Executive Officer seems content to stay, and concerns about whether raising the issue of succession might be upsetting to the current Executive Officer or other staff. However, by failing to make succession planning a routine, ongoing process, a board risks making future Executive Officer transitions more difficult, increasing the amount of time to find and orient an appropriate successor.

Particularly when an Executive Officer has been in that position for a long time and the board has not engaged in succession planning, broaching the subject of succession, even in the context of strategic planning, can be sensitive. A possible starting point is for the Board Chair to begin discussions with the Executive Officer as part of the performance evaluation process, or in other one-on-one meetings. The Board Chair can report on such discussions in executive session with the board or an appropriate committee and then work with the Executive Officer and the board (or committee) on succession planning. Periodic review and updating of the Executive Officer's job description is another useful tool to assist in succession planning. Keeping a current description of the key functions of the Executive Officer provides a starting point for evaluating skill sets needed in a new Executive Officer.

Initiation of Succession Planning by the Executive Officer. Sometimes it is the Executive Officer who is concerned about lack of succession planning and who must determine how to raise the subject with the board or the Board Chair without creating adverse reactions. In such cases, the Executive Officer may wish to start by suggesting one or more ways to approach succession planning while at the same time indicating that his or her concern is being raised in the interests of good governance rather than related to his or her intention to leave the organization. It is ultimately the board's responsibility to determine how to prepare for succession in the Executive Officer position or other senior officer positions.

Emergency Planning. Larger and more complex nonprofits sometimes create specific succession plans for emergency situations in which the Executive Officer is unavailable. This type of succession planning is closely associated with disaster planning, but may also be useful in a crisis involving only the Executive Officer, such as incapacity or sudden death. Emergency succession planning usually involves designation in the organization's disaster plan of an interim successor or acting Executive Officer (usually designated by position rather than by name) to serve in specified emergencies. Typically, the time and conditions under which the individual should continue to serve in the position are also spelled out in these plans. Depending on the organization, such emergency Executive Officer designations might be incorporated into the organization's bylaws.

Use of Job Descriptions in Succession Planning. An often overlooked tool in succession planning for the Executive Officer and other key staff is the job description. Development of job descriptions for key staff can provide a nonthreatening entry point for discussions about the skill sets needed for critical positions within the organization. Regular reviews of such job descriptions help ensure they remain current as jobs evolve over time. Periodic board review of the Executive Officer's job description may help focus the board on the need to provide the Executive Officer with professional development or other training opportunities to meet changing job requirements or, in some cases, help crystallize the need to make a change in the organization's leadership.

Risk Management and Disaster Planning

Insurable and Uninsurable Risk. All organizations are exposed to risks, including risk of material loss of assets; risk of injury to employees, members of the nonprofit, volunteers, or members of the public; risk of interruption of programs; and litigation and other legal risks. Insurance can often be purchased to help mitigate such risks. Some risks may involve the essence of the organization's operations, such as the risk of loss of audience for a performing arts organization or risk of loss of membership because an organization has lost its relevance to its targeted participants. These types of risks cannot be insured against, although effective management and governance are apt to reduce the likelihood of an organization suffering a loss from these risks.

Both insurable and uninsurable risks are important for a board to understand and, from a governance perspective, risk management is one of the board's primary oversight functions. Many nonprofits have limited assets and may not have the ability to sustain a significant financial loss or disruption to operations. Even if losses are covered by insurance, the very fact of a loss may significantly damage the organization's reputation, affecting donor or other constituency support. An organization that understands its critical risks can allocate funds and attention to these areas to help forestall problems that might lead its intended beneficiaries to desert it or avoid problems that may endanger the organization's ability to fulfill its mission. The Executive Officer and the board can help assure that the organization takes such risks into account by developing and maintaining a process for recognizing both common and uncommon, but potentially devastating, risks and developing risk management and mitigation strategies, including purchase of insurance.

Risk Oversight. Depending on the size of the organization and the nature of its risks, the board may assign oversight of the risk management process to a board committee, such as finance, or create a separate risk management committee. Other nonprofits may rely on periodic reporting on risks and risk management activities directly to the board. A larger or more complex nonprofit may use outside advisors to assist the board in satisfying its duty of care in assessing the nonprofit's risk profile and taking steps to mitigate those risks.

Reports to the board or a board committee on risk management typically include a full description of the organization's risks and its mitigation efforts, including the nature and extent of any insurance coverage, as well as discussion of uninsurable risks. A cost-benefit analysis is an integral part of any risk management assessment. For instance, while insurance may be helpful in mitigating some risks, the organization must balance the cost of insurance (including the costs of different levels of coverage) with the likelihood and the economic impact of certain types of losses. Considering changes to the political, economic, and other environments in which the nonprofit operates is also important to effective risk assessment.

Disaster Planning. Another component of risk management is advance disaster planning or emergency preparedness planning. Despite an organization's best efforts, from time to time, risks become reality. Disaster plans are intended to help organizations survive significant emergencies, such as major fire damage making facilities unusable, earthquake, flood, hurricanes, or civil unrest. Many of these sorts of risks may affect not only the organization but the community in which it operates. How such crises are actually handled may make the difference between an organization that survives and one that is irretrievably damaged.

Disaster or emergency preparedness plans set forth steps that may need to be taken if and when a disaster or emergency occurs, so that the impact of the disaster is minimized and the organization is able to return to normal as quickly as possible. The board's role is to help ensure that the nonprofit has the ability to withstand an actual disaster, and advance disaster planning can help the organization survive should such an event occur. From a governance standpoint, the board will be less interested in the details of the plan than in the fact of its existence and what the process is for training and internalizing procedures and for updating the plan. Additionally the board itself will want to know what it and individual board members, as well as management, are expected to do (or not do) during an emergency. The Executive Officer and the board may also want to consider including emergency governance and management procedures in the organization's bylaws, setting forth who has authority to make emergency decisions on behalf of the organization if the board or senior officers are unavailable. Most state nonprofit corporation laws permit such emergency bylaw provisions to be adopted.

Regular Discussion of Risk. Because of the significance to nonprofits of risk management issues, the Board Chair and Executive Officer may find it helpful to consider risk management issues as one of the areas for frequent discussion between them, as well as for regular reporting to and discussion with the board.

The Practical Advice Section of this Chapter has additional suggestions about risk management and disaster planning. See pages 105–106.

Facilities and Real Estate

Not all nonprofits have significant facilities or real estate issues, other than the amount of rent that they pay for an administrative office. However, some nonprofits do own or rent significant real property for which they are responsible. In such cases, the board directly or through a board committee needs to have a general understanding of the costs and other risks associated with such ownership or lease arrangements. For example, the board may ask the Executive Officer to establish a capital budgeting process for handling depreciation and planning for major capital expenditures, including needed facility improvements and upgrades. The board may also ask the Executive Officer to inform it of any significant environmental issues, such as the presence of asbestos, which could endanger employees or others in an owned building, be potentially expensive to correct, or adversely affect the property's market value. Major real estate purchases or sales typically require full board approval.

Critical Relationships

If a nonprofit has operations or relationships with customers, clients, vendors, or suppliers that, if lost, could substantially adversely affect its continued viability or its ability to continue to fulfill its mission, the board will want to assure itself that these operations or relationships are being handled so as to ensure their ongoing benefit to the organization. Often such relationships will be discussed as part of a general overview of risk management issues, but sometimes a relationship is so important it warrants individual discussion at the board level, as, for example, if an organization receives all or the bulk of its funding from a single source.

The Practical Advice Section of this Chapter lists a number of questions to consider with respect to an organization's critical relationships. See page 107.

Compliance

Increased Importance of Compliance Issues. Board oversight of an organization's compliance with laws and regulations is an important governance responsibility and boards have a fiduciary duty to assure that a reasonable compliance program exists and is followed. Boards that assure reasonable compliance programs are in place and updated periodically, and that monitor these programs, are likely to be protected from liability even when the compliance program fails to detect or prevent wrongdoing. Boards generally have the responsibility to assure that there are mechanisms in place to promote compliance with applicable laws and regulations, including requirements to protect whistle-blowers who bring instances of noncompliance to the attention of the organization and requirements related to retention of documents. While much of Sarbanes-Oxley is not applicable to nonprofits, the provisions related to protection of whistle-blowers and retention of documents are applicable. The Form 990 also requires nonprofits to report whether they have written whistle-blower and document retention policies in place.

Compliance oversight is also important for nonprofit boards in light of their special responsibility to help assure their organizations fulfill their tax-exempt missions and do not violate the public trust. As nonprofits grow in size and complexity, the need for focus on compliance issues also increases. What is reasonable for a small local nonprofit probably will be insufficient for a large regional or national nonprofit. The substantive area in which the nonprofit operates also will determine the scope and complexity of its compliance program. In a highly regulated area, such as health care, the establishment of a robust compliance program may well be required.

To fulfill their duties of compliance oversight, boards need information on who in the organization is responsible for compliance; how risk areas are monitored; what procedures have been instituted and are followed when potential compliance problems are identified; and what policies and procedures are in place to not only protect against significant instances of noncompliance but also to protect whistle-blowers. Boards will also want to know how well the organizational culture supports compliance efforts and will expect the Executive Officer to support compliance efforts in the organization and to be familiar with key organization compliance risks as well as industry trends in managing compliance efforts and risks.

Tone at the Top. Compliance begins with the tone at the top of an organization. The expectations of the board and senior management shape the ethical culture of an organization. These expectations are communicated in many ways, often in codes of conduct and conflict of interest policies and the manner in which these policies are enforced. Codes of conduct and conflict of interest policies are commonly used by both nonprofit and for-profit corporations to establish baseline standards for ethical and legally compliant conduct by employees and board members. Their use is encouraged by many commentators and regulators, including the IRS. Codes of conduct and conflict of interest policies are usually approved and periodically reviewed and updated by the board.

Scope. Because enforcement is critical to how an organization implements compliance with policies and procedures, board oversight of compliance usually includes the adoption of and periodic review of the organization's code of conduct, conflict of interest policies, whistle-blower protection policies, and other key compliance-related policies. It also includes review and approval of other procedures and processes designed to ensure the organization's compliance with specific laws and regulations. Compliance reviews may be a responsibility delegated to an audit or risk management committee. Presentations on compliance to the board or a board committee help assure the board that appropriate procedures are in place and have been tested, by audit or other means, to ensure adherence to policies and that a process is in place that can reasonably be expected to detect deviations and take appropriate steps to remedy any such deviations.

Tax-Exempt Status. For tax-exempt nonprofits, compliance issues are particularly important, as failure to comply with laws and regulations may affect an organization's tax-exempt status. For example, compliance issues fundamental to an exempt nonprofit's eligibility for tax-exempt status include not engaging in lobbying as a substantial part of its activities, not participating in political campaigns, not providing improper private benefit to any person or excess compensation to employees or board members, not providing loans with no, or below-market, interest to board members, or paying vendors more than fair market value for goods or services.

The Practical Advice Section of this Chapter contains additional suggestions for assessing the board's compliance oversight. See pages 107–108.

Advocacy and Lobbying

Importance of Oversight. Oversight of advocacy and lobbying activities warrants particular scrutiny by nonprofit boards. The missions of nonprofits often involve activities that are affected by public policy decisions, such as public funding designated for support of the arts, tax deductions for contributions, or policy changes affecting education, health care, or other areas. Not only may changes in public policy significantly affect the nonprofit's activities, but public policy changes may originate in efforts led by nonprofits. As a result, many nonprofits do engage in activities designed to influence public policy.

Activities designed to influence public policy may be considered "lobbying" under the IRC, the Federal Lobbying Disclosure Act, applicable state lobbying statutes, and, in some instances, local lobbying ordinances. The IRC also limits or, in the case of Section 501(c)(3) organizations, outright prohibits involvement in political campaigns by various types of nonprofits. Unfortunately, nonprofits that engage in these activities are faced with multiple sets of rules, including multiple registration and reporting requirements. If the activities are considered "lobbying" as defined in the IRC, then the nonprofit will be subject to a variety of limitations. Such limitations vary depending on the type of nonprofit and are most strict for nonprofits that are tax-exempt under Section 501(c)(3) of the IRC. If the activities are considered "lobbying" as defined in federal, state, or local lobbying laws, the nonprofit may be required to register and report its lobbying activities.

Failure to understand or comply with limitations on lobbying and involvement in political campaigns may, in certain circumstances, affect the organization's tax-exempt status or result in imposition of excise taxes. Failure to register and report lobbying activities under applicable federal, state, or local lobbying disclosure laws may subject the nonprofit, or individuals within the nonprofit, to civil and/or criminal penalties. It is, therefore, critical for a nonprofit board and management to understand the potential benefits and possible drawbacks of public policy advocacy, the legal restrictions on various types of activities, and any applicable registration and reporting requirements for those activities. It is also important that the Executive Officer and the board, directly or through a board committee, monitor the organization's compliance with the various federal, state, and local legal guidelines for engaging in such activities.

The Practical Advice Section of this Chapter has a number of questions to consider when an organization is contemplating engagement in public policy advocacy, or in reviewing existing activities in this area. *See pages 108–109.*

Definitions of Lobbying, Political Campaign Activity, and General Advocacy and Educational Activities. The IRC defines lobbying as efforts to influence legislation—whether on the national, state, or local levels. It divides lobbying into two types: grassroots lobbying, defined as efforts to influence legislation by influencing the general public, and direct lobbying, defined as efforts to influence legislators. The definition of lobbying does not include advocacy or educational efforts unrelated to specific legislation; therefore, such activities are generally permitted. General advocacy and educational activities include activities to influence public opinion on issues (but not specific legislation), to influence nonlegislative governing bodies, to educate the public on issues, and to encourage voter participation.

In contrast to the IRC definition of lobbying, the Federal Lobbying Disclosure Act applies to paid activities involving legislation, regulations, and the administration and execution of federal programs, including grants. Under this federal statute, a lobbyist is an individual employed or retained by a client for compensation, who makes one or more "lobbying contacts" and whose lobbying activities constitute 20 percent or more of his or her services' time on behalf of that client during any three-month period. A "client" is a person or entity that employs or retains another person for compensation to conduct lobbying activities on behalf of that person or entity. An organization employing its own lobbyists is considered its own client for reporting purposes.

There are three factors to be considered in determining whether registration is required under the Federal Lobbying Disclosure Act: lobbying contacts; lobbying activity; and whether certain monetary thresholds are met. An individual is a lobbyist if he or she makes more than one lobbying contact and his or her "lobbying activities" constitute at least 20 percent of the individual's time in services for that client over any three-month period. To be required to register, however, the amount received or expended must exceed certain monetary thresholds.

State law and local ordinances often define "lobbying" in a manner that is significantly different from the definition in the IRC or in the Federal Lobbying Disclosure Act. Thus, nonprofits may need to understand and comply with multiple different lobbying registration and reporting requirements at the local, state, and federal levels.

Campaign Prohibitions and Lobbying Limitations for Section 501(c)(3) Nonprofits. Nonprofits that are tax-exempt under Section 501(c)(3) may engage in general advocacy (not tied to specific legislation) and educational activities without limitation. However, they may not under any circumstances engage directly or indirectly in any political campaign or activity for an elected office or align with a political party. Prohibited involvement in political campaigns, which is prohibited for any 501(c)(3) organization, includes any partisan political activity directly related to an individual's candidacy for political office, including endorsement, opposition to, contributions to, working for, or support for such candidacy in any form. Special care needs to be taken in an election year with respect to what might otherwise be considered routine contacts by a 501(c)(3) nonprofit with its elected representatives. In nonelection years, asking a state senator to speak at an organization's luncheon would not trigger any concerns, while in an election year, care would need to be taken that providing such a forum without the presence of other candidates for the same office did not appear to be an endorsement for the incumbent.

Section 501(c)(3) nonprofits are permitted to lobby, but only so long as such activities do not constitute a substantial part of the organization's activities. There is a generally accepted rule of thumb that lobbying is not a substantial part of a nonprofit's activities if its efforts to influence legislation represent less than 5 percent of the organization's total activities. However, circumstances vary, such that for some Section 501(c)(3) organizations a greater or lesser percentage may be appropriate.

Section 501(h) Election. Determining which activities and how much activity are within legal and regulatory parameters for advocacy and lobbying efforts can be complex. Organizations that do not want to run any risks of being found to engage in excessive lobbying can take advantage of IRS rules that essentially provide a safe harbor for lobbying activity: the ability to make a "Section 501(h) election." Section 501(h) of the IRC allows tax-exempt Section 501(c)(3) nonprofits to safely incur lobbying expenses within defined parameters. These parameters vary based on the size of the organization, since they are based on percentages of the organization's annual budget, up to a maximum of $1 million per year. These parameters are frequently referred to as the "expenditure test."

Section 501(h) specifically defines which activities do and do not constitute lobbying for purposes of the Section 501(h) election. It also provides proportional sanctions for violations in the form of various levels of excise tax on excess expenditures, although persistent violations could result in loss of tax-exempt status. Churches and private foundations may not make a Section 501(h) election.

Other organizations with large budgets, for example, large educational institutions or health organizations, may prefer not to limit their lobbying expenditures to the $1 million annual cap. These organizations must then determine, based on their individual circumstances, the level of lobbying they may engage in without these activities being deemed a "substantial part" of their total activities. Put another way, they may not spend more than an insubstantial amount of their annual expenditures on lobbying activities. A determination that an organization has engaged in excess lobbying subjects the organization to a potential loss of tax-exempt status. Under certain circumstances, managers may also be subject to personal financial penalties for excess lobbying by their organization.

Limitations on Lobbying and Political Activities for Other Nonprofits. Nonprofits that are exempt from taxation under other sections of the IRC, such as Section 501(c)(4) civic leagues or social welfare organizations, Section 501(c)(5) labor, agricultural, and horticultural organizations, and Section 501(c)(6) trade associations and business leagues, are not subject to the same restrictions on lobbying as apply to Section 501(c)(3) organizations. Such nonprofits may engage in unlimited lobbying and general advocacy activities as long as they are related to and in furtherance of their exempt purposes. However, each such nonprofit is subject to applicable lobbying registration and disclosure statutes at the federal, state, and, perhaps, local level.

Political campaign activity by such nonprofits is permitted so long as that is not the organization's primary activity. However, any political expenditure incurred by such organizations may be subject to tax under Section 572(f) of the IRC. Limitations on lobbying and partisan political campaigning for other types of nonprofits can be found on the IRS website: www.irs.gov.

Reporting and Tracking. For IRS purposes, lobbying activities of tax-exempt nonprofits must be reported annually on the organization's Form 990 (other than churches, which are not required to file Form 990s), which means that organizations that engage in lobbying must have a mechanism for keeping track of lobbying activities and expenditures. A more detailed report (and hence greater underlying tracking effort) must accompany the Form 990 for organizations that choose not to make a Section 501(h) election.

In contrast to annual reporting for IRS purposes, under the Federal Lobbying Disclosure Act and various state laws and local ordinances, lobbying activities are often required to be reported more frequently than annually. Reporting typically is required to be done on a quarterly basis. Nonprofit boards must make certain that their organization is meeting applicable lobbying disclosure deadlines.

For organizations not large enough to maintain an internal government relations function responsible for oversight of advocacy activities, the tracking task can be particularly difficult since activities of all parts of the organization will need to be identified and tracked. Tracking may also be necessary to be sure that certain funds received by the nonprofit are *not* used for lobbying. For example, charities are prohibited from using government funds for lobbying purposes. Similarly, some foundation grants may restrict or limit use of funds for lobbying purposes. Organizations that engage in lobbying may find it useful to maintain a template for recording advocacy activities. This tracking may also be done in conjunction with the organization's accounting personnel.

Information Management, Technology, and the Internet

Information management, technology, and the Internet are related areas that may have significant implications for organizational effectiveness and delivery of a nonprofit's mission and, therefore, are of interest to boards as they exercise oversight over operations.

Information Management

Definition. Information management generally refers to an organization's ability to access and process information relevant to its operations. It encompasses both electronic and hard copy information storage systems, as well as systems for records management and organizational policies and practices related to information-sharing and protection. Information management may also encompass an organization's approach to effective communication and sharing of information.

Importance of Access to Relevant Data. Information management is important to nonprofit boards and management because an organization's ability to easily retrieve, sort, and mine its data for financial information, trends, and benchmarking can make a material difference in the organization's success and fulfillment of its mission. Access to clear, concise, and relevant information is critical to support the board's efforts to identify important issues and to govern effectively. Communication and analysis of relevant information among nonprofit employees and with the board can be critical to effective operations. Thus, establishing a culture and infrastructure that facilitates such information-sharing and analysis can be an important element in effective management.

Legal Aspects of Information Management. In recent years, there has been a proliferation of laws relating to information use, including laws imposing responsibility for maintaining the privacy of customer, patient, and employee information, and laws regarding the gathering and use of personal data. Laws also prohibit the destruction of documents pertaining to investigations or litigation. It has become important for organizations to have appropriate policies, procedures, and systems in place to comply with these laws. Provisions in the 2002 Sarbanes-Oxley Act, for example, impose liability for destruction of information relevant to a governmental investigation, and these provisions apply equally to for-profits and nonprofits. The Form 990 now specifically asks whether the reporting nonprofit organization has a written document retention policy.

Nonprofits also need an effective process for identifying information that can be slated for destruction. Failing to regularly destroy or eliminate obsolete, duplicative, or other unneeded documents can result in unnecessary clutter, at best, and expensive document storage costs and nightmarish litigation discovery obligations, at worst. An important role for the Executive Officer is to help ensure that the organization's document retention policies are designed and applied in a way that complies with applicable legal requirements and that there is routine destruction of unneeded documents.

The Practical Advice Section of this Chapter lists a series of questions to help determine whether an organization's information management systems and policies are effective. See pages 109–111.

The Practical Advice Section also contains information on developing a records management system and on actions to be considered in complying with records retention requirements. See pages 112–115.

Technology

Importance. Since most nonprofit organizations use computers and rely heavily on electronic access to data and communications, policies for management of computer systems, including policies prohibiting improper personal use of organizational systems, are important to effective operations. Because of the importance of technology to the operations of most organizations, boards typically want assurance that the organization's technological assets are being appropriately managed and protected and that systems are in place to protect data and to restore equipment and data in the event of an interruption in service. Board oversight in this area is often assigned either to a board technology committee or a board committee that monitors risk.

Technology and electronic communications are areas of rapid growth and change. As they evolve, board and management policies will need to address new issues such as, for example, how involved the organization should become in organization-based blogs or social networking initiatives, the use of flash drives to store organization information, employee blogging or posting information on personal social networking sites, or use of other forms of electronic communication to provide personal or organizational information. Executive Officers have a significant role in management of technology by establishing and monitoring the internal process for periodic review of information technology policies by staff and, as appropriate, by hiring external experts to assist in these reviews or to make recommendations for changes in systems, processes, or policies.

Technology Gap. Despite the growing importance of technology generally, studies continue to document significant differences in how nonprofits and for-profit companies use technology and deal with technological issues. Lack of money for hardware or software or to hire personnel to create or manage systems may account for some of this difference. However, lack of familiarity and reluctance to change old methods or to understand the importance of technology to an organization could seriously hamper its ability to fulfill its mission.

The Practical Advice Section of this Chapter contains a list of questions that may help in developing an organization's capacity to embrace technology and understand the impact of technological change. See page 111.

The Internet

Importance. The Internet has dramatically changed how most organizations, including nonprofits, communicate with their constituencies. It is difficult to imagine a nonprofit that doesn't use e-mail or have a website. The Internet is an effective tool for fund-raising, for communicating about mission, activities, products, and other organizational information, for sourcing volunteers, and for obtaining constituent feedback, among other things. Social networking sites are increasingly useful to organizations in disseminating information about programs or in connecting with people who share an interest in the mission of the organization. The Internet has also helped increase accountability by providing an easily accessible mechanism for distribution of comparative information about nonprofit organizations. Informational returns (Forms 990 and 990PF) filed by tax-exempt nonprofits are available at guidestar.org and allow donors, community members, and other nonprofits to review and compare nonprofit organizations with respect to their net program revenues, expenses (including executive compensation), and other operating data. Many nonprofit organizations now also post their most recent Form 990 or form 990PF on their own websites.

The Internet also provides a way for organizations to communicate more frequently and at lower cost with board members. Some organizations maintain a password-protected section on their website for the exclusive use of board members and senior staff. The nonprofit's website may be a good source of information for new board members who are not yet familiar with the organization's activities, history, and traditions.

Time, Cost, and Legal Issues. Creating and maintaining a useful website take both time and money. Creating and posting blogs, keeping up with social networking communications, and responding to e-mails or messages on websites also take time and may require quality control systems and management oversight. Federal, state, and local laws regulate fund-raising online, advertising on websites, Internet sales, and retention of electronic documents.

Board Focus. From a governance perspective, boards typically focus on legal compliance and security issues related to the Internet, generally acting through whichever board committee focuses on risk or legal compliance issues. However, a board may also be interested in how effectively an organization is using the Internet for marketing and other communications with constituencies.

Regulatory Accountability

Regulators and Regulatory Filings. Like for-profit entities, nonprofits are subject to laws and regulations of various federal, state, and local agencies. IRS rules impose significant compliance responsibilities on tax-exempt and other nonprofits. State attorneys general have some level of oversight and enforcement responsibility for nonprofits. Most nonprofits must make annual filings with the IRS and state officials or agencies. While many nonprofits will never experience a challenge from the IRS or a state regulator, audits do occur, and boards need to be assured that the organization is making timely and accurate filings with government bodies, complying with legal requirements, and keeping apprised of regulatory and legal changes that may affect the organization's status or operations.

Depending on the size, sophistication, and tradition of the organization, regulatory filings may be reviewed and discussed with the board in advance of filing, or just made available as an information item to the board after filing.

The current version of the Form 990 makes it likely that advance reviews of that Form will be conducted by the full board or a board committee. The new Form asks whether the organization provided a copy of the Form 990 to the board before filing. The Form also asks the organization to describe the process used to review the Form 990. This description is to include a summary of who reviewed the Form 990, when the review was conducted and the extent of the review. For many larger nonprofits, the Form 990 may be reviewed by the organization's Chief Financial Officer and outside accountants along with the organization's counsel and Executive Officer, along with a review by the board or a board committee.

For other filings, a board will often rely on the Executive Officer and other management staff to know and submit timely regulatory filings, but may, if it has doubts about the organization's handling of filings, require advance board or committee review, or even engage the services of legal or other experts to review filings and the organization's compliance with filing requirements.

Awareness of Issues. Boards will expect management to establish an ongoing reporting process for advising the board of any tax or state regulatory issues and concerns.

Internal Revenue Service

The IRS has the power to revoke a nonprofit organization's tax-exempt status for failing to comply with exemption requirements. Loss of tax-exempt status may prevent a nonprofit organization from achieving its mission, or even continuing its existence. There is no constitutional or statutory right to tax-exemption, and the IRS is a serious watchdog, ready to challenge an organization's exempt status if there is an indication that the organization is not meeting the requirements for that status.

Challenges from the IRS are particularly common in connection with elections and alleged politically partisan activities by nonprofit organizations, especially churches and other religious organizations. However, tax-exempt nonprofits have from time to time come under IRS scrutiny for various other reasons. Issues of particular concern to the IRS include significant unrelated business income, high salaries for nonprofit executives, fringe benefits, excessive fund-raising costs, and conflicts of interest involving board members and officers. In light of recent changes to IRS Form 990, governance issues have joined the list of issues inviting IRS scrutiny.

As nonprofit organizations consider additional forms of revenue generation, it is increasingly important for boards to consider the tax implications of these changes. An IRS challenge or audit does not necessarily need to be predicated on fraud or criminal activity or a material issue within the organization. The IRS may scrutinize or question long-standing activities that may not have previously been considered to pose any risk as well as any new activities adopted to increase efficiency or generate revenue that might be considered inconsistent with the organization's tax-exempt status or that the organization might not have reported properly as unrelated taxable business income.

State Attorneys General

At the state level, oversight and enforcement responsibility for charities and other exempt organizations tends to reside with the state attorney general. Actual enforcement authority varies from state to state. For instance, California and New York attorneys general have broad authority over nonprofits and enforcement actions against nonprofits are not uncommon. In many states, enforcement authority is more circumscribed. In many states, attorneys general have investigative and subpoena power to review possible wrongdoing in a nonprofit organization and the right to bring legal action, which may include, in serious cases, a petition to remove officers and board members. State attorneys general may also take legal action against a nonprofit organization or its board to obtain an accounting, to appoint a receiver or require dissolution, to redress or prevent negligent management or fraudulent use of assets, or to prevent use of assets in a manner inconsistent with designated charitable purposes unless approved by a court. In some states, prior approval of the state attorney general is required for certain transactions involving charitable funds or significant change in organization activities or structure.

State Annual Report Filings

Most states require corporations to file a report annually with the secretary of state or other official of the state in which the organization was formed (or in which a foreign corporation conducts business). This annual report typically lists the directors and officers, registered agent, and, in some cases, some minimal financial information. A nominal fee usually must be paid in connection with the filing. These annual filings are a prerequisite to obtaining a Certificate of Good Standing or Certificate of Existence from the state, a document that indicates that the organization is in existence, has complied with state organization formalities, is authorized to do business in the state, and has paid its state taxes. Certificates of Good Standing or Certificates of Existence are often required by banks and by other third parties in connection with banking and other major business transactions. Although the annual filing is not burdensome, failure to make the filing will prevent the issuance of a Certificate of Good Standing or Certificate of Existence and ultimately may result in termination of the right to do business in the state or involuntary dissolution. The process of achieving good standing after it has been lost may require the assistance of legal counsel and the payment of penalties.

Handling Crises

Advance Preparation. Boards play a role in overseeing and managing the handling of significant organizational crises. Such crises can erupt at any time, often when least expected. Crises may arise from various types of events, including the sudden death or departure of the Executive Officer; a fire or flood or other natural disaster affecting the organization or the entire area in which it operates; embezzlement or other financial impropriety; thefts of property; investigations by federal or state authorities; negative publicity as a result of any of the above; or loss of confidence in the organization arising out of its handling of a particular matter. From the board's perspective, the most important aspect of crisis management is how well the organization and the board itself are prepared to and actually deal with a crisis.

Effective Approaches. While there is no single best way to handle a crisis, there are a number of approaches that have proven to be effective components for reducing or controlling the impact of a crisis. These include:

- Reacting promptly as an organization, but not going beyond the known facts. If more information is needed, ensuring that a process is quickly established to gather the facts.

- In developing responses, erring on the side of transparency and openness.

- Limiting public comments, as much as possible, to a single spokesperson for the organization. The spokesperson might be the Executive Officer, the Board Chair, or a senior staff person, depending on the situation and the skill of the individual in dealing with media and the public. Regardless of the spokesperson designated, it is advisable to be prepared for either the Board Chair or the Executive Officer to be available and prepared to represent the organization with public comments or in press conferences.

- Identifying a main contact within the organization for staff and board members to obtain information from or to pass along information to. This would usually be the Executive Officer (unless, of course, the Executive Officer is a factor in the crisis).

- Making sure the board is fully aware of the problem and that each board member knows who will speak for the organization. If necessary, convene a special board meeting to review progress or problems in addressing the crisis.

- Cautioning board and staff members against speaking out on their own either publicly or off the record. The Board Chair may need to emphasize this with directors.

- Using outside advisors, such as legal counsel or a public relations firm, to advise the organization or the board, if the situation warrants.

- Conducting a board post mortem after the crisis concludes so that missteps and lessons learned can be used to improve how the next crisis is handled and procedures to minimize the likelihood of similar future crises can be implemented.

The Practical Advice Section of this Chapter has additional suggestions on handling crises. See pages 115–117.

Practical Advice on Dealing with Substantive Issues

Developing the Knowledge Base

A critical role of the Executive Officer and the Board Chair is to provide opportunities for directors to understand the nonprofit's organization and functions in sufficient depth to facilitate sound decision-making by the board. The following suggestions may help with this process:

- *Develop Background Materials.* Develop background materials on the activities of the organization that can be included in orientation materials for new board members and made available to current board members periodically.

- *Develop a Board-Only Website.* Develop a password-protected secure website (or section of the main website) just for board members containing general information on the organization and its activities; important documents such as the organization's mission statement, articles, bylaws, strategic plan, most recent Form 990, and committee charters and membership; biographical and contact information on board members and staff; board and committee meeting materials, including minutes and reports; and updated information from management about previously posted or distributed reports.

- *Schedule Mission-Related Presentations.* Schedule regular presentations to the board throughout the board year on various aspects of the organization's mission, business operations, and strategic plan.

- *Emphasize the Mission and Strategic Plan.* Tie all board presentations back to the mission of the organization and its strategic plan.

- *Visit Locations or Constituents.* Schedule visits by board members to various locations served by the organization or with various constituencies.

- *Introduce the Staff.* Arrange meetings between board members and senior staff.

- *Rotate Assignments.* Rotate committee assignments (with due regard to the benefit of individual experience in some areas) so that board members have an opportunity to work on different issues affecting the organization and with staff from different parts of the organization.

- *Suggest Reading Assignments.* Alert board members to articles and other publications that may provide insight into the area in which the organization operates.

- *Discuss the Competitive Environment.* Bring in outside experts or representatives from similar or competing organizations to talk with the board about the environment in which the organization operates.

- *Present Updated Information.* Provide regularly updated presentations on operations, financial resources, and the competitive environment to help ensure that new and existing board members have the same basic understanding of both.

Additional suggestions for the Executive Officer related to building the board's knowledge base are included below, under "The Mission."

The Mission

Build Understanding. Making sure that all directors and staff understand and support the organization's mission is an important function for both the Executive Officer and the Board Chair. Organizations that have been operating for a long time may find it necessary to reacquaint the board and staff with the mission, particularly during times of growth and periods of substantial staff or board turnover. Often organizations assume that board members and staff have a solid understanding of the mission and are surprised to find that this is not true.

Danger of Not Understanding. The danger of directors and staff not having a firm grasp on the organization's mission is that programs and priorities may drift away from the focus of the mission, or misunderstanding may develop on where resources should be deployed. Focus on mission-related issues in board and committee meetings may help prevent such misunderstandings and the inadvertent drift of programs and priorities away from the mission.

Questions to Consider. Considering questions such as the following may help determine whether the mission is adequately understood by the board and throughout the organization:

- Is there a mission statement and does it reflect the actual mission of the organization as it is now being performed?
- When was the mission last reviewed and reaffirmed or modified by the board?
- If the board and senior staff were asked to state the mission, unaided, would the answers be substantially the same, as well as reasonably close to the mission statement?
- Is discussion of the mission central in strategic planning?
- What actions might the organization take to make it easier for board members to understand and remember the mission so that it is kept in focus in board deliberations?

— Does each director have a copy of the mission statement?
— Does or should each board meeting start with some acknowledgement or discussion of the mission?
— Is the mission highlighted in board materials or within the board room or the building in which the organization operates?
— Is the mission incorporated into marketing materials?

Role of the Executive Officer. One of the Executive Officer's important responsibilities is to ensure that the board receives regular information about the organization's operations presented in a manner that facilitates the board's understanding of how the organization is fulfilling its mission—in short, by tying performance and all other information presented to the board to key elements of the mission, using measures approved by the board.

There are many ways in which the Executive Officer fulfills this responsibility. One important way is to develop and present historical trend information so the board can place current performance in context. Other methods of tying performance to accomplishment of key elements of the mission include:

- Arranging the organization of financial statements and other reports on operations in a way that highlights key revenues and expenses related to delivery of the mission;
- Aggregating key performance indicators from the organization's computer systems into easy to read and interpret charts and reports, sometimes referred to as "dashboards," which can be used to track multiple aspects of performance;
- Structuring summaries or cover letters accompanying material presented to the board so as to link performance or information to key aspects of the mission; and
- Arranging for onsite visits to locations where the organization's activities occur so board members have a chance to experience how the organization is delivering its services.

Another way in which an Executive Officer facilitates the board's understanding of how the organization is fulfilling its mission is through oversight of the preparation of the organization's annual Form 990 information return, including review and discussion of the Form with the board or a board committee in advance of filing. While others in the organization, such as the Chief Financial Officer, may take the lead in preparing the Form, the Executive Officer's role is to make sure not only that the Form presents an accurate description of the organization's activities, but that those activities are consistent with the organization's exempt purposes. This is a significant management function that requires constant attention, not just at the time of preparation of the Form. Tying regular board reports to the substance of what must be included in the Form 990 not only helps make the annual Form 990 review process easier but also may assist the board and the Executive Officer in keeping the organization focused on its mission and acting consistently with its tax-exempt purposes.

The Form 990 review process has become more important given the recent expansion of the Form 990.

Strategic Planning

Perhaps the most critical factor in successful strategic planning is the willingness of both board and staff to think creatively and strategically and not become overly concerned with process. The Executive Officer and Board Chair have leadership roles in keeping both board and staff focused on ideas, raising possibilities, asking questions, and suggesting alternatives.

Matters to Consider Before Getting Started. Prior to implementing a strategic planning process, it is important for the Board Chair and the Executive Officer to be sure that both the staff and board members recognize the importance of strategic planning to the organization. If either group is hesitant or dubious, the process is unlikely to be successful.

The Board Chair or other member of the board charged with the strategic planning process and the Executive Officer will also want to discuss what type of process is likely to be most effective in developing a strategic plan, given the composition of the board and the management team and the organization's resources. Who will lead the process? Will an outside facilitator help or hinder the process, and can the organization afford a facilitator's fee? Will committees be involved? How many meetings may be necessary? What data must be gathered? Will only board members and senior staff participate in the process, or will external constituents or lower level staff be included? What timeline seems feasible for development, review, and adoption of the plan?

In addition to the above considerations, the following questions and issues may help avoid pitfalls that can cause the strategic planning efforts to flounder:

- If the organization has previously engaged in strategic planning, how successful was the exercise, and what factors made it so, or kept it from being so?
  - What do participants in previous strategic planning processes have to say about those efforts? Being honest in evaluating any problems with past efforts can help minimize any problems with a new strategic planning effort.
- If the organization or the Executive Officer has never previously participated in a significant way in a strategic planning process, what resources are available to help educate the Executive Officer, staff, and the board about the strategic planning process?
  - Is there a board member or other volunteer who can educate the staff or the board, or who might donate the services of his or her company to assist with the strategic planning process?

- Is there affordable outside training or assistance available for the Executive Officer or other senior staff, such as, for example, consultants who could assist with the process?
- Is the need for strategic planning clear to both staff and the board? If not, what more is required to clarify the need?
  - Clarity of purpose is essential to a successful planning process.
- Should the work of developing a plan for board approval be primarily led by the staff, or by the board, or should it be a joint process?
  - The answer depends on many factors, but level of trust is a critical one. Does the board trust the staff? Does the staff trust the board? If trust is lacking, a joint planning process may have the best chance of success.
  - Does the staff have the expertise and the resources to develop key elements of a strategic plan for board consideration? If staff is inexperienced or lacks resources, board leadership of the process may be critical to success.
  - Are board members sufficiently knowledgeable about the organization and the environment in which it operates to provide constructive leadership in a planning process? If the board is inexperienced, staff leadership of the process may be essential.
  - Will certain individuals on the board or staff further the planning process or interfere with it? Use of a facilitator may be necessary to keep the process moving forward effectively.
- Is there a need for an outside consultant or facilitator to assist the board and the staff with their strategic thinking and to help with development of the plan or to lead discussion of the plan at the time it is presented for approval?
  - Use of outside consultants can be counterproductive if their credentials and professional style are not respected by those engaged in the process. Any facilitator selected will need a style that is compatible with that of the organization, its board, and its staff.
  - Once hired, if it becomes apparent that such compatibility does not exist, changing consultants or limiting their participation is advisable. It is rare for compatibility issues to resolve themselves in the course of the planning process. More often, such problems become a major hindrance to a successful process.
  - Outside consultants who lack familiarity with the organization may require considerable time to understand the organization well enough to be of real assistance in strategic planning.
- Is the time frame for strategic planning and creation of a plan consistent with the organization's skills and resources?
  - The fact that priorities may need to be changed in order for work on strategic planning to proceed is often overlooked.

- Can strategic planning be accommodated within the organization's existing budget, or is additional funding needed and if so, who will be responsible for obtaining such funding?
  — Grants are sometimes available to facilitate strategic planning processes.

Monitoring Execution after the Plan has been Approved. Once a strategic plan has been approved, it is important to consider how and by whom and how often implementation will be monitored. Possibilities include:

- Assigning monitoring to a board committee;
- Creating time on board agendas on a regular basis for reviewing progress on implementation of the plan;
- Creating objective criteria to measure performance towards the plan;
- Working to ensure that individual staff performance objectives and evaluations are tied to achieving various aspects of the plan; and
- Comparing and discussing current organizational performance and programs in light of plan priorities when information on performance or programs is presented to the board.

Financial Performance

Basic Issues. Directors need to understand the organization's sources of revenue, how stable these sources are, and the principal drivers of changes in revenues. They also need to understand the drivers of expenses and, in particular, how direct and indirect expenses are both allocated and interconnected. Numerical line items on financial statements generally do not make such important information clear, particularly to new board members.

Because many nonprofit board members will not be experts in finance or accounting, particularly accounting for nonprofits, they will also need information on major accounting principles and practices that affect how the nonprofit is required to account for revenues and expenses on its financial statements.

There are a number of ways to assist board members in understanding a nonprofit's financial statements and financial performance:

- *Orientation Presentations.* Hold a financial performance briefing/ educational seminar for new board members as part of an orientation program and include, in a form they can keep and refer to in the future, a written glossary of terms and concepts used by the organization in discussing financial performance and in creating financial statements. Provide explanations in lay terms of the various accounting standards that affect the organization's financial accounting and reporting.

- *Refresher Briefings.* Invite longer-term board members to attend orientation briefings on financial performance, or hold separate refresher briefings apart from board meetings, since many board members may find a refresher briefing a useful way for them to ask basic or more detailed questions they may not feel comfortable asking during board or committee meetings.

- *Presentations on Financial Accounting/Reporting at the Board.* Periodically (i.e., once a year, or every other year) have a presentation at the board (and similar, perhaps more detailed, presentations for the finance or similar committees) on financial accounting and other financial reporting issues that have the potential for significant effect on the organization (for example, requirements to adopt new accounting standards, or a recommendation by the management to change the organization's capital budgeting process).

- *Assume More Explanation is Needed.* Always assume that board members need more explanation and more information than the financial statements themselves provide:
  — Include an executive summary cover sheet with all financial statements, providing highlights of important issues or background explanations for major changes that appear on the financial statements;
  — Create a column on the financial statements for explanation of major changes (for example, changes up or down from prior statements, or from budget or forecasts, of more than $x or x% of the budget or prior forecast);
  — Compare performance to prior periods and provide trend information;
  — Provide forecast information so the board has a sense of how financial performance may change in the future;
  — Spend time at board meetings discussing the assumptions underlying financial statements and budgets and be up front about changes or problems with such assumptions;
  — Try to anticipate questions that board members are likely to have and include answers in the executive summary or a financial statement column highlighting changes, or as part of the oral discussion on financial performance;
  — Make statements easy to follow in discussions by numbering each column or row, as well as numbering all pages.

Beyond the Basics. Focusing the board's attention on high-level financial statement review is only one aspect of developing a complete picture of an organization's financial status and issues. Here are some other issues and actions to consider as part of financial statement reviews, or as part of other board or committee level discussions:

- *Balance Discussions of the Past and the Future.* Balance the time spent at board meetings on discussion of past performance as reflected in the financial statements, and anticipated performance in the future. It is important to make clear what past performance may or may not indicate about future performance.

- *Point Out "Shortcomings" or Problems that Might be Masked.* Take the time at board or committee meetings to discuss factors which, although accounted for correctly, may mask important issues of which the board should be aware—for example, a one-time major contribution to annual earnings that may mask an overall decline in contributions expected in the future, or price increases that may mask a trend in declining sales.

- *Highlight How the Organization Handles Issues That May Be Governance Hot Buttons or That Have Been Problems for Other Organizations.* Periodically surface potential "hot button" issues that are related to review of financial performance, but are not necessarily visible in the statements themselves—for example, the level of CEO pay (either alone or in comparison to pay of others in the organization); monitoring/management of expense accounts; reliance on a single service provider (such as an investment advisor); employee morale or turnover (which can be common at nonprofit organizations); and integrity of systems that provide information used in building the financial statements.

- *Educate the Board on Systems and Controls.* Make periodic presentations at board meetings or finance or audit committee meetings on the organization's financial accounting/reporting, budgeting, and internal control systems so the board understands these processes and any weaknesses that need to be addressed.

- *Discuss and Review Investment Policies.* Even if the board has an investment committee, periodically provide the full board with a presentation on the organization's investment policies and practices and how current investments comply with those policies. Consider engaging an independent investment expert or other consultant to assist the board in its review of the organization's policies and practices to help the board understand
  — The level of risk to the organization permitted/taken under current policies and procedures;
  — How risk might be mitigated, e.g., by diversification;
  — What specific risks have been assumed either because the risks are believed to be justified by the potential reward, or because they cannot practically be eliminated; and
  — How the organization's policies and practices compare to those of other comparably situated organizations, and to generally accepted investment policies and practices.

Fund-raising

Governance Implications. The governance implications of fund-raising and donor relationship management are varied, numerous, and dependent, in part, on whether management, the board, or an auxiliary organization, or some combination of the three, is responsible for soliciting donations and grants. When management is principally responsible for the fund-raising process, the board's involvement is one of oversight of those processes, including management of the risk associated with a sudden, substantial decline in donated funds. If some or all of the board is expected to be actively involved in fund-raising, board members become both fiduciary overseers of the process as well as participating donors, solicitors, relationship builders, and advocates, requiring careful attention to the differences in these roles. When auxiliary organizations handle or assist with fund-raising, either generally or in connection with special events, they may have their own boards or steering committees, sometime with substantial independent powers. The interaction between the auxiliary board or steering committee and the nonprofit organization's board often requires the attention of the Executive Officer and the Board Chair.

Because fund-raising takes many forms and may require different skills and processes to conduct as well as to monitor, boards often need ongoing education to stay current on fund-raising-related issues and complexities.

Types of Fund-raising. To create a board that is effective in its fund-raising as well as in oversight of fund-raising activities, Executive Officers and Board Chairs need to make sure that everyone on the board understands the various types of fund-raising that an organization is involved in, or may become involved in, and the governance implications of each.

- *Annual Fund Drives:* Many nonprofits have an annual fund-raising drive that helps support operations by raising large and small contributions from a variety of sources. The process of soliciting for the annual fund may take place over the entire period of an organization's fiscal year, or be concentrated at particular times of the year. Multiple or follow-up requests throughout the year are not uncommon, and with the advent of the Internet, it is fairly easy and inexpensive for organizations to have the capability to be continually soliciting and accepting donations. Many tax-exempt organizations expect board members to be directly involved in solicitation of annual fund gifts from major donors. They may also expect board members to be major contributors to the annual fund or to obtain funds equal to a specified amount from others (sometimes referred to as a "give or get" policy). A major role for Board Chairs and Executive Officers is to make sure that board members understand their role in the annual fund drive.

- *Special Events:* Although many organizations treat special fund-raising events, such as galas, auctions, raffles, etc., as something separate from their annual fund drives, these events often raise funds for annual operating support. These events also may be produced by auxiliary organizations, or by including other non-board member volunteers. Board members may be involved in leading these special fund-raising efforts or in finding community leaders to be involved and board members will almost certainly be expected to support such events with their presence as well as by donations. Board members may need to be educated about the importance of their participation.

- *Grants:* Many nonprofits actively seek funding in the form of grants from other nonprofits, governmental agencies, foundations, or corporations. These grants typically require an application from the nonprofit. Many organizations have grant writers on staff; others use the services of freelance writers. Producing a grant application may require the nonprofit to do considerable work, not only in articulating the basis for the request for funds, but also in articulating the organization's mission and strategy so as to be very clear how the grant will facilitate that mission. In addition, not all grants are budget-relieving, that is, they may be given for specific projects which the organization might be interested in, but may add further stress or require additional operational capacity to handle, without providing any funds for ongoing activities that also require monetary support. Finally, grants are typically for specified periods with no guarantee of renewal. Organizations that rely heavily on funding through grants need to avoid undue reliance on specific granting organizations.

  Developing alternative or multiple sources of funding helps protect against unexpected nonrenewals of long-standing grants that might substantially affect the organization's ability to function. Board Chairs and Executive Officers can help this process by periodically including presentations or discussion on the board agenda about the importance of grants to an organization's financial stability and soliciting board members' advice on potential new sources of donations.

  Many grant-making organizations also are interested in knowing about the board governance practices of applicants, another reason why board and management leadership will want to focus on effective governance. The level of individual board member financial support can also be a factor of importance to grant-making institutions.

- *Endowments and Capital Drives:* Larger nonprofits often fund raise to establish endowments—a more permanent aggregation of funds that can be invested so that earnings on the endowed funds are available to support ongoing operations or special programs. A capital or other special purpose campaign may be carried out to obtain funds to buy a building or land or to fund other needed long-term capital improvements. This type of fund-raising usually requires significant involvement of board members, both by way of major personal financial contributions and by active participation in cultivation and solicitation of donors. Boards often use the services of outside experts or consultants to help determine the feasibility of raising funds for endowments and capital campaigns. Executive Officers, heads of development, Board Chairs, and other directors frequently find they must spend considerable time working with such consultants. In addition, if board members have never participated in an endowment or capital campaign, the Executive Officer and Board Chair will need to make sure the board fully understands the process and the role of individual board members, including the level of personal donation that might be required of them, before the organization embarks on such a campaign.

- *Planned Giving Programs:* Under these programs, donors arrange to leave funds or other gifts (typically appreciated assets) to the organization at a specified time, frequently, but not always, upon the death of the donor. Occasionally, a donor makes a gift during his or her lifetime, but has the right to receive income for a specified period, or retains a life estate in the property. The complexities of planned giving often require the services of a bank or trust company or other consultant to help manage the program and legal counsel to review any arrangements reached with donors.

Legal and Accounting Issues. In addition to understanding the various ways that organizations raise funds, there are many legal and accounting issues related to fund-raising that boards and management also need to understand.

- *Acknowledgements.* Nonprofits are required by federal tax law to provide acknowledgements as well as certain disclosures and notices to donors, including information on benefits provided in return for the donation.

- *Federal Solicitation Law.* Federal law may prohibit certain activities as being misleading or fraudulent solicitations.

- *State and Local Solicitation Laws.* State and local laws also may affect the process or substance of solicitations for donations and may require the organization to register with a government agency, even for solicitation of funds over the Internet.

Appendix 7 has a summary of state charitable solicitation and registration requirements and forms.

- *Anti-Spam Laws.* Anti-spam laws may impact an organization's solicitation over the Internet. "Do not call" laws may affect an organization's ability to use telemarketing or reduce the effectiveness of this mechanism.

- *Noncash Contributions.* Noncash contributions (such as securities, art work, interests in property, historical writings, and the like) raise additional legal and accounting issues related to valuation and appraisal procedures and create a need for the board to adopt policies covering whether to keep or sell such items, and whether to accept donor restrictions on sales. The Form 990 requires additional disclosures regarding these contributions.

- *Accounting Requirements.* Planned gifts and pledges must be in writing and meet certain other criteria in order to be accounted for properly.

Educating and Reassuring the Board. Boards that raise funds need to feel assured that the organization's staff is competent to manage these types of matters. When board members are expected to solicit funds on behalf of the organization, they themselves also need to be competent fund-raisers. Executive Officers and Board Chairs typically have a major role to play in developing board member expertise in these areas.

Continually weaving fund-raising and donor relationship issues into board agendas as well as into new director orientations is a good way to educate the board and may also help ensure that board members with fund-raising and donor cultivation responsibilities understand that such responsibilities are integral to their individual duties as board members. There are a number of other practical steps that can help:

- *Be Explicit.* Be explicit about the financial expectations of board members and the role that the organization expects them to play in cultivating donors or in asking others to make contributions. In order to be explicit, the board will need to consider and agree upon such expectations. This can be a time-consuming process, as it often raises other issues related to board membership criteria or the role of the board or the effectiveness of the board or individual board members. However, being explicit on financial and fund-raising expectations helps avoid unpleasant surprises such as board members who are not prepared to make personal contributions at the level expected, or are not prepared to ask others for donations. Occasionally, there may be informal, unstated expectations which are greater for some members of the board (for example, those with substantial wealth or connections that might be utilized on behalf of the organization). The Board Chair and Executive Officer often play a role in making sure such differing expectations are raised with the board members in question.

- *Put Expectations in Writing.* Consider creating a written document that can be distributed to prospective and current board members specifying the personal financial contribution and fund-raising expectations for board members. This helps avoid the problem of individuals saying or hearing different things when talking about board membership requirements or expectations. While such a document can be helpful, care needs to be taken that it does not appear to imply that board membership can be "bought" by means of donated or solicited funds. Board members are fiduciaries with obligations that extend well beyond donation or solicitation of funds. For these reasons, it is important that any list of board member expectations extend beyond just those that are financial and fund-raising-related.

- *Obtain Board Approval.* Obtain board approval of any written document spelling out financial contribution and fund-raising expectations. Board approval reinforces the importance of financial contributions and fund-raising and each subsequent reapproval or amendment provides further reinforcement.

- *Personalize Requests.* Personalize all requests for donations from board members. Keep track of all types of contributions a board member makes, financial as well as nonfinancial, and acknowledge their total level of support to the organization every time financial support is requested. Tracking all types of contributions not only helps make board members feel valued, but also helps minimize the possibility that they may feel the organization is only interested in them for their financial donations.

- *Emphasize in Orientation Materials.* In board orientation materials, emphasize the organization's fund-raising process and structure and the board's role in fund-raising. Remind board members that donations are never assured and must be continually earned by hard work of the board and the organization.

- *Offer Training and Education.* Provide board members with a variety of opportunities for education and training in donor cultivation and so-licitation and the importance of fund-raising to the organization. Not all board members are intuitively good at fund-raising and donor cultivation and many will not have a good grasp of everything that is encompassed within the process of "development" (the common organizational title for fund-raising/donor cultivation). Even those with fund-raising skills may need training in effective communication of organizational priorities and messaging and/or changing priorities and interests of donors. Ways to provide training include:
  — Formal sessions apart from board meetings, which may be particularly helpful for those who are new to fund-raising or donor cultivation;
  — Regular reminders, explanations, and suggestions at board and com-mittee meetings, or in board or committee materials;
  — Sharing success stories involving members of the board who have been actively participating in donor solicitation or cultivation;
  — Sharing lessons learned so everyone on the board has the benefit of un-derstanding particular circumstances which are best avoided and the fact that the fund-raising process does not always run smoothly or as expected; and
  — Reviewing fund accounting and the requirements for managing and adhering to restrictions on donations. This helps increase director un-derstanding of these issues when reviewing the organization's finan-cial performance and also provides information on how such issues may specifically relate to the process of solicitation or cultivation. To a volunteer board filled with individuals who do not work daily with the intricacies of fund accounting or management of endowments or

restricted funds, these concepts may need considerable ongoing reinforcement and explanation.

Facilitating Board Efforts. Another important way to help boards with fund-raising efforts is by making cultivation or solicitation assignments clear and logistically easy for board members. Because asking others for money is not easy for many people, making it as painless as possible often helps. For example:

- *Ask Staff to Draft Letters.* The Executive Officer can prepare, or have staff prepare, drafts of solicitation and thank you letters that board members can personalize as appropriate, rather than simply asking board members to create their own letters from scratch.

- *Provide Background Information.* The Executive Officer, staff, or a board member who knows the potential donor can provide background briefings to board members on the individuals they are expected to cultivate or solicit; the Internet can sometimes be a useful tool for finding out information on individuals.

- *Suggest Topics of Interest.* The Executive Officer, staff, or board members experienced in donor cultivation efforts can suggest topics or issues that might be of interest (or perhaps should be avoided) when talking to particular donors or donors in general.

- *Track Information.* The Executive Officer, staff, or a designated board member can follow up with board members after their interactions with donors and keep records of information gleaned in such interactions. Debriefing, whether with staff or a designated board member, is an important way to keep track of donor reactions and interests and such tracking need not require a computer data base; simple file notes that can be shared with board members can also be helpful.

- *Use Staff to Arrange Appointments.* Rather than provide general exhortations to "cultivate" donors, the Executive Officer, staff, or a designated board member can help arrange meetings or events involving board members and donors and make clear to the board members being asked to participate exactly what they are expected to do at such meetings or events.

- *Accompany Inexperienced Board Members.* The Executive Officer, staff, or an experienced board member can accompany board members who are less experienced on fund-raising calls.

- *Tailor Assignments to Individual Strengths.* As the Executive Officer and staff get to know board members, they can steer them to assignments that fit their individual strengths.

- *Seek Board Members with Cultivation Experience.* The Board Chair and Executive Officer can work closely with the nominating committee to source new board members who may have experience in cultivation and fund-raising and need less training and personal attention to carry out these tasks.

Use of Affiliate Fund-Raising Organizations. Sometimes nonprofit organizations create legally separate organizations to raise contributed funds. Such organizations may relieve the board and staff of the nonprofit organization of many time-consuming fund-raising tasks. Individuals who enjoy and are skilled or interested in fund-raising are often willing to join an affiliated fund-raising organization that enables them to put their talents to work in this area but does not require them to participate in other mission-related activities or to assume other responsibilities. In addition, an affiliated fund-raising organization may become a potential source of board member candidates for the nonprofit, as the individuals on the board of such organizations, or otherwise working with such organizations, often become devoted advocates of the nonprofit organization and their skills can be closely observed as they work on fund-raising. These affiliated fund-raising organizations sometime are referred to as auxiliary organizations.

From a governance perspective, there are three major issues to keep in mind in using these affiliated organizations:

- The use of a separate organization creates additional governance responsibilities since the other organization will require a separate board and at least some separately dedicated staff;
- Control of the affiliated organization becomes important if it holds significant assets; and
- A separate organization also means another set of relationships for the Executive Officer and the Board Chair to manage.

Performance Evaluations for the Executive Officer

Performance evaluation processes vary among organizations and can be adapted to organizational needs and culture.

Key Elements for a Successful Evaluation Process. Successful evaluation processes usually:

- Establish a time frame for formal written performance appraisals;
- Are based on goals and objectives that have been agreed upon in advance by the employee and manager and which reflect the organization's needs in light of current circumstances;
- Reflect actual performance of the individual;
- Recognize and reward achievements;
- Identify areas for improvement and spell out specific actions expected to address areas identified for improvement;

- Provide the opportunity for respectful give and take between the reviewer and the employee and constructive feedback;
- Encourage periodic discussions on performance between formal evaluations, particularly for employees struggling with performance issues; and
- Have consequences that are implemented consistently by the organization (e.g., promotion, increase in responsibility, growth/training opportunities, salary increases/bonuses and/or nonmonetary recognition in the case of strong performance, or alternatively, in the case of poor performance, change in responsibilities, reduction or no increase in salary, or termination).

These factors are applicable to performance evaluations for employees generally as well as for the Executive Officer.

Development and Delivery of Evaluations. Actual development and delivery of an evaluation for the Executive Officer may take several forms. Responsibility for the process generally rests with the Board Chair, but may also be undertaken by the chair of a committee which has been assigned responsibility for the evaluation process.

For those who have not previously been involved in performance evaluations, the suggestions below, which are important elements of any performance evaluation process, may be helpful.

- *Agree on Goals.* Specific performance goals are developed, documented, and agreed upon, typically after consultation with the board or a committee of the board. In some organizations, the Board Chair drafts the initial performance goals for the year (or longer period) for the Executive Officer, based on his or her experience in working with the Executive Officer and input from the full board or a board committee. In others, the Executive Officer drafts initial performance goals, discusses them with the Chair and the board or a board committee, and then the Executive Officer and the Board Chair finalize the objectives. Either approach is workable as long as both the Executive Officer and the Board Chair are involved in setting the goals. It is also important that goals be prioritized and limited to a reasonable number, and when possible, measurable against criteria also established by the Board Chair and the Executive Officer.

- *Review Progress During the Year.* Progress in meeting the goals is reviewed by the Chair with the Executive Officer periodically during the year and, if needed, goals are adjusted depending on organizational circumstances. While interim meetings are particularly important if there are concerns about the Executive Officer's performance, they can also be useful when there are no such concerns. Regular interim reviews or conversations help keep the Executive Officer and the Board Chair focused on priorities and on accomplishments or problems that surface during the year.

- ***Prepare Draft Evaluation.*** Near or following the end of the performance evaluation period, the Board Chair drafts a written performance review, usually after requesting input from other board members. The draft evaluation may be shared with a committee of the board prior to finalizing it for delivery to the Executive Officer. In some organizations, the Executive Officer may be asked to draft his or her own self-evaluation, which may serve as the basis of the final evaluation or as an addendum to one drafted by the Board Chair. Regardless of who prepares the initial draft, it is important that accomplishments as well as any failures or concerns be highlighted and that the language used be respectful.

- ***Meet with the Executive Officer.*** The Board Chair, alone or with one or more senior board members, meets with the Executive Officer to review the evaluation. As with the written evaluation itself, it is important for the discussion to be respectful, to focus on accomplishments as well as shortcomings, and to highlight goals and expectations for the future, including discussion of resources and support needed by the Executive Officer to accomplish the goals and meet expectations.

- ***Discuss and Clarify.*** The Executive Officer may ask for clarification or express disagreement with certain aspects of the evaluation, which perhaps may require reconsideration of aspects of the evaluation, or the need to provide the Executive Officer the opportunity to note his or her disagreements, concerns, or explanations in writing.

- ***Sign the Evaluation.*** The Executive Officer and Board Chair both sign the evaluation, and it is filed in the Executive Officer's personnel file or, if desired in order to maintain greater confidentiality, in a separate file held by the Chair. If the Board Chair holds the file, the file will need to be transferred to the new Board Chair when he or she takes office.

- ***Report Results.*** The Board Chair shares the results of the meeting and the evaluation with the full board or a board committee in executive session, reminding all participants of the importance of maintaining the confidentiality of the evaluation as well as the Board Chair's report to the board or committee.

- ***Agree on New Goals.*** The goal-setting process begins again, unless new objectives were already developed in the course of finalizing the performance review and agreed upon during discussion of the prior year's evaluation.

Terminating the Executive Officer

Terminating an Executive Officer, or any other senior officer, can be difficult and unsettling, especially if the individual is the founder or has been a long-term employee. A number of things may be helpful to keep in mind regardless of the actual circumstances of any termination:

Role of Counsel. Engaging counsel as soon as termination appears advisable or necessary is one of the best ways to help prevent or minimize legal complications. Counsel can assist the board and the Board Chair in many ways, including:

- Reviewing the legal issues the organization may face in connection with the proposed termination;
- Recommending actions the organization might take to reduce potential legal problems;
- Serving as an intermediary between the Board Chair and the Executive Officer if there are personal animosities or difficulties;
- Providing advice on common terms of severance or termination agreements;
- Assisting with negotiation of a termination agreement;
- Drafting an agreement and release; and
- Helping to manage communication with external (and maybe internal) constituencies.

Not all of these forms of assistance may be needed. The relationship with counsel can be structured to fit the circumstances.

Role of the Chair. The Board Chair generally is the director responsible for addressing the issues associated with the termination of the Executive Officer. The Chair's handling of the termination may have a significant effect on how the organization weathers a change in executive leadership.

- *Sharing Opinions and Listening.* Because the Chair usually works closely with the Executive Officer, he or she typically understands the Executive Officer's strengths and weaknesses better than most other board members and will have a strong sense of whether the individual is the right person to continue to lead the organization. Sharing such knowledge and opinion with the full board or an appropriate board committee is an important governance function of the Chair. Executive sessions of the board can be used for such discussions and have the benefit of allowing the Chair to listen to opinions about the Executive Officer from other board members.

- *Confronting Performance Issues.* Confronting poor performance issues of the Executive Officer or addressing the fact that an individual does not have the skills needed to lead the organization is a critical Board Chair function. Performance or skill problems would normally be addressed first in the Executive Officer's performance review. However, the Chair is also responsible for apprising the board of the Executive Officer's progress in addressing performance issues and for alerting the board to problems that may arise which may not have been covered in previous performance reviews. When the Chair fails to confront performance problems, or to share with the board his or her concerns about the Executive Officer's leadership, it is a governance failure that may not only delay needed changes, but also make such changes much harder to implement in the future.

- *Taking Charge.* When termination appears to be necessary, the Chair is usually the board member who presents the matter to the board or a board committee for discussion and ultimate approval and who helps shape the terms of the termination arrangement based on his or her knowledge of the organization's needs and the circumstances.

- *Delivering the Message.* The Chair is typically the board member responsible for meeting with the Executive Officer to inform him or her of the board's decision on termination. Particularly in difficult or contested terminations, it may be useful to have a written script for the meeting; a script can help the Chair stay focused on the key points to be made, and avoid diversions into less relevant issues. It may also be advisable to have counsel or an additional member of the board present, so that there is a witness to the discussion.

- *Exercising Judgment.* Sometimes circumstances arise which present the Chair with the opportunity or necessity to suggest resignation or retirement to the Executive Officer prior to having the approval of the board. This places the Chair in the difficult position of having to use his or her own judgment in negotiating with the Executive Officer and in deciding when to bring the matter to the board for approval or ratification. With rare exceptions, acting without prior consultation with counsel and at least some key board members on such a critical matter is inadvisable and best avoided.

- *Working with Counsel.* The Chair typically works directly with attorneys in negotiating any termination agreement.

- *Acting as Spokesperson.* The Chair may serve as the organization's spokesperson if it becomes necessary to discuss the termination with the press or major funders or other constituents.

- *Interim Management Leadership.* In connection with any termination of the Executive Officer, the board will need to consider appointment of an Interim Executive Officer. Sometimes the choice will be apparent from within the management ranks, but in other cases there may not be anyone in management who has the skills to assume the responsibility. Unless other arrangements can be made quickly, the Chair may need to act as the Interim Executive Officer for a period of time.

Compensation of the Executive Officer

Establishing the Executive Officer's compensation is a complex process, especially because of IRS procedures for documenting the reasonableness of compensation, public concern with the level of compensation for executives generally, the possible difficulty of obtaining comparative compensation information, and possible media attention.

Questions to Consider. The following questions may help in reviewing and establishing appropriate compensation of an Executive Officer:

- What skills are desirable or required?
- What level of pay is competitive for the needed or required skill set? (Large nonprofits may survey for-profit organizations as well as nonprofits, although some commentators question whether for-profit compensation levels are relevant or appropriate for the nonprofit sector.)
- What benefits and other nonmonetary perquisites are commonly offered or are expected by executives in similar positions, and are these perquisites important to the particular candidate or employee or are other factors of greater importance?
- How much can the organization afford and what combination of salary and perquisites or other nonmonetary benefits fit the organization's culture?
- How will the size of the total compensation and benefits package provided to the Executive Officer affect compensation, perquisites, and other benefits for the rest of the organization?
- Will the size of the total compensation and benefits package provided to the Executive Officer cause embarrassment to the organization as being much higher or lower than compensation and benefits packages of similar organizations or the level of expectation of the organization's other senior staff, supporters, and other constituencies?
- In light of the answers to the above questions, how realistic are the organization's expectations? How appropriate is the level of compensation being paid or proposed to be paid? Are there any adjustments to expectations, job descriptions, organizational structure, or mission that might be necessary?
- Is a portion of Executive Officer compensation tied to performance, and if so, what are the performance standards that are to be considered?
- What is the Executive Officer's level of performance with reference to the performance standards set by the board?
- Does the level of compensation reflect the level of performance?

Outside Consultants. Answers to some of the questions may require the services of an outside consultant who is a human resources or compensation specialist. A great deal of information can also be gathered on the Internet, although the most current data may not be available. Informal or formal compensation surveys of similar organizations can also be helpful.

Role of the Board and the Executive Officer. Whether or not consultants are used or surveys conducted, the real work in setting and managing Executive Officer compensation is done by the board or a board committee assessing organizational needs and the Executive Officer's skill sets and his or her performance in relation to stated needs. The Executive Officer's job is to make sure the board is provided with the facts needed to facilitate those deliberations.

Board or Committee Approval. Once a compensation package has been proposed for the Executive Officer, the governance trend is for the board or a committee of the board to specifically approve the compensation package and to document in minutes the process used to determine the level of compensation, including the use of objective, third-party information. This approval process helps the board or a designated board committee meet the "rebuttable presumption of reasonableness" established by the IRS, and meeting the requirements for this presumption helps a nonprofit defend itself from a later challenge that the Executive Officer's compensation is excessive.

Risk Management and Disaster Planning

Risk Management. In evaluating a nonprofit's risk management, it is important to consider both insurable and uninsurable risks and the organization's ability to mitigate risk at reasonable cost and with reasonable effort. Consideration of the following types of questions may be helpful:

Insurable Risks

- Does the organization have adequate insurance for its insurable risks?
- For those risks for which insurance is available but very expensive, is it reasonable for the organization to forego such insurance or to accept a substantial deductible? Could the organization afford to pay for a loss arising from such risks? Can such risks be mitigated?
- What steps is the organization already taking to mitigate the most common types of insurable risks including:
  — Property loss;
  — Personal injury loss;
  — Theft or defalcation or other illegal activity; and
  — Employee claims.
- What procedures does the organization have in place to reduce potential liability risks from claims of employee or vendor fraud or other wrongdoing or violation of law which might be raised by employees, recipients of the organization's goods or services, or the IRS or other regulatory bodies?

Uninsurable Risks

- What steps is the organization taking to mitigate or anticipate uninsurable risks such as:
  — Loss of funding from a major supporter of the organization;
  — "Mission creep" that results in fragmented and ineffective use of organizational resources;
  — Technological or scientific breakthroughs that eliminate or reduce the need for the organization's services; or
  — A change in government policy or public sentiment or need or expectations affecting delivery of the nonprofit's services in accordance with its mission.

Disaster Planning. In preparing an organization to cope with disaster, there are many publications and websites with helpful information on disaster planning. There is no single plan that is appropriate for all organizations. Key elements of a good disaster plan include the following:

- *Broad Scope.* The plan takes into account a wide variety of possible disaster scenarios.

- *Wide Involvement.* The plan involves a number of people throughout the organization considering not only what might happen, but also how to address a problem should it arise and to minimize the possibility of a problem arising.

- *Flexibility.* The plan has sufficient flexibility to allow for on-the-spot decision-making by people at the scene when those normally in charge are not available or when circumstances render the plan unworkable.

- *Constituencies.* The plan considers the potential effect on external as well as internal constituencies.

- *Mock Training Exercises.* The plan is tested and retested in mock disaster training exercises.

- *Accessible.* The plan is accessible to employees and, as appropriate, to board members in a variety of forms (online, hard copy, detailed, and summary versions).

- *Updated.* The plan is updated periodically, particularly after an actual disaster, to include any modifications required by experience.

- **The plan is tested again, and again, and again.**

Emergency Bylaws. Because the advent of cell phone and wireless technology has improved the ability to communicate in major disasters, the need for emergency bylaws may be less critical than in the past for many organizations. But organizations that operate in areas such as healthcare or disaster relief, or that have large boards which may complicate obtaining a quorum in disaster situations, may still find it helpful to adopt emergency bylaw provisions specifying how governance decisions may be made in such emergency circumstances. Since the nature and extent of an emergency cannot be predicted in advance, a critical feature of emergency bylaws is to provide flexibility to adapt procedures as circumstances may require. For example,

- **Definition of Emergency.** Emergency is typically defined as some sort of catastrophic event in which normal conduct of business is impossible. State law may define what constitutes an emergency so it is important to consult state law as well as counsel in crafting a definition to be included in emergency bylaws.

- **Quorum for Board Business.** Emergency bylaws often reduce the quorum to conduct board business to a lower level, for example 33 percent of the board rather than 51 percent. Alternatively, they may delegate additional authority to an organization's Executive Committee to act in place of the full board in an emergency. They may also specify that if it is impossible or impracticable to obtain even the reduced quorum, or for the Executive Committee to act, then any member of the board (perhaps acting with one or more board members or the Executive Officer or other senior staff member) may be authorized to take action on behalf of the organization.

- **Acting Executive Officer, Board Chair, and Others.** Emergency bylaws often specify a mechanism for someone to be designated Executive Officer or Board Chair if either becomes incapacitated or otherwise unavailable during an emergency, and for other individuals to be appointed as officers or board members in such circumstances.

- **When Emergency Provisions No Longer Needed.** Emergency bylaws are intended only to apply during an emergency as defined. But it may be helpful to include provisions that make it possible to specifically terminate the special powers granted to individuals or the other special provisions that may become applicable in an emergency. For example, the bylaws may specify that reduced quorum requirements cease once a quorum of the full board becomes available.

These sorts of provisions not only enable an organization to continue to function during an emergency, but also help protect those acting on behalf of the organization from liability based on later claims of unauthorized actions during an emergency.

Appendix 12 has a sample emergency bylaw provision.

Critical Relationships

Critical relationships are often taken for granted. In many cases, such relationships are of long standing and with organizations and others the nonprofit considers sympathetic and supportive of its mission. A nonprofit may assume that certain critical relationships are part of the fabric of its operations. However, major suppliers, contractors, lessors, donors, foundations, government agencies, and others with whom the organization may have significant relationships can and sometimes do change their focus abruptly, regardless of how important the mission of the nonprofit may be or how long the relationship has existed. For example, a grant-making organization which has routinely provided operating funds to well-established organizations may decide it will only provide such funds to help new organizations begin operations. Grants from government agencies can stop suddenly if newly elected legislators or executives have different policy objectives or if the granting agency is subject to across-the-board budget cuts. To help prevent a crisis situation should such a change occur, and to help determine whether the board should be reviewing certain of an organization's critical relationships, it may be helpful to consider the following types of questions:

- Have the organization's critical relationships all been identified?
- Who in the organization is responsible for managing these relationships?
- If one or more of these relationships were to terminate, what would be the effect on the organization?
- How might the effect on the organization be mitigated in the event of a loss of such a relationship?
- Is the risk of possible loss of such relationships being monitored as part of the organization's risk management programs?
- Does the board understand and has it considered the importance of such relationships to the organization?
- Should monitoring these relationships be the responsibility of a board committee?

Compliance

Role of the Board. The board's compliance oversight role is to assure that adequate controls are in place to promptly identify and address any compliance issues and to avoid compliance issues from arising in the first place. Some governance experts have expressed concern that board compliance oversight efforts may tend to take valuable time away from other important work of the board. Board Chairs and Executive Officers have the responsibility to help assure a proper balance in the board's focus.

The following suggestions may assist in assessing whether compliance oversight is appropriate:

- *Self-Audits.* Conduct a self-audit which considers the nature and extent of the compliance issues in each part of the organization, how such issues are identified and managed, and whether and how compliance efforts are supported.

- *External Risk Assessments.* Consider engaging an expert to conduct a general risk assessment to identify material organizational compliance risks.

- *Internal Compliance Function.* Consider whether establishing an internal compliance function or, in smaller organizations, appointing a senior employee as compliance officer, might help improve compliance efforts.

- *Committee Oversight.* Discuss whether the board's compliance oversight can be effectively handled by the finance or audit committee, or whether a separate compliance committee might be warranted.

- *Compliance Expertise on the Board.* Consider whether the board has members with compliance expertise who might be helpful to the organization, either as members of a committee charged with compliance oversight or as advisors to management on establishing effective compliance efforts. If such expertise is not currently available on the board, consider what resources the organization might access to provide guidance to the board, a board committee, or senior management on compliance issues.

- *Reporting to the Board.* Determine whether written reports to the board highlight compliance issues and efforts as a matter of course, and provide sufficient detail to allow the organization to engage in appropriate oversight without overwhelming the board with operational detail.

Advocacy and Lobbying

Questions to Consider. Focusing on the following questions may be useful for nonprofit management and boards when contemplating engagement in public policy advocacy, or in reviewing the efficacy of already existing activities:

- How do current laws, regulations, and government funding decisions affect the organization's mission-related work and the people whom the organization serves?
- What goals, policies, laws, regulations, and funding priorities would the organization want various governmental entities to adopt or change?
- What changes to existing laws and regulations or policies might help or harm the organization's mission, and are any such changes likely?

- What are the potential benefits to the organization of engaging in advocacy activities?
- What are the potential risks to the organization of engaging in such activities?
- Does the organization risk alienating key supporters or other constituents if it engages in advocacy or lobbying on a specific issue or is perceived as too closely aligned with a particular political faction or perspective?
- What types of advocacy activities do management and the board support or recommend (e.g., research; analysis and dissemination of educational materials on major policy issues; direct or grassroots lobbying on legislation; public initiatives or propositions; political appointees; interaction with elected officials on regulations or legislation)?
- What resources would be needed for the organization to engage in such activities and how would allocation of resources to these efforts affect resources allocated to other mission-related activities?
- Who in the organization would be responsible for/manage these activities?
- Are there other organizations, such as trade associations, that might do the job better, or with which this organization can ally itself to increase the effectiveness of its efforts?
- What tax consequences might there be if the organization engages in lobbying (e.g., private foundations may be subject to excise taxes on lobbying expenditures)?
- Should the organization consider making a Section 501(h) election? Should the organization use other mechanisms to assure that its lobbying activities do not constitute a substantial part of its overall activities? What does tax counsel advise?
- What level of internal staffing as well as board involvement or guidance would be needed on a regular basis to monitor these activities?
- What level of reporting to the board on advocacy activities is necessary and appropriate?

Information Management, Technology, and Records

Information Management. The development of information systems and policies is a management function. However, because effectiveness in information management is becoming more critical to operations, boards are increasingly interested in how the organization manages information and uses technology. There are a number of useful questions which Board Chairs (or other board members) and Executive Officers may ask to help determine whether an organization's information management systems and policies are effective or are in need of attention.

- With respect to information that the board receives:
  - How easily is the information understood by all members of the board?
  - Is the information focused on major issues and does it provide information on trends in key areas?
  - Does the information cover both good and bad news?
  - Is the information presented consistently over time?
  - Can changes to previously supplied information be tracked easily and are any such changes explained?
  - Are management explanations clear, plausible, and supported by facts and circumstances?
  - Does the information received by the board facilitate discussion of the future of the organization or only its past?
  - Does the information provide the board the data necessary to make strategic decisions and exercise its oversight function effectively?
  - Is information furnished in a timely manner?
  - Does the organization maintain a board "intranet" site, with access to the site controlled by use of a password, which can be used to post financial information, board material, notices, and other board documents, and to maintain and update information needed by board members?
- With respect to information used by management:
  - What is the culture in the organization with respect to information sharing and analysis (e.g., bottom up, top down, bias for openness, bias for limited access, or only if there is a need to know) and is the culture appropriate for the organization?
  - Does the organization have and follow clear guidelines for retention or destruction of information and do such guidelines incorporate legal requirements for retention of certain records and other documents that might pertain to current or anticipated lawsuits or investigations?
  - How is information most often shared/analyzed within the organization?
  - Is there an organizational system as to how to file information, including whether to retain hard copies or use online storage, which employees understand and are expected to adhere to? Is the system enforced?
  - How is information most often stored, and are storage costs reasonable?
  - Does the technology used to develop, analyze, store, and share information support organizational needs as well as organizational realities?
  - Does the organization have an "intranet" for management, with access to the site controlled by use of a password, which can be used to post financial information and other important information which is useful to share among managers?
- With respect to the overall process of information management:
  - Whose responsibility is it?

— What is the scope of the job (or jobs)?

— How are information management policies and practices coordinated throughout the organization?

— How is access to data controlled within the organization?

— How safe are the organization's computers and other electronic systems from hackers, viruses, or systems failures?

— What policies and procedures does the organization have that relate to information management?

- Is there a privacy policy to protect confidential information?

- Is there a records management (retention and destruction) policy?

- Are there data protection policies and procedures (in case of computer systems failure, fire, flood, or other catastrophic events)?

- Do information management policies cover electronic data, including e-mail and the organization's website?

- Is the organization in compliance with anti-spam laws?

- Are there policies against personal or improper use of organizational information or systems?

- How are policies and procedures communicated to employees and others throughout the organization?

— How are information management policies monitored, enforced, and updated to meet new legal or organizational requirements?

Technology. With respect to technological hardware and software, Board Chairs and Executive Officers may have meaningful influence on an organization's use of technology by working to develop the organization's capacity to embrace technology and understand the impact of technological change. The questions below may prove useful in starting this process. These questions might be used simply as the basis for discussion with staff or as a basis for discussion at one or more regular board meetings, or as part of meetings devoted to long-term planning. While these questions do not specifically address the issue of cost, when technological issues are seen as integral to the mission of the organization, technology becomes one of the many issues requiring prioritization. Spending dollars on technology without such prioritization frequently leads to erratic decision-making and dissatisfaction with the end result.

- What is available in technology that is now affecting or might in the future affect the organization?

- How are insights on the effect of technology on the organization shared and addressed?

- For what purpose(s) and how does the organization currently use technology?

- How do the organization's competitors use technology?

- What aspects of current technology are critical to the organization's successful delivery of its mission?

- How might changes in use of technology assist fulfillment of the organization's mission?

- How are technology and technological issues built into the strategic planning process, or should they be?
- What do the actual users of technology in the organization say about how the organization:
  — Currently uses technology?
  — Might use technology?
  — May be affected by technological change?
- When changes in technology are contemplated:
  — Are changes user-driven or technology-driven?
  — Who has input into or can initiate technology changes?
  — Who has final decision-making authority over technology changes?
  — How are priorities established or adjusted?
  — How might changes in one area affect users in other areas of the organization?
  — How is information about changes shared?
  — How is success measured?
- Does or can the organization share technological resources or ideas with other entities or groups?
- What technological changes might increase program effectiveness?
- Does the organization provide online donation opportunities for supporters?
- Does the organization have guidelines for staff use of the Internet on organization time or covering employee uses of organization information or discussion about the organization in blogs and social networking sites?
- Has the organization ever had a review of its use of technology:
  — In comparison to how others use similar technology?
  — In comparison to what is currently available?
  — In comparison to foreseeable changes in technology?
  — In terms that are meaningful and understandable to the nonprofit staff?

And, if not, should it?

- Is any board member able to offer, or to connect the organization to, technological assistance (training, tech-savvy volunteers, expanded knowledge, brainstorming about technological change)?
- Are users of the organization's systems and technology trained in their use and are such systems and technology designed with the users' needs and skills in mind?

Records Management and Records Retention. Records management is a part of an organization's information management system. It deals with the inventory, categorization, access, protection, retention, and destruction of records, whether paper or electronic. Records management systems are useful in assisting organizations with accessing information effectively and for purging information that is no longer useful. There are also important legal reasons for establishing and maintaining an effective records management function.

Records management for nonprofits acquired new importance in light of the requirements of Sarbanes-Oxley in 2002. This law makes it a crime for any organization to intentionally alter, falsify, or destroy records related to a federal investigation. "Record" is defined broadly by Sarbanes-Oxley and covers records contained in e-mail and other electronic forms, which increases the complexity of tracking, storage, and retrieval systems that are needed in connection with records management. Not all information is considered a "record." Therefore, clear guidelines need to be established to help staff distinguish between records that need to be retained for specified periods and other information that does not need to be retained. Other federal, state, and local laws also set forth requirements for the production and preservation of documents in actual and anticipated investigations and litigation.

Developing a records management system is usually considered a management function. However, Sarbanes-Oxley and other laws and standards have made the existence and management of such a system a matter for board concern. Many boards have adopted policies, or required management to adopt policies, specifically addressing document retention obligations both in general and in connection with lawsuits and investigations.

Because such policies can be effective only if there is a system for identifying and accessing records throughout the organization, such policies may contain specific details on the records management system of the entire organization.

Appendix 13 has a sample short form record retention and destruction policy.

Following is a checklist which can be used to assist in starting to create a records management system or for evaluating an existing system.

- ***Make Someone Responsible.*** Appoint someone to be responsible overall for records management in the organization and appoint others within various departments to be responsible for records management issues within each department.

- ***Define Record.*** Depending on the law or circumstances, a "record" may be broadly defined to mean any business information. Records may be contained in electronic form (such as e-mail, word processing, or other computer documents, and computer programs) as well as in paper documents. The definition includes information held in personal files as well as organizational files. Any document retention system will need to address all records, in whatever medium they reside.

- ***Inventory records throughout the organization.***
  — What records exist?

— Where and how are they kept?
— How old are they and are they active or inactive?
— In what medium are they kept? (paper, electronic)?
— How long are they kept under current practices?

- *Categorize Records by Importance or Type.* For example,
  — **Vital Records:** Those essential to the survival of the organization and which, in case of disaster or interruption of operations, allow it to carry on critical services and functions;
  — **Legal Records:** Corporate documents such as articles of incorporation, bylaws, board minutes, contracts of all sorts, audit reports, and other records that may support the organization's actions in legal disputes; and
  — **Operational Records:** Official financial statements and accounting records, customer information and donor information, internal memoranda, policies and procedures, communications with vendors or other constituents, and other records that relate to day-to-day operations.

- *Set up filing systems that readily identify documents by appropriate category.*

- *Determine how long each type of record needs to be retained to meet legal and operational requirements.*
  — Retention times for certain records may be specified by federal law; other record retention periods may be governed by state law.
  — Different types of organizations may have different needs with respect to retention or protection of information. For example, hospitals have very different needs to retain and protect information than arts organizations, although both need information management systems.

- *Determine what records or other information constitute personal information of the organization's donors, patients, or patrons.* To avoid liability for inadvertent disclosure of personal information, nonprofits must assure adequate protection mechanisms are in place for donor, patient, and patron identifying information.

- *Determine if it is necessary to preserve software and/or hardware in order to access certain data when computer systems change.* Consider whether it may be more economical to simply save paper copies of records which are likely to be kept for decades.

- *Document Processes.* Document the process for categorizing, accessing, and protecting information and the retention/destruction schedule and make sure these processes and schedules, including any exceptions, are understood throughout the organization. Exceptions generally relate to situations involving litigation or investigations. Federal law (Sarbanes-Oxley, for example) requires that documents not be destroyed in particular circumstances.

- *Establish Procedures.* Establish procedures and timelines for ongoing destruction of information that are legally appropriate and commensurate with the categorization of such information (for example, special procedures will likely be needed for the destruction of confidential information).

- *Support the Process.* Support the information management process with an organizational policy that sets forth management's support for the system.
  — Policies typically state and reflect management's commitment to an effective information management system that both supports organizational needs and complies with legal requirements.
  — Policies usually also specify that information and records belong to the organization not to individuals within the organization (including e-mail correspondence and documents stored on an employee's computer "C" drive).
  — Make it clear that everyone in the organization is expected to understand and comply with the policy and with related records management procedures (e.g., identification, protection, retention, and destruction procedures) and specify the process by which exceptions are to be handled in case of litigation or governmental investigations or other circumstances specified in the policy.
  — Require annual employee certification of compliance with such policies.

- *Monitor Compliance.* Create a process for monitoring compliance with the policy and its underlying procedures, including enforcement of consequences for compliance failures.

- *Revise Periodically.* Establish a process for revising information management policies and procedures on a periodic basis as needs or legal requirements change.

Handling Crises

Dealing with the media can be one of the most important and difficult aspects of managing a crisis. Establishing a crisis communications policy can help ensure that employees, donors, clients, and other important constituents are provided with information to help them understand how the organization is managing the crisis. Establishing a separate media response policy can help avoid missteps with the media that might exacerbate negative public perception of a crisis or the board's handling of a crisis.

Media Response Policy. A media response policy might include some or all of the following:

- Identification of the person or persons authorized to speak for the organization in the event of a crisis;
- Statements that the organization will take certain actions during a crisis, including
  - Scheduling regular briefings with media;
  - Attempting to correct misconceptions;
  - Staying with known facts and telling the truth, without stonewalling or denying the existence of a crisis;
  - Refusing to provide information about victims until families are notified;
  - Attempting to protect families from media and outside sources until approval by appropriate persons;
  - Maintaining positive media relations;
  - Treating all media equally, with no exclusives; and
  - Monitoring media coverage.

Crisis Communications Policy. While a media policy is narrowly aimed at dealings with the media, a crisis communications policy is broader and addresses how an organization will communicate with employees, clients, donors, and other important constituents during a crisis. Such communications can be as important as communications with the press. The elements of a crisis communications policy may be similar to those included in a media policy. For example:

- Identification of the person or persons authorized to speak for the organization with specific constituencies in the event of a crisis;
- Statements that the organization will take certain actions during a crisis, including
  - Providing regular communications to employees and, as appropriate, to donors, clients, and other constituents;
  - Staying with known facts and telling the truth, without stonewalling or denying the existence of a crisis;
  - Refusing to provide information about victims until families are notified; and
  - Attempting to protect families from communication with employees and others until authorized by appropriate persons.

Keep Records. In addition to establishing and following media and crisis communication policies, it can be important to keep records of all replies to media and communications with employees, clients, donors, investigators, and government officials (institution, group, or individual name, reporter/individual name, date, time, person responding, summary of response or communication, and any follow up request) as such replies and communications are made.

These records can be useful if it subsequently becomes necessary to clarify or prove what was said or provided at a particular time.

Provide Written Instructions to Anyone Authorized to Speak for the Organization. Make sure that designated spokespersons understand the media and crisis communications policies, but also consider creating simple written directions, in a format that can be easily distributed in a time of crisis, to remind them to

- Stick to the facts;
- Tell the truth;
- Limit statements to the immediate problem;
- Respond "I don't know" when that is the case, and offer to investigate and respond at a later time;
- Avoid saying "no comment"; and
- Not respond to any regulatory or law enforcement officials but refer such officials to those specifically designated to speak on behalf of the organization or, as appropriate, to legal counsel.

Provide Instructions to Board Members and Staff. Make sure that all board members and staff know to refer all media inquiries immediately to the designated spokesperson within the organization and understand the importance of refraining from making any comments themselves.

Learn from Experience of Others. Any organization may experience a crisis, and there is ample evidence that the existence of a disaster plan and media response policy does not assure that every crisis will be handled effectively. Much can be learned by watching how others handle crises.

Chapter 3: Governing Documents, Board Structure, and Operations

Governing Documents, Board Structure, and Operations

Governing Documents and Certain Filings

Articles of Incorporation

A nonprofit corporation's basic organizational structure is set forth in its charter document, the document that establishes the organization under state law or other jurisdiction as a corporation. Depending on the state of organization, the charter may be referred to as the articles of incorporation, certificate of incorporation, or certificate of organization. Whatever the official name, this organizational document is often referred to simply as an organization's charter or articles.

Provisions of Articles. The matters that must be contained in the charter are determined by the laws of the jurisdiction in which the organization is formed. As a practical matter, some provisions are relevant just to the initial formation of the entity, such as those naming the incorporators and initial directors. (Incorporators are those individuals who create the organization by signing and filing the original articles with the appropriate state officer.) But many provisions that may be included in articles are relevant to ongoing operations, such as those setting forth:

- The name of the organization;
- The purpose for which it is being formed;
- Minimum and maximum number of directors;
- Any special limitation of liability or indemnification provisions, to the extent permitted by law; and
- Special approval requirements for fundamental changes, such as mergers or dissolutions or distribution of substantially all the organization's assets, or significant amendments to the articles themselves, such as a change in the organization's purpose.

The articles of particular types of nonprofits, such as membership organizations, may have additional provisions relevant to the rights of members to vote on directors, mergers, dissolution, amendments to articles, or other matters. Often the articles of member organizations simply state that members will be defined in and have such powers as are listed in the organization's bylaws.

Filing of Articles. Articles are filed with the Secretary of State or, depending on the jurisdiction, another state officer. In some states publication of the filing may be required as well. Banks, the Internal Revenue Service (IRS), state and local agencies, and others may require copies of the articles as evidence of the nonprofit's existence. Often such authorities require a certified copy issued by the Secretary of State or other appropriate state officer.

Bylaws

A corporation's bylaws provide day-to-day "rules of operation" for the organization's governance structure. While bylaws must be consistent with state law requirements, they can be tailored to specific organizational needs and preferences.

Bylaw Provisions. Bylaws essentially provide the structure and roadmap for corporate governance and other material operational matters. Bylaw provisions are generally more specific and detailed than the provisions contained in articles and often elaborate on matters touched upon in the articles, such as:

- The nonprofit's purpose;
- The required minimum and maximum numbers of directors;
- The extent of indemnification provided to officers and directors; and
- Provisions related to the rights of members, for membership organizations.

Other bylaw provisions address ongoing governance matters related to:

- Directors (number, terms, qualifications, procedures for election, removal and filling vacancies, duties and responsibilities);

- Meetings (annual, regular, and special meetings, required notices, quorums, voting requirements, ability to hold telephonic or electronic meetings);
- Officers (titles, roles and responsibilities, terms of office, procedures for election or appointment, removal and filling vacancies, approval of compensation, if any);
- Committees (types of committees, appointment of committee members and chairs, roles and responsibilities of committee members, notices, quorums, and voting requirements); and
- Administrative or Other Issues (process for amending bylaws, actions by written consent, maintenance of books and records, determination of fiscal year, delivery of annual reports and financial statements, limitations on liability, prohibitions on certain activities (such as loans to directors or officers, or issuance of guarantees), and specific authority for certain activities (such as creating or working with affiliated entities).

The style and level of detail in bylaws vary greatly from organization to organization and state law generally allows considerable flexibility with respect to governance choices. For example, boards may choose whether all directors must be elected annually, or whether terms will be staggered. They may decide whether to have director term limits or not, whether to use the title Chair or President for the presiding officer at meetings, whether to include committee charters within the bylaws, or allow committees to develop their own charters subject to board approval.

Risks of Inconsistent Provisions in Articles and Bylaws. Bylaw provisions need to be consistent with provisions in the articles—a fact that is important to remember when amendments are made to bylaw provisions. In case of a conflict between the articles and bylaws, the provisions of the articles legally control. For example,

- Amending the purpose provision in the bylaws but not in the articles can result in management and board action inconsistent with the purpose set forth in the articles and upon which basis the organization obtained state and federal tax exemption. If a nonprofit organization's purposes as set forth in the bylaws materially deviate from the purposes set forth in its articles, actions taken in accordance with the bylaws purposes may be subject to challenge as inconsistent with the purposes for which the organization was formed and was entitled to exempt status.
- Inconsistent indemnification provisions in the bylaws and articles may result in unintended limitations on the extent of indemnification available to directors. For example, if an organization's articles and bylaws are specific as to details of indemnification (e.g., by simply repeating provisions of existing state law on indemnification) and the bylaws but not the articles are subsequently amended to provide for "indemnification to the full extent of the law," the more detailed provisions of the articles will con-

trol, even if narrower than the coverage that would be available under the language of the amended bylaws.

Board Adoption. Bylaws and amendments to bylaws are usually adopted by the board and/or the members, as specified in the bylaws. They do not need to be filed with state authorities to be effective, although it may be necessary to file copies with other governmental filings, such as filings for licenses, permits, or state or local tax exemptions. Grant-making organizations often request a copy of a nonprofit's bylaws as well as its articles, including any amendments.

Bylaws may also provide that a specific group, such as members or others, must approve amendments to certain provisions. Bylaws tend to be amended, or even restated in their entirety, far more often than articles as they are meant to be adapted to changing governance needs of the organization.

Drafting and Review of Articles and Bylaws

Consulting Legal Counsel. Articles and bylaws generally are drafted by or with the assistance of legal counsel because of the need to make certain they comply with state law requirements and because counsel can help tailor provisions to reflect the specific nature of the organization and its goals.

Periodic Review. Because laws applicable to nonprofits may change, it is important that these governing documents be periodically reviewed by legal counsel and updated to conform to such changes.

Potential for Disconnect with Actual Practices. The Executive Officer, Board Chair, and other board and management leadership will want to make sure that bylaw provisions are consistent with the actual practices of the organization. Understanding and frequently consulting bylaw provisions help ensure that the board is operating within the governance structure set forth in the document and help minimize the possibility of a disconnect between bylaw requirements and board practices.

Failure to adhere to bylaw provisions may have unfortunate consequences, ranging from possible embarrassment for failure to follow board procedures, to time-consuming and distracting legal challenges to actions taken by the board, to personal director liability for acting improperly.

Distribution of Copies. Copies of articles and bylaws usually are distributed to directors in orientation materials or the organization's "board book" when a director joins the board. Posting updated copies on the organization's intranet or website eliminates the need to send revisions in paper form.

Other Documents and Filings

Registration to Do Business. An organization that conducts operations or otherwise engages in activities in states other than the state in which it is incorporated is likely to be required to qualify as a foreign corporation in order to operate in each such state. Legal counsel can assist in determining whether registration as a foreign corporation is necessary and in ascertaining the specific state filing requirements.

Doing Business Under Another Name. In addition to its corporate name set forth in the articles, some nonprofits find it beneficial to conduct their affairs under a different or "assumed" name. Such assumed names are often referred to as a d/b/a (doing business as) names. Organizations doing business under a different name often determine that it is advantageous to make an assumed name filing with the Secretary of State (or other state office) in each state in which the organization operates to protect the organization's right to use the d/b/a name and avoid confusion in litigation, banking relationships, and other matters. Assumed business name filings may also be required at the local or municipal level. Such filings may require notice by publication in a newspaper to be deemed effective. D/b/a names must also be checked in advance for availability in the jurisdictions in which they will be used to avoid name infringement claims. A nonprofit using a d/b/a name may consider registering the name as a trade name under state and federal law.

Tax-Exemption. If a nonprofit organization seeks to be exempt from taxation under Section 501(c) of the Internal Revenue Code (IRC), it generally must file an application with the IRS to obtain an exempt determination. An exception to this is made for churches, and certain church-related organizations, which are considered tax-exempt automatically. Organizations that are not required to file for exemption may still want to file an application in order to receive a determination letter. A Form 1023 is filed for organizations seeking tax-exemption under Section 501(c)(3) of the IRC, and a Form 1024 for those seeking tax-exempt status under most other sections.

Some states require nonprofits to apply for and obtain a tax-exempt determination from the state as well. Legal counsel can advise on this issue, as well as on the extent of state tax-exemptions available for other taxes, such as property taxes, sales or use taxes, and business license taxes.

Board Structure Issues

Board Composition, Officers and Committees

A nonprofit board generally consists of a specified number of directors, sometimes including the Executive Officer. Directors are usually nominated and elected or appointed by members of the current board or, if there are members with voting rights, by the members. The board generally elects the organization's officers, although in nonprofits with members, the members may elect the officers. The officers may or may not be members of the board.

In organizations in which the offices of President, Vice President, and other officers are held by full-time management employees, such officers, other than the President, do not typically also serve as directors. In other organizations, especially those with small administrative staffs, officers are often selected from among the board members. The Board Chair typically is elected by the board; however, in some nonprofits a designated individual, such as the President (often when the President is also the Executive Officer), serves as the Board Chair. The Board Chair is always a member of the board.

Typical officers of a nonprofit might include a President (sometimes called by a different title, such as CEO), a Treasurer, and a Secretary, and often one or more Vice Presidents. Other organizations have a Chair, a Treasurer, a Secretary, and one or more Vice Chairs, but no President. Individuals holding Vice President or Vice Chair positions may, or may not, be designated as (or informally assumed to be) the successor to the current Board Chair or President, respectively, when his or her term expires.

Board members are usually expected to serve on one or more board committees and may be asked to chair one or more committees.

Board Size, Length of Service, and Other Structural Basics

The size of the board, the period of time for which directors are elected or appointed, staggering of board terms so only a portion of the board is up for reelection in a single year, limits on the age of board members, term limits, and limits on the number of consecutive terms a board member may serve all affect board governance.

Board Size

Parameters. Most states require a specified minimum number of directors (typically three, although some allow for one director), and many organizations provide in their articles or bylaws for a range within which the number of directors may be set, such as between 10 and 15. Within this range, the board (or membership, if members elect the directors) determines the actual number of directors to serve at a given time.

Optimum Size. Current trends in the for-profit world generally favor smaller boards. The optimum size for a nonprofit board is a matter of debate among governance commentators as well as within and among nonprofit organizations and may vary depending on the nature of the organization. Many commentators recommend a board size of from 9 to 15 board members as optimum for providing an effective governance and oversight structure. However, many nonprofit organizations depart significantly from these numbers. A large arts organization, for example, may have a much larger board because board members often form the core of major donors and fund-raisers. A small social services organization with a limited mission in a small community may function adequately with a much smaller board, particularly if it receives most of its funding from donor groups other than the board.

Because there are inherent difficulties in managing a large board, those organizations that have one frequently make use of an active and much smaller executive committee. However, a large board's reliance on an executive committee does not relieve board members who are not on the executive committee of their fiduciary duties. Other directors can be subject to suit or challenged for breach of fiduciary duty if the executive committee is found to have been acting inappropriately and the board's reliance on decisions of the committee appears to have been unreasonable. In recent years, some organizations with traditionally large boards have reduced the size of their boards and created advisory or honorary boards with no governance or fiduciary responsibilities. Such alternative bodies allow members formerly on the fiduciary/governance board to stay connected to the organization and play a community leadership role for the organization while avoiding potential liability for board decisions made by the fiduciary board.

Director Terms, Staggered Terms, Term Limits

Term Length. Bylaws typically specify the term for which directors are elected, for example, one, two, or three years. If not specified, director terms are typically one year. Term length depends on the needs and nature of the nonprofit as well as the tradition of the organization. Some organizations like the flexibility of one-year terms, while others prefer longer terms in order to give directors more time to grow into their board member roles.

Staggered Terms. If a director's effectiveness on the board of a particular nonprofit is enhanced by a certain amount of continuity of board membership, this is usually achieved by having staggered board member terms of three years, with one-third of the directors being elected in each year. Not only does this arrangement give a new director an opportunity to learn and become a more effective board member, but it also helps ensure institutional knowledge and continuity by avoiding a majority of the board turning over in any particular year. Newly organized nonprofits creating a staggered board typically divide the initial group of board members into three groups, with some directors elected for initial terms of one year, some for two years, and the rest for three. Directors with the initial shorter terms are generally eligible to subsequently serve one or more full terms, if specified in the bylaws.

Term Limits. Some nonprofits limit the number of terms a director may serve. This restriction can be an effective way to ensure that people with new ideas are rotated onto the board on a regular basis, which can be helpful in maintaining an organization's vitality. However, term limits may also result in the loss of some board members with substantial expertise, passion, and knowledge of the organization and its mission, a reason some nonprofits prefer not to impose such limits.

A common way to obtain the benefit of both new ideas and organizational experience is to limit the number of consecutive terms for which a board member may serve, but permit the election to the board of a former board member who has not been a board member for one or more years. The benefit of this approach is that it gives the board time to develop a new dynamic without the participation of the former board member and allows more time for an objective evaluation of the benefit to the board of asking the former board member to return. The drawback of this approach is that once a board member has left the board, he or she may become involved in other areas of interest or may be unwilling or no longer have time to return. Governance trends encourage boards to find ways to keep regenerating themselves and to bring new perspectives and approaches into the board room.

Age Limits

In addition to limiting the number of consecutive or total terms a director may serve, a nonprofit organization may also have an age limitation policy or bylaw provision which limits nominations or renominations to persons under a certain age, such as 70 or 72. Such a policy is not merely to ensure more youthful board members, since experienced members are often significant contributors in many different ways, but an age limitation gives the board an opportunity to bring in and develop younger members who may have many years of productive service ahead of them. Nonetheless, as the population ages, some nonprofits are raising retirement ages to 75 or higher, or eliminating them altogether.

Some nonprofits with age limitations for directors permit exceptions in unusual circumstances, although it is important that the nonprofit not use the exception routinely to extend the terms of its older members. Otherwise, the age limitation is meaningless and it can become difficult to remove older members who may have become ineffective without the removal being considered an insult and resulting in an unnecessarily unpleasant break.

One way of retaining the expertise of older directors or directors who have served several terms is to have an honorary, nonfiduciary board in addition to the legal governing body.

Board Membership

Directors are typically considered as "independent," "inside or interested," or "ex-officio" based on their relationship to the organization. There are important governance implications related to each of these director designations and the characteristics of individuals elected or appointed to fulfill a particular classification will also vary.

Independent Directors

Independence Trend. Current governance standards encourage nonprofits to have boards that are composed substantially of independent directors, that is, those who are not employees of the nonprofit, nor so closely involved in its activities or allied with its founder or staff, that their objectivity may be questioned. This preference for independent outside directors is shared by many funders of nonprofit organizations, based on their presumption that when nonprofit directors are wholly or substantially independent, with no expectation of financial or other personal benefits from the organization, they are more likely to make decisions based purely on the best interests of the organization.

Tax-exempt nonprofits under Section 501(c)(3) of the IRC are generally expected to have boards composed of all, or almost all, independent board members who (and whose immediate family members) are not employees of the organization or vendors to the organization. There are exceptions to this general rule, for example, family foundations, in which only a portion of the board or management are individuals without a connection to the family, and churches, in which all directors are church authorities or members. However, the IRS takes the position that tax-exempt nonprofits are more likely to be well-governed if most of the members of the governing body are independent. The Form 990 definitions section specifies the conditions that must be met for a board member to be considered "independent."

Transition Issues. Despite the governance trend toward independent boards, some smaller or newly formed nonprofits may still have boards composed largely of paid staff, the organization's founder, his or her close friends, or others with a close personal relationship. Moving from this structure to an independent board structure can be a significant challenge for an organization.

In some cases, an organization may determine that despite one or more directors' technical lack of independence as defined by the IRS or other governance standards, such directors are valuable members of the board and should continue serving. In other cases, the board may determine that it would be helpful if the board consisted of a greater number of independent board members as defined by the IRS and others, requiring those who do not fit such definitions to resign or retire from the board. Nonprofit organizations facing such a transition often struggle to retain the fervor of their former board members and service providers as they move to gain the oversight of independent board members. In such instances, the transition may be considerably less disruptive if the board and management leadership understand the problems and issues, and are both diplomatic and firm in moving from one model to the other.

Interested and Inside Directors

Directors employed or compensated by the organization are considered interested or inside board members. Most commonly, if staff is represented on the board, it is the Executive Officer who serves. Directors who are not paid by the organization, for example, a founder still closely allied with the organization or a board member with substantial business ties to the organization, may also fall within the definition of an interested or inside board member for certain legal or governance purposes. Form 990, in particular, has expanded the concept of "interested" board members. In addition, state law or the organization's conflict of interest policies may impose restrictions on membership of audit committees or on the ability of interested directors to be involved in certain decisions, such as those relating to the compensation of the Executive Officer.

Ex Officio Directors

Ex officio directors are those whose position on the board is as a result of holding or formerly having held a particular position with the organization or an affiliate entity. For example, the organization's Executive Officer may be an ex officio member of the board—serving on the board as a result of holding, but only for so long as he or she holds, the position of Executive Officer. The immediate past Board Chair might also be an ex officio board member for a year or more following his or her service as Chair. In other cases, ex officio board positions may be held by individuals associated with organizations affiliated with the nonprofit, such as the chair of an auxiliary fund-raising organization.

Voting Rights and Duties. Depending on an organization's bylaws, ex officio directors may or may not have voting rights at board meetings. The fiduciary duty of nonvoting ex officio directors falls in a gray area, but they may be deemed to be as subject to fiduciary requirements as voting directors. Sometimes organizations rely on *Robert's Rules of Order* in determining whether ex officio directors have voting rights or must be counted in determining a quorum. *Robert's Rules of Order Newly Revised (10th ed. 2000)* provides that ex officio members of boards and committees have all the same rights as all other board and committee members, including the right to vote, but in certain limited cases are not counted in determining a quorum. However, *Roberts Rules of Order* is not binding (or necessarily appropriate) except for those organizations, such as very large membership organizations, that have explicitly chosen to adopt *Robert's Rules of Order* as part of their meeting or parliamentary procedures. Therefore, to avoid uncertainty, it is helpful for a nonprofit's governing documents to state specifically whether ex officio directors have voting rights and whether they count in determining a quorum.

Issues Raised by Ex Officio Status. There are many valid reasons for creating ex officio board positions. The former Board Chair may have a great deal of institutional knowledge that may be useful to current board members. An ex officio President or Executive Officer can serve as a bridge between the board and management and allowing them to serve as ex officio directors enhances their ability to do so. The chair of an affiliated fund-raising organization or committee may have valuable information to share with the board and may learn things about the nonprofit that are valuable to the affiliated organization's or committee's fund-raising activities.

However, ex officio positions also raise a number of issues. For example, will the presence of a former Board Chair tend to undermine the authority of the current one or instead lend support to the leadership tradition by offering a certain level of continuity to the board? For how long should a former Chair or President or Executive Officer be given ex officio status on the board? Should ex officio board members have a vote on board matters when they have not been elected or appointed in the same manner as other board members—and if they cannot vote, what is their role on the board? Are the interests of ex officio board members narrower than those of the rest of the board or potentially in conflict with the organization as a whole? Will the presence of ex officio board members at board meetings interfere with the functioning of the board? Will the individual serving as an ex officio board member of one organization and a board member of an auxiliary organization be able to fulfill his or her fiduciary duties to both organizations? Are the reasons for creation of the ex officio position clear? Have alternatives been considered which might achieve similar benefits without some of the potential drawbacks?

Honorary, Emeritus, and Advisory Directors and Special Recognition Boards

Boards often name various individuals as honorary, advisory, or emeritus board members and may also create honorary, advisory, emeritus, or other special recognition boards. Honorary, advisory, or emeritus board members are not directors of the nonprofit unless they have a vote on the nonprofit's board and honorary, advisory, emeritus, or other special recognition boards are not boards of directors unless they vote on matters and their vote obligates the nonprofit.

Honorary, Advisory, or Emeritus Directors. The titles Honorary Director (or Honorary Board Member), Advisory Director, or Emeritus Director are often bestowed on board members who have retired from the board due to term or age limits. However, consideration needs to be given to the implications of such titles as well as to whether they are to be offered to all retiring directors or only in specific cases. Some issues to consider are:

- If such titles are granted, what are the roles associated with these titles?
- Are such honorary, advisory, or emeritus board members welcome to or expected to attend board meetings? If so, do they sit at the board table?
- Are they allowed to participate in deliberations, or are they expected to act primarily as observers who may add occasional comments?
- Do the bylaws of the organization make clear that honorary, advisory, or emeritus board members do not have voting rights and are not counted for purposes of determining a quorum?
- Do honorary, advisory, or emeritus board members and the organization have a clear understanding of the degree to which such individuals would still be deemed to retain fiduciary obligations regarding nondisclosure of confidential information?
- With respect to any discussions with the organization's attorney that may be subject to attorney-client privilege, will the Board Chair remember to ask any honorary, advisory, or emeritus board members to leave the room in order to avoid waiver of the privilege?
- Are such honorary, advisory, or emeritus board member titles held indefinitely or are they granted for a specific period of time?

Special Recognition Boards. Beyond the designation of an honorary, advisory, or emeritus director title for retired directors, some nonprofits seek to encourage the continued interest of valued retired board members through establishment of a separate honorary board or advisory board (sometimes called an emeritus board). Honorary or advisory boards may meet periodically, but have no official governance responsibilities or duties. Their meetings are usually designed to inform, entertain, or recognize certain accomplishments of the retired board members and to encourage their continued support of the organization.

Members of such honorary or advisory boards will generally be invited to and given prominent places at major events involving the organization or at fund-raising or other social activities involving the board in order to reward their prior service and encourage their continued participation. Some organizations invite their honorary or advisory board members to attend one or more regular meetings of the board during the year, or some portion of such meetings, although they may limit such participation to sections of the meeting that do not involve confidential information or board decision-making.

There are a number of issues to be considered in creating a special recognition board:

- Will membership on the honorary or advisory board be automatic for all board members who, because of age or term limits, can no longer serve or is appointment to the special recognition board by invitation and only for those who have been in some way exceptional board members during their tenure?

- What will the function of the special recognition board be and to what degree will its members be asked to participate in regular board activities? Will the function of the board be documented in a written charter?

- Will members of the special recognition board be invited and encouraged to attend meetings of the regular board, or will the special recognition board itself have one or more separate meetings a year at which its members can be informed about the organization's activities? If the former, will attendance of members of the special recognition board interfere with regular board deliberations, or expose that person to confidential information that is not generally available or encourage their participation in deliberations that would typically be limited to those with legal responsibility for governance? If the latter, what kind of information will be shared and by whom, what extra time and expense will the separate meetings entail, and who in the organization will be responsible for assuring that they are of sufficient value to keep the interest of the honorary board members?

Criteria for Board Membership

Criteria for nonprofit board membership are usually determined by the board or a committee of the board, although the bylaws or funding sources of some organizations may mandate that certain types of expertise be represented on the board or certain board committees. In addition, governance trends encourage not only board member independence, but also certain types of expertise for certain committees (e.g., financial expertise for audit committees), as well as diversity of backgrounds among board directors (e.g., based on age, geography, ethnicity, and experience with different aspects of the organization's activities).

Individual Characteristics. Because board composition is such a critical factor in the effectiveness and success of a nonprofit board, it is useful for Executive Officers and Board Chairs to regularly discuss the composition of the board and to work together to make sure the board's process for establishing and monitoring membership criteria remains effective. As a starting point, certain fundamental individual characteristics are often included as board member criteria, including:

- *Vision, Leadership, and Independence.* the ability to see the big picture and to help create and, if necessary, reset strategy and policy to help the organization achieve its mission; the ability to be objective and independent of management and to focus on the overall best interests of the organization;

- *Advocacy, Stewardship, and Integrity.* the ability to serve and promote the best interests and goals of the organization without forgetting the interests of the public and the organization's intended beneficiaries, and without being distracted by extraneous facts or factors or having a conflict of interest;

- *Knowledge.* the willingness to become thoroughly familiar with the mission and how the organization actually carries out the mission on a day-to-day basis through its structure and operations, as well as the willingness to understand and adhere to applicable governance principles, including fiduciary duties and responsibilities;

- *Personal Commitment and Diligence.* the willingness to take the necessary time and make the necessary effort to fulfill board member responsibilities, including regular attendance at board and committee meetings, understanding the strategic, financial, and operational issues facing the organization, asking questions and following up as needed, engaging personally with the organization, whether through financial support, advocacy, networking, personal service, or other personal support activities;

- *Financial Support.* the willingness to support the nonprofit financially, either by direct contributions or by attracting other supporters or contributors; and

- *Collegiality.* the ability to work well with others and to show respect for the ideas and views of fellow board members and staff, and the understanding that a board operates as a body.

Life Experience and Expertise. Beyond these fundamental individual characteristics, nonprofit boards typically seek directors who can help provide leadership to the organization based on their experience and expertise (e.g., business or technical skill), their personal financial capacity or connections (for organizations that fund-raise), their positions in the community, or their access to key constituents or professionals who can be helpful to the organization. Directors are expected to use their expertise/experience in their service on the board. In line with governance trends in the for-profit sphere, in recent years there has been a trend for nonprofit boards to seek individuals representing specific ethnic and minority groups, women, and younger individuals, so that the board has a diverse membership.

Written Criteria can be Helpful. One way to help ensure that a board is effective in considering members who meet the organization's needs is for the board or its nominating committee to create and maintain written criteria for board membership, focusing on key characteristics being sought. The board should also conduct an annual review to determine if the board and its committees are following the board's established criteria and board members are meeting expectations and responsibilities. Review of the criteria and the strengths and weaknesses of the existing board may help focus future recruiting on the organization's needs.

Director Recruitment

Sources. Once the specific criteria for board membership have been determined by the board, the nominating committee or the board serving in the capacity of nominating committee has the responsibility of finding the individuals who both satisfy the agreed upon criteria and have an interest in joining the board. The sources of potential candidates vary widely and may include:

- Community leaders;
- Persons of stature known to have interests compatible with those of the nonprofit;
- Persons who have served in volunteer capacities on board committees or with affiliated organizations, in fund-raising activities, or in other volunteer capacities with the nonprofit;
- Donors or other supporters of the nonprofit;
- Persons who have been beneficiaries of the services provided by the organization;
- Individuals employed by or otherwise affiliated with organizations that have been active in supporting the nonprofit; and
- Individuals employed by noncompetitor organizations in the same or a different field as the nonprofit, such as a curator at an art museum in another city serving as a board member of a newly established women's history museum (although staff may be uncomfortable with such a selection).

Often an organization maintains a list of individuals considered viable potential directors and updates that list periodically to reflect responses to recruitment efforts with such individuals and to add other potential candidates.

Solicitation of Interest. Once the board or its nominating committee has identified a particular individual as a viable candidate for board membership, normally the nominating committee or its chair will contact the individual and explore the person's willingness, interest, and ability to serve. This initial contact provides both the potential candidate and the nonprofit's representative an opportunity to discuss the nonprofit, its mission, and its governance scheme, as well as any expectations for board members, including meeting attendance and any required financial contributions and other fund-raising responsibilities. Creating a list of board responsibilities that outlines what the organization expects of board members (including committee membership and board and committee meeting attendance) in a format that can be given to potential candidates helps ensure that all candidates understand the level of commitment expected of them.

The Practical Advice Section of this Chapter contains suggestions on how to develop a written list of board expectations and responsibilities. See pages 175–176.

Appendix 14 has samples of documents describing expectations and responsibilities for board members.

Information Provided to Candidates. Another critical part of the recruitment process is to furnish the individual being considered with sufficient information about the nonprofit to enable him or her to understand the basic parameters of the organization's operations and financial condition, any major issues the organization may be facing, and, as appropriate, the specific reasons the board is interested in the candidate (for example, because of his or her legal or human resources expertise or prior nonprofit board experience) and how he or she may be particularly helpful to the board or one or more of its committees. Some organizations provide prospective board members with a packet of information regarding the nonprofit's mission and history, current challenges and strategic plan, composition of the current board, calendar of events, and director and officer insurance coverage. Such information can be provided in hard-copy or electronically, including via a dedicated website for board candidates. It is important to remember, however, that providing confidential or privileged information to prospective directors risks such information becoming public or losing its attorney-client privileged status. For this reason, some organizations require candidates to execute nondisclosure agreements, which provide some measure of protection.

Appendix 15 has a list of informational documents that are often provided to prospective board candidates.

Candidate Evaluation. It is common and usually desirable for an individual being considered for board membership to meet with a number of representatives of the nonprofit, including nominating committee members and perhaps additional board members, the Executive Officer, and sometimes other key staff. These discussions assist both the nonprofit's representatives and the potential director to determine if that person's participation with the nonprofit is likely to be an appropriate fit.

Once the nominating committee has determined that the candidate would likely be a useful contributor to the board and the candidate has indicated his or her interest in joining the board, the nominating committee nominates the individual for board membership and recommends that the full board approve the nomination (or, for a membership organization, that the members do so, if members appoint the directors). The committee will usually provide background information on the individual in advance of the board (or membership) meeting at which he or she is to be considered. The chair of the nominating committee may speak about the nomination at the meeting and answer any questions prior to a vote. If there is no nominating committee, the Board Chair may either present the individual's name for board or member approval (with appropriate background information) or ask another member of the board to do so.

Officers

Directors as Officers. Nonprofit corporations typically have the following officer positions: a Board Chair or President (or sometimes both), one or more Vice Presidents or Vice Chairs, a Secretary, and a Treasurer. State law usually requires that the organization have at least certain officer positions, such as President, Secretary, and Treasurer, although the titles may vary.

In some nonprofits, officer positions may be filled by board members. In many nonprofits, individuals serving in positions other than the Board Chair or Vice Chair are often paid employees of the organization and, as such, are part of the staff who report to the organization's Executive Officer rather than serving in a board governance or oversight role. For nonprofits in which the officers also serve as board members, such officers are sometimes referred to mistakenly as "board officers." However, this is a misnomer. State law provides only for officers of the organization (i.e., President, Secretary, Treasurer), with specific responsibilities and powers to be exercised on behalf of the nonprofit organization itself, not on behalf of the board. Organizations are free to determine whether the individuals holding officer positions may also serve as board members.

In organizations in which officer positions such as Vice President, Secretary, and Treasurer are held by board members rather than paid staff, such officers are generally viewed, together with the Board Chair, as the principal leadership group of the board and often succession to the Chair position follows board member service in one or more of these officer positions.

Bylaw Provisions Regarding Officers. The basic responsibilities of officers of nonprofit organizations are set forth in the organization's bylaws, with the level of detail in the description of duties and powers varying among organizations. At a minimum, most nonprofit bylaws state that the Board Chair presides at meetings; the Vice Chair presides when the Chair is unavailable; the President, Executive Officer, or Board Chair serves as the chief executive officer or management officer; the Secretary is responsible for board minutes, as well as safekeeping of key organizational and board documents; and the Treasurer is responsible for overseeing the financial condition of the organization and its management of funds.

Roles and Titles Vary Among Organizations. The actual roles of, and titles used by, nonprofit officers will depend on the nature of the organization and its particular needs at a given time. For example, in large, complex organizations, there may be separate officer positions for a Board Chair and a President, with responsibilities for external relations, for example, handled by the Board Chair, and responsibilities for leading or working with staff handled by the President. The two might share the function of chairing meetings, or that function might be assigned solely to the Chair. The President might also serve as Executive Officer.

Not all nonprofit corporations have Vice Chairs. Those that do typically provide that the Vice Chair presides at meetings and otherwise assumes the responsibilities of the Board Chair when the Board Chair is unavailable. In many organizations, the Vice Chair is designated or assumed to be the successor to the Board Chair when his or her term expires. The Vice Chair may also be asked to assist the Board Chair with committee oversight or other duties, or to play a leadership role on specific matters, such as strategic planning. The role of Vice Chair often changes depending on who is Chair and how much assistance that person needs or desires. The term Vice President is used in place of Vice Chair in organizations in which the presiding officer is denominated President rather than Chair.

The Secretary's and the Treasurer's basic duties help assure that the board has sufficient information to exercise its fiduciary duties and that board actions are appropriately documented. The Secretary, although often not the original drafter of minutes, is responsible for making sure that minutes are accurate and that the organization has a process for maintaining them, as well as other important corporate records. The Treasurer may or may not be the Chief Financial Officer of the organization, but he or she has the responsibility for understanding the organization's financial condition and monitoring its financial reporting. The Treasurer and the Secretary may each be called upon to certify the accuracy of various corporate documents or reports. Organizations also may have Assistant Secretaries and Assistant Treasurers who may take actions when the Secretary or Treasurer, respectively, is unavailable and who also may be assigned certain functions or specific tasks.

Board Committees

The board's responsibilities may be carried out either by the full board or by committees it has established and to which it has delegated particular responsibilities or functions. Subject to any superseding provisions of applicable law, which may require certain significant actions to be taken by the full board, delegation to committees is both appropriate and useful. An active committee structure gives individual board members an opportunity to become knowledgeable about specific areas of the organization or about issues requiring board oversight and provides an opportunity for more concentrated discussions in smaller groups.

The number and type of board committees typically depend on the size of the nonprofit and the board, the nonprofit's immediate needs and longer-term plans, legal requirements, and, often, organizational tradition. The Executive Officer and Board Chair have important roles to play in reviewing the committee structure periodically to help assure that the committees that exist continue to be appropriate and work effectively, and that new committees are formed and old ones dissolved when circumstances suggest that an alternative structure may be more useful.

Creation and Membership

Determination of committees, their membership, and responsibilities are the legal function of the board. However, as a practical matter, suggestions as to structure and membership are likely to be first discussed by the Board Chair and the Executive Officer and then proposed to the full board or to a board committee. Considerations in determining which committees to create and which board members should become committee members include

- The functions necessary for or helpful to effective operation of the board and the organization;
- Legal requirements and governance trends;
- The specific talents and experience of individual potential committee members; and
- The staffing required for committee support.

Delegation of Authority and Committee Charters

Committees are created by the board and have only the authority delegated by the board. Sometimes that delegation comes in the form of a short resolution of the board. Sometimes the committee is established by a bylaw provision.

Whether established by resolution or a provision of the bylaws, a board committee's operations are greatly facilitated if it has a detailed written charter which delineates its specific functions, including whether the committee has authority to take certain actions on its own or solely the authority to make recommendations to the full board. Committee charters may also provide flexibility for the board to add additional responsibilities to the committee from time to time. However, state law places limits on actions that can be undertaken by a committee, reserving some actions to the full board. Committee charters also may address matters such as committee composition, number of meetings, and procedural matters such as quorums and notices. Governance experts recommend that committees periodically review their charters and have the board periodically review and approve the charters well.

Types of Committees

Standing Committees and Ad Hoc Committees. There are generally two basic types of board committees: standing committees (typically those with important governance functions) which are expected to continue indefinitely or until their responsibilities are assumed by a different committee, and ad hoc committees, which are formed for a specific, short-term purpose. Standing committees typically include committees with specific governance-related functions, such as:

- *Finance-Related Committees.* Finance, audit, budget, and investment committees monitor the work of the nonprofit's internal and external auditors and financial personnel to address any issues that may have arisen in the course of their work and to help the board assure the nonprofit's compliance with financial and accounting policies and procedures (and other policies and procedures that may have an effect on financial results, such as budgeting, investment management, compliance, and risk management).

  Larger organizations often have separate finance and audit committees, and some states, such as California, require such a separation for organizations over a certain size. In such cases, the audit committee works principally on audit, risk, and financial integrity or compliance issues, while the finance committee recommends or develops financial policies and procedures and monitors their application, oversees financing plans for the organization, and generally monitors the organization's financial health. The finance committee also typically reviews income and cost projections for the organization's programs for its fiscal year and reviews the organization's performance in comparison to its budget, although some organizations delegate these matters to a separate budget committee.

  In organizations with endowments, employee benefit plan assets, or other liquid assets to invest, there may also be an investment committee which oversees and establishes policies for investing the organization's endowment or significant cash or other liquid reserves.

  In most cases, these finance-related committees review the areas assigned to them in great detail, but may not actually approve the audit, the budget, or investment policies. Such actions are generally taken by the board based on the recommendations of the committees. For very small nonprofits, if there is no annual or other regular audit, the board will be more active in overseeing matters relating to the financial statements of the nonprofit and its adoption of and adherence to its policies and procedures.

- *Nominating Committee and/or Governance Committee.* A nominating committee is often used to identify and screen potential candidates for the board and to recommend nominations to the full board (or membership, if the organization has voting members). It often nominates the slate of board officers as well. A nominating committee usually follows a selection process and criteria for board membership or officer status which either it or a separate governance committee has previously developed and submitted to the board for approval. Occasionally, the nominating committee is responsible for the initial work in connection with the hiring, evaluation, and, if necessary, firing of the Executive Officer, although this responsibility may be given to the executive committee or an ad hoc committee created just for such a purpose.

In some nonprofit organizations, the nominating committee may also have the responsibility for corporate governance matters. In others, a separate governance committee may be established to handle such matters. The governance responsibility delegated to either the nominating or governance committee generally includes developing, subject to board approval, and implementing a process for evaluating the effectiveness of the board and its individual members; recommending changes to board structure, operations, and membership based on such evaluations; periodically reviewing and suggesting revisions to the organization's articles, bylaws, committee charters, and governance policies; assisting the Chair with committee assignments; helping individual directors improve their effectiveness; conducting exit interviews with directors who resign or retire; developing a process for succession planning for officers; planning board educational programs and retreats; and keeping apprised and advising the board of governance developments generally.

- *Executive Committee.* An executive committee takes action on behalf of the board if required between meetings of the full board; handles certain routine matters on behalf of the board in order to free up time on board agendas for strategic discussions; and serves as a sounding board for the Executive Officer or Board Chair on various issues, including those not yet ready for full discussion by the board. Under some state laws, executive committees are not permitted to exercise certain powers of the board (relating mainly to fundamental changes to the organization).

An executive committee may also be useful in providing a smaller forum for important discussions that help build board member support and understanding, since it is possible to discuss issues in greater depth in smaller meetings, or over the course of several meetings devoted to a single topic.

While these functions of an executive committee are important, use of an executive committee requires care to ensure that the nonprofit has not, in effect, established a two-tiered board or created the perception among board members of having done so. Such a situation may exist when the smaller executive committee begins actually to perform significant functions of the board, fully discussing and essentially deciding issues, with the larger full board becoming merely a rubber stamp for actions taken or recommended by the executive committee. In such situations the organization, in effect, has created one class of board members—those on the executive committee—who are fully informed about important issues, and another class—those on the larger board—who have access to less information and a lesser opportunity to participate in meaningful discussions.

In situations in which the executive committee is essentially functioning as the nonprofit board, the members of the full board may still have liability for the committee's actions unless it is clear that the board has fully delegated authority over certain matters to the executive committee (as long as such delegation is not prohibited by state law). Aside from legal concerns, board member perceptions of first and second class status may be a significant issue, with board members not on the executive committee feeling as if their contribution to discussion of major issues is not as valued as that of members of the executive committee.

Ensuring that regular written reports or minutes of the executive committee are provided to the full board, as well as providing the full board the opportunity to review and discuss executive committee actions, can assist in mitigating legal and interpersonal issues that might otherwise arise with extensive use of an executive committee. Executive Officers and Board Chairs can help reduce the possibility of such problems arising by actively reviewing how the executive committee is functioning in relation to the board and other committees. If it appears that that the full board is not routinely being provided with the opportunity to participate fully in major decisions, the Executive Officer and the Board Chair can then take action to remedy the situation. For example, they might consider recommending a bylaw amendment or other board action to reduce board size or to move some directors to an honorary or advisory board with no official governance responsibilities, so that the full board can be the main decision-making body. Alternatively, executive committee membership might be rotated more often, or other committees might be utilized to handle some of the issues being brought to the executive committee.

- *Compensation or Human Resources Committee.* A compensation or human resource committee typically develops, subject to board approval, and oversees implementation of a compensation philosophy and guidelines for compensating the Executive Officer and sometimes for others in the organization's senior management. The committee may be delegated authority by the board to approve the Executive Officer's compensation within board-approved guidelines. It may be responsible for career development and succession planning for the Executive Officer and senior staff and it may oversee other human resources programs or compliance issues.

The foregoing committees perform governance functions that are specifically within the board's oversight responsibility. They do not normally include non-board members but may, of course, request information or other input from non-board members. Sometimes non-board members may be regular guests in the meetings of these committees.

Committees with Non-Directors as Members. An issue that often arises with nonprofits, which does not have a counterpart in the profit-making sphere, is whether certain committees may include non-board members. Many states limit voting membership on committees, such as those described above, which are delegated governance responsibilities by the board, to board members. Other states require that these committees have a majority of directors. However, depending on state law, membership on advisory, non-governance committees such as development (fund-raising), facilities, marketing, community outreach, or advisory committees related to specific programs or operations may include non-board members. These committees generally are not considered committees of the board and merely have advisory functions under most state laws.

The following are examples of types of advisory committees (or other committees if permitted under state law) that might include non-board members:

- *Development (fund-raising and/or endowment or capital campaign) Committees.* A development committee generally deals with annual giving campaigns and works on or oversees annual fund-raising efforts and events. While a capital or endowment campaign would normally be undertaken by a separate and special committee focused on the particular campaign, in smaller organizations, the same committee may undertake both the annual and special appeals.

- *Planning Committees.* A planning committee is often used to consider and make recommendations to the full board as to the organization's overall mission, long-term objectives, and key strategies and structures. It may also consider new programs and monitor and assess ongoing programs and projects. This committee may monitor progress in achieving an existing strategic plan and may also form the core group for initial planning leading to a new strategic planning effort by the board.

- *Membership Committees.* For a membership organization, a membership committee helps recruit members and reviews and suggests changes in qualifications for membership. It may also be the primary source of communication between the organization and its members.

- *External Relations or Public Affairs Committees.* This type of committee organizes and oversees external public relations and materials. If the nonprofit engages in advocacy activities, this committee may be the interface between the nonprofit and outside advisors on these activities. It may also assist the staff in marketing efforts, or a separate marketing committee may perform that function.

Many nonprofits believe that having persons in addition to board members on these types of committees enables the organization to obtain the input of various constituencies in certain aspects of the nonprofit's operations and funding, helps encourage volunteers already involved with the organization, expands the pool of volunteers available to assist with vital nonprofit functions, and, ultimately, provides an opportunity to assess whether any of these individuals is a potential candidate for board membership. Nonetheless, since laws in this area vary from state to state, whether and to what extent these committees may include non-board members is a matter that typically requires legal advice.

Ad Hoc Committees. Occasionally, the board may want a special or ad hoc committee to deal with a specific project, such as a major fund-raising campaign, the evaluation of a specific transaction, or the development of a new strategic plan. As with any other committee, a special or ad hoc committee has only those functions and responsibilities delegated to it by the board. While the duration of an ad hoc committee is expected to be short, its operations will be facilitated and the potential for misunderstandings minimized if its powers and responsibilities are set out in a written charter approved by the nonprofit's board.

Board Operations

Board and Committee Meetings

Most of the actions taken by boards and committees occur at meetings. Because meetings are so critical to the functioning of the board and its committees, state law and the organization's charter and bylaws usually have a number of provisions related to meetings. It is important for Executive Officers and Board Chairs to understand these provisions not only because of their importance to board administration but also because failure to follow these provisions may cause board or committee actions to be ineffective.

Types of Meetings

Regular, Special, and Annual Meetings. Regular meetings are those that occur on a regularly scheduled basis, with the schedule (place, date, and time) usually set well in advance to facilitate greater attendance. Special meetings are generally called for a particular purpose between regular meetings. Annual meetings are those that are required by law to be held every year or other period for the purpose of taking certain actions, such as electing directors or officers. In some states, one or more meetings may need to be open to members of the general public or to the nonprofit's members, if any.

Face-to-Face, Telephone, and Online Meetings. Most meetings are held face-to-face, that is with members of the board or the committee in the same room. Such meetings facilitate the opportunity for discussion and help assure that directors receive the same information at the same time. However, states allow board members to attend a meeting by telephone, provided that all attendees can hear one another and provided that the organization's bylaws do not prohibit telephone participation. Some states also permit online meetings through web-based technologies. Usually the critical factor in whether non-face-to-face meetings will be allowed is whether the technology used allows directors to be able to communicate directly with all directors attending and to participate in an interactive group discussion.

Actions Between Meetings. Occasionally action is needed between meetings at a time when it is inconvenient or difficult to schedule a special meeting. In such cases, the action may be taken by a duly constituted executive committee which has been delegated the authority to take the action contemplated, or by a written document, commonly called an "Action by Unanimous Written Consent," in which the action sought is approved by all members of the board. The consent document is then filed in the minute book. Written consents are generally useful only for fairly routine matters that do not require discussion and that are not subject to a near-term deadline. In most states, the document must be signed by **all** board members (in original or counterpart) before the action is approved and effective.

Appendix 16 has a sample "Action by Unanimous Written Consent."

Notices

Required Board Notices. To help assure that directors are aware of meetings, state law and bylaw provisions usually provide specific requirements for meeting notices. For example, most bylaws have provisions

- Requiring board members to be notified in advance of meetings;
- Requiring that notices be given a specified number of days in advance;
- Requiring that notice be given in one or more specific manners (mail, personal delivery, electronic (e-mail), telephone, or fax); and
- Specifying whether or what specific information must be detailed in the notice.

If a meeting is a regularly scheduled meeting, the schedule for which has been set and communicated well in advance, a specific meeting notice may not technically be required but, as a practical matter, most organizations routinely furnish notice of all meetings.

Waiver of Notice. Sometimes there is no time to give proper notice, for example, in an emergency, or the notice may have been inadvertently defective for some reason. Most states allow for a "waiver of notice" in these situations. Those attending the meeting are usually deemed to have waived notice by virtue of their attendance. But, in order for any actions taken at such a meeting to be valid, those unable to attend must sign a document stating that they waive notice and consent to the actions taken at the meeting. These waivers are then filed with the minutes of the meeting in question. In minutes of meetings for which proper notice was not given, it is advisable to include a statement that those present waived notice by attending the meeting.

Appendix 17 has a sample Waiver of Notice.

Quorum

For a board or a committee to conduct business, a specified number of board or committee members must be present. This required number of board members is called a quorum. State laws vary on what constitutes the quorum. Typically, state laws provide that unless otherwise specified in the bylaws, at least ½ of the board or committee members must be present for a quorum, but permit the bylaws to specify a lower number, down to a minimum such as 1/3 of the board members then in office. For small boards, quorum minimums may allow two directors to constitute a quorum.

Vacancies usually must be counted in calculating a quorum, so that, if the number of board members has been set at 15 and a quorum is 1/3, but there are three vacancies, the quorum would be five, 1/3 of the full board number of 15, not four or 1/3 of the actual number of board members. Under some states' laws, once a quorum is obtained, the meeting may continue, if not challenged, even if a quorum no longer exists because one or more board members have left the meeting. In other states, a quorum must be maintained whenever a vote is taken so even temporary departures from the meeting room may affect the board's ability to take action.

It is important for the Board Chair, the Executive Officer, and the Secretary to be aware of quorum requirements to avoid situations in which absence of a quorum prevents a board or committee from taking needed action.

Effective Meetings

Because so much of a board's effectiveness depends on the actions taken at meetings, an important role for the Board Chair and Executive Officer is to establish and implement a process and procedures that facilitate the board's consideration of substantive issues. Generally, the potential for effective board and committee meetings is maximized when the following guidelines are followed:

- *Create Written Agendas.* Develop written agendas for each meeting, supported by complete yet concise informational materials for each agenda item.

- *Deliver Materials in Advance.* Deliver agendas, along with supporting information, to each board or committee member sufficiently in advance of the meeting to enable each director adequate time to consider thoroughly the information and actions proposed.

- *Limit Distributions at Meetings.* Minimize distribution of new or amended materials during the board meeting to avoid confusion and facilitate director understanding of issues.

- *Provide Time for Discussion.* Provide sufficient opportunity and resources at the board or committee meeting for full discussion of the material and actions proposed, but consider time limits so that extended discussion of one topic does not prevent consideration of the next items on the agenda.

- *Keep Discussion Relevant.* Manage the board or committee meeting in such a manner as to enable relevant discussion and avoid unnecessarily extended or irrelevant discussion.

- *Keep Discussion Respectful.* Ensure respectful and thorough consideration and decision-making by setting appropriate ground rules and emphasizing the importance of respectful discourse.

Agendas

Purpose of Agendas. While there is no legal requirement to provide an agenda, written agendas help focus board and committee members, as well as staff, on the issues to be considered. If prepared with careful consideration of the full spectrum of board responsibilities and the organization's operations, the agenda also helps ensure that the board or committee is covering matters that are important to the board's exercise of its duty of care.

Many organizations find that assigning times to specific items on the agenda helps keep meetings on track by signaling the amount of time expected to be devoted to each item. Including times for each item also may help the Chair make decisions during the meeting to re-order items on the agenda or shorten times allotted, or even to defer some items for later consideration, if discussion of a particular matter extends substantially beyond the time allotted.

The process for creating agendas varies with each organization. Often the Executive Officer's secretary or administrative assistant prepares an initial draft, based on input from the Board Chair and the Executive Officer. Frequently, input is solicited from senior staff and also from committee chairs.

Agenda Calendars. To help ensure that agendas cover important issues throughout the course of a board year, it can be helpful to create a calendar indicating various items that warrant inclusion on specific agendas or at certain times during the year. Some organizations create draft agendas in advance for the full year, a practice which gives the Executive Officer and the Board Chair the opportunity to look ahead to make sure that important matters are scheduled for discussion, that agendas are consistently tied to the board's own goals and to the organization's strategic needs, and, to the extent feasible, that meetings are of more or less equal importance and length.

Ordering the Agenda. There are no rules for ordering items on an agenda. Some organizations prefer to start with routine or repetitive items that can be handled quickly. Others prefer to start with major or unusual items that need substantial time for discussion. To maximize time for discussion on important items, many organizations utilize the procedure of a "consent agenda" for routine items that usually require little or no discussion by the board or committee. The items contained in the consent agenda are typically voted on as a group. Examples of such items might include routine bank resolutions, ceremonial resolutions (of appreciation, wishing someone well, etc.), or resolutions acknowledging receipt of certain regulatory or other reports. Some organizations include routine committee reports and even board minutes on their consent agendas. Inclusion of an item on the consent agenda does not mean that it cannot be discussed; simply that it is not likely to require significant discussion.

It is often helpful to indicate on the agenda which items require discussion, which are for information, and which require a vote of the board.

Appendix 18 has two examples of agenda formats.

MATERIALS

Advance Delivery. Bylaws often specify the number of days in advance of a meeting that materials and agendas must be delivered to directors. Even when there is no such requirement, advance delivery helps facilitate the ability of a board or committee to handle business effectively. The exercise of due care requires that directors have information and materials on which to base a decision as well as time to understand and discuss such information and to ask questions. Increasingly, board and committee materials are provided electronically by e-mail or on a secure website.

Relevance and Comprehensiveness. A board or committee member's ability to understand and act upon information will be greatly enhanced if the information furnished is complete and accurate but not overwhelming. Voluminous information often sacrifices comprehension to detail: relevance, not technical detail, is a useful standard to apply and follow.

Retention of Meeting Materials. Retention and filing of all meeting materials in an official file is common practice as these materials may need to be referred to after the fact as evidence of what the board or committee considered in taking a particular action, or as evidence supporting the board or committee's exercise of due care.

The Practical Advice Section of this Chapter has additional suggestions on actions that may help improve the usefulness of board and committee materials. See pages 178–180.

Conduct of Meetings

Role of the Chair. The Chair is responsible for ensuring that discussion at the board or committee meeting is relevant, but the Chair's role is to control discussion without directing it. This means the Chair is usually an active listener, rather than a dominating speaker. It also means that the Chair's own views on a particular matter under discussion be expressed carefully, so as not to bias the board or committee discussion. Board or committee members need sufficient opportunity to have their questions answered and to express their views. At the same time, the Chair needs to ensure that the time schedule for the meeting is maintained and that individual board or committee members do not introduce irrelevant matters or interfere with the opportunity of other board members to ask questions or engage in discussion.

Importance of Collegiality. Collegiality and mutual respect among board members are critical to effective meetings, although it is important to realize that collegiality does not always mean agreement by all directors. The Chair's major role is maintaining firm but polite control of the meeting and making it clear that personal attacks, attempts to dominate, and other negative and nonconstructive behavior will not be tolerated.

The Practical Advice Section of this Chapter has additional suggestions on issues and actions that may improve the effectiveness of board and committee meetings. See pages 180–186.

Executive Sessions During Board or Committee Meetings

Meeting with Staff Present. Board and committee meetings generally include, in addition to board or committee members, the Executive Officer (even if not a board member) and perhaps other members of management whose areas of responsibility are relevant to the board's consideration of particular issues or oversight responsibilities. Including senior staff also gives the board opportunity to become familiar with the organization's senior managers. For some matters, board and committee meetings may include outside auditors or other advisors or other guests as well.

Meeting in Executive Session. It is increasingly common for the board or its committees to meet in executive session periodically, if not at every meeting. These executive sessions include only board members, although the board may invite a non-board member, such as the outside auditors, counsel, or a member of the staff to attend some or all of the executive session. The purpose and benefit of executive sessions is to provide a forum for board members to

- Discuss issues they may be otherwise reluctant to raise in the presence of non-board members;
- Discuss particular issues with the Executive Officer or other individual members of management or an outside consultant that are best discussed privately between the board and the individual in question;
- Share candid views with each other about management's or the organization's performance and future;
- Discuss or take action on personnel matters or other potentially sensitive or confidential issues involving members of management or the future of the organization;
- Discuss the effectiveness of board operations; and
- Discuss certain issues raised during the board meeting and the performance of staff at the meeting.

To help keep discussions on point, it may be helpful for the Board Chair to prepare a separate agenda for the executive session that can be distributed at the outset of the session.

Executive Sessions Governance Trend. Governance trends encourage frequent use of executive sessions as a means of emphasizing the level of independence of the board from management. Some Executive Officers may feel uncomfortable or threatened if they are excluded from executive sessions, particularly if they are used to being included in all board discussions or they actually serve on the board. Having such sessions at each board meeting or on a regular schedule throughout the year helps reduce the level of anxiety of staff, as conducting such sessions then becomes a routine matter.

Depending on state law, it may not be possible to exclude an Executive Officer who is also a board member from an executive session of a board meeting without his or her specific consent. Nonetheless, boards commonly make such requests, and it would be highly unusual, and potentially a sign of trouble, if the Executive Officer were to refuse such a request.

Briefing the Executive Officer After an Executive Session. Following an executive session, the Board or Committee Chair may brief the Executive Officer generally on what was discussed. Establishing this practice helps reduce the potential anxiety which an Executive Officer may feel as a result of being excluded from the executive session. Often the board or committee will request that the Chair inform the Executive Officer specifically on certain requests or concerns that arose during the executive session. Because of the potential sensitivity of discussions during an executive session, minutes are not typically kept of such sessions, except to note that the executive session was held. However, if the board takes official action during an executive session, any resolution adopted will need to be included in the minutes of the meeting. Also, if the board makes personnel decisions during an executive session, a record of such actions may need to be made in the appropriate personnel files.

Appendix 19 has a sample executive session agenda.

The Practical Advice Section of this Chapter has additional suggestions for managing the process of holding executive sessions. See pages 185–186.

Motions, Resolutions, and Voting

Boards and committees take action by voting on motions that have been made and seconded by members of the board or committee. A motion is a suggestion or proposal that the board or committee take a particular action. Proposed actions, particularly complex or important ones, are often detailed in written resolutions. A resolution is simply a statement of the action to be taken and may or may not include background reasons or information as to why the board is taking the action.

Formal Resolutions. There are no absolute rules, and state laws differ, on items that require a formal written resolution of the board. A motion to adjourn does not require such a resolution. A motion to buy or sell a building or other significant asset typically requires a written resolution. Other actions may or may not be documented by a written resolution. Resolutions are often used when it is likely that third parties will need evidence of a particular board action or when a broader group, such as employees, may need to be informed of the action taken and use such information in their daily duties (for example, a delegation of authority). Resolutions often contain specific delegations of authority to specific individuals to take specific actions or to carry out the intent of the resolution.

Several Common Formats. There are no universal standards for the format to be used in drafting resolutions. Many organizations use the traditional "whereas…., resolved that…" format, where the background information is contained in "whereas" clauses and the action is detailed after the words "resolved that" or "further resolved that." Others use phrases such as "the board authorizes and determines that…" as the lead-in language for the specific action being approved and dispense with "whereas" clauses. Clarity rather than form is the most important quality in drafting resolutions. Often specific language will be required by an organization, such as a bank or brokerage firm, requesting adoption of a particular resolution. There may be little room for discussion of the wording required in such instances, but the board or committee may request clarification or changes to the wording if the proposed language raises concerns.

Advance Distribution Advisable. Drafting and distributing proposed resolutions in advance of the board or committee meeting at which the resolution will be considered can be helpful in assuring that those voting have a clear understanding of what they are being asked to consider.

Changes Often Required. Often the draft resolution will require changes based on discussion at the board or committee meeting. If the changes are extensive, it may be preferable to delay voting until the revised resolution can be redistributed.

Voting Process. Voting on resolutions is typically done by voice vote and, unless the bylaws otherwise require, an affirmative vote of a majority of the board members constituting a quorum for the meeting is sufficient to adopt a resolution.

Index. For ease of reference and keeping track of board and committee actions over time, it is useful to keep an index of resolutions adopted by the board or its committees and to maintain a separate file with copies of all resolutions adopted.

Certifications. Resolutions often need to be certified by the board Secretary and delivered to third parties. The certification typically includes the full text of the resolution, states the date the resolution was adopted, and certifies that it is still in effect.

Appendix 20 has a typical Secretary's Certificate and formats for resolutions.

Minutes of Meetings

In order for directors and the board to receive the benefit of the business judgment rule and to show that the duties of care and loyalty have been satisfied, it is important that accurate records be kept of board and committee deliberations and actions. Minutes summarize the actions taken at meetings and, once approved by the board or committee, constitute the official record of the legal actions taken by the board or committee. Minutes are often reviewed by auditors and regulatory authorities and may have to be produced in litigation. They set forth, at a minimum, the date and time of the meeting, which board or committee members attended and which ones did not, who served as Chair and Secretary for the meeting, the topics discussed and what actions were taken. When resolutions are adopted, the text of the resolutions is included in the body of the minutes or as an attachment.

Minute Writing is an Art. Clarity and accuracy are very important, as minutes may be referred to long after the fact. Confusing or nonessential details in minutes can also create legal problems. The degree of detail required to be included in the minutes is a matter of discussion among attorneys and between organizations and their regulators. Directors may reasonably require that minutes be sufficiently detailed to support the availability of the business judgment rule by summarizing important discussions and reflecting that board members engaged in a reasonable deliberative process before taking action, taking into account the information given them and having considered possible alternatives. Minutes are not intended to be a verbatim transcript nor do they need to attribute particular opinions to individual board members. However, board members voting against an action or abstaining are within their rights to have their abstentions or negative votes noted in the minutes and many nonprofits identify dissenters as a standard practice.

Guidelines Based on Experience. While minute writing is somewhat of an art, many corporate secretaries and lawyers recommend a few simple guidelines which can help simplify and demystify the process. It may facilitate not only the process of drafting, but the ease of subsequent review, to develop a template that can be used as the basis for each set of minutes.

Appendix 21 has minutes guidelines and templates.

Taking Notes. Taking notes at a meeting is often done by a staff member rather than the board-appointed Secretary. The main function of the note taker is to keep track of actions taken and the matters discussed. A verbatim transcript is not needed. Occasionally, the individual responsible will want to record the meeting on tape, although this is generally not advisable for a number of reasons: audio quality is generally poor, making subsequent transcription difficult; it usually takes more time to transcribe from a tape and then to draft from handwritten notes and the prepared agenda from the meeting; board members may be uncomfortable stating their views when the meeting is taped; and tapes that are not destroyed once minutes are finalized may create legal issues.

Drafting and Reviewing Minutes. For most nonprofits, the person who takes the notes at the meeting also creates the first draft of minutes. The draft is then reviewed by the Executive Officer, the Board Chair, and the Secretary prior to submission to the board or committee for further review and approval, usually at the next meeting. Depending on the matters considered at the meeting, legal counsel may also be involved in the review.

Attorney-Client Privileged Matters. If any part of the minutes is considered to contain attorney-client privileged material, counsel will probably be involved not only in the drafting and review of such minutes, but also in establishing and implementing a procedure to avoid inadvertent loss of the privilege once the minutes are filed in the minute book.

The Practical Advice Section of this Chapter has additional guidelines for drafting minutes. See pages 186–188.

Committee Reports. In addition to documenting committee activity in minutes, committee work is also typically reported on a regular basis to the full board either by distribution of committee minutes or committee reports or by oral presentations by committee chairs during board meetings. Board members are entitled to rely on committee minutes and reports in their own deliberations of matters brought before the board following committee action or consideration.

The Practical Advice Section of this Chapter has additional guidelines for drafting committee reports. See pages 188–189.

Delegation

Board members are entitled to rely on others to assist them in discharging their duties, and boards routinely delegate to others the duty of handling various matters on their behalf. Those on whom they may rely and to whom they may delegate include board committees, outside advisors and experts, members of management, and, in certain instances, others not as closely affiliated with the legal structure of the organization, such as volunteers. Delegations may be made only to the extent permitted by applicable law and the organization's governing documents. Board member reliance on those to whom it has delegated duties or responsibilities must be reasonable in order for the board to satisfy its duty of care and to receive the benefit of the business judgment rule for its decisions.

Delegation to Management

General Delegation. Most nonprofit boards do not manage day-to-day operations but delegate operational management to the Executive Officer and other senior staff. Such delegation may be authorized in part by the nonprofit's bylaws, for example, as part of the description of the role of the Executive Officer. Additionally, the board's approval of the nonprofit's strategic plan and its approval of the annual operating budget have the effect, as between the board and staff, of giving the staff authority to operate within the parameters of the approved plan and budget.

Specific Delegation. There are, however, types of delegations or responsibility that require a specific delegation or board approval, either as a matter of law or because another party to a transaction, such as a bank, demands it. For example, committing the nonprofit to significant action such as a major asset purchase or sale generally requires board approval. Boards often specify the

Executive Officer, CFO, or other responsible representative who is authorized to sign documents or take other necessary action. Outside the context of a specific transaction, a board may want to impose certain limits on the general authority of the Executive Officer to act without specific board authorization. In such a case, policies and procedures approved by the board or the description of the Executive Officer's role in the bylaws or in specific board resolutions may require that the Executive Officer obtain specific authority to act under certain circumstances (such as before committing the organization to a long-term lease or before hiring a senior staff person).

Clarity is Important. From a governance perspective, the important issue regarding delegations and limits on authority is that they be clearly understood and articulated. Executive Officers and boards may have differing expectations relating to delegated authority, which are often unarticulated. Putting delegations and limitations on delegated authority in writing, whether in the nonprofit's basic documents, its policies and procedures, or in specific board resolutions, helps to assure that both board and staff understand the parameters under which they operate.

Appendix 22 has a sample general delegation of authority and a sample of delegation for a specific transaction.

Use of Advisors and Outsourcing

There are various kinds of expert advisors the board or management may engage.

- Many nonprofits have outside auditors and rely on their auditors to assist in the board's oversight responsibilities.
- Nonprofits with substantial endowments may hire outside money managers to invest funds and investment advisors to review the effectiveness of the money managers.
- The board or senior leadership may also from time to time retain attorneys to advise and assist in understanding legal responsibilities and to perform certain tasks or to assist with certain transactions, such as the purchase or sale of major assets.
- In the event of a strategic evaluation, the board may retain an outside firm or a facilitator to assist in its planning sessions.
- Tax advisors may also be retained, and these may or may not be the same as the outside auditors.
- A valuation company may be used to appraise assets being purchased or sold to help assure that the nonprofit does not pay more than fair market value or receive less than fair market value for real property or other material assets.
- An organization may use outside marketing or public relations firms to propose and/or implement specific projects.

- Advocacy or lobbying efforts may also require the use of experts not normally found on the nonprofit's staff.
- Various administrative functions, such as payroll and benefits administration, may be outsourced to for-profit organizations or to individuals with expertise in specific administrative areas.

In many cases, such experts are engaged by management with reports reviewed by both management and the board. In other cases (such as with auditors and compensation consultants) the board or a board committee may select and engage the expert.

Legal Responsibility cannot be Delegated. While engaging independent experts may be a useful, or even necessary, way for a nonprofit's leadership or the board to assure that the organization is meeting its legal obligations and maximizing its resources for the benefit of its mission, unquestioning reliance on such experts may constitute an improper delegation of the board's or management's fiduciary duty of care. The board cannot delegate its decision-making functions to outside experts or to management, although directors are entitled to reasonably rely on the opinions of such experts. Before relying on an expert's opinion, directors must be satisfied regarding the expert's qualifications, process, and overall conclusions and have the opportunity to review reports and ask questions. In addition, while in many cases engaging an outside expert or consultant is a necessary expense, excessive use of outside experts may be a drain on the organization's resources. Therefore, the use and selection of experts for significant levels of service may itself be a matter for board review and consultation.

Conflicts and Related-Party Transactions. In some cases, nonprofits, especially smaller ones, may obtain a needed service from friends or family members of officers or board members or companies owned by board members or their friends. Such related-party services raise concerns about conflict of interest and the payment of fair value for services rendered. However, related-party transactions are not inherently wrong nor bad for the organization, and often a nonprofit's leaders have a greater degree of confidence in dealing with individuals or companies that have other connections with the nonprofit. However, related-party transactions and other conflict situations need to be managed to avoid legal problems and public perception issues. Careful adherence to conflict of interest policies and procedures, such as disclosure and recusal, and recording such adherence in board minutes, may help avoid the appearance of impropriety that often accompanies such related-party transactions.

See pages 171 and 183 for additional discussion of conflict of interest issues.

Liability for Actions of Third-Party Service Providers. Organizations can be liable for actions or inactions of an individual or company hired to perform services on the nonprofit's behalf. Ongoing and careful monitoring of service providers is important, particularly in situations in which outside parties might not be aware that the applicable service is being conducted by an individual or entity separate from the nonprofit organization. (Fund-raising is one area in which the actions of overzealous outside agents have been known to harm an organization's reputation or create liability for the organization.) For this reason, nonprofits often ask service providers to provide indemnification and/ or insurance protecting the nonprofit against such potential liability.

Delegation to Auxiliary Organizations

A very common form of delegation to an affiliate organization is the use of auxiliaries or other volunteer organizations for fund-raising events. Such organizations may or may not be separately incorporated entities and may or may not be wholly controlled by the nonprofit organization or under common control through a parent organization. Occasionally, an auxiliary may appear to have a separate legal structure with a charter and a board but in reality be just a separate division within the nonprofit organization. Regardless of actual structure, the possibility of role confusion is inherent whenever multiple groups or entities engage in similar activities on behalf of an organization. Periodic board review of the relationship of the auxiliary and the nonprofit, as well as careful attention to, and documentation of, the desired roles and relationships between the auxiliary organization and nonprofit at the time the auxiliary is created, may help minimize confusion and problems.

Limits of Delegation to Auxiliary Organizations. While it may be useful to have an affiliated organization undertake the myriad details surrounding a major fund-raising event or other fund-raising activities, there are potential negative aspects of working with such an organization, such as having to ensure that the organization does not become more independent from the nonprofit and its mission than is legally acceptable or practically useful. Many nonprofit organizations have experienced the awkwardness of having to explain to a volunteer organization, whether or not separately incorporated, that it exists in connection with the greater whole and has duties and responsibilities that tie it closely to the main organization it was formed to support.

Auxiliaries and affiliated organizations that are separately incorporated will generally have separate tax-exempt status, but their organizational purposes, as reflected in their articles of incorporation, typically specify the operating nonprofit as the sole beneficiary of the auxiliary's operations. The funds raised are generally solicited in the name of and in accordance with the tax-exempt status of the nonprofit or that of the affiliated or auxiliary organization.

The affiliated or auxiliary organization cannot divert funds to its own use but must ensure that its fund-raising activities and use of funds are in accord with the overall mission and subject to accounting procedures and review in the same manner as all other activities of the nonprofit. Nonetheless, there may be conflicts between a nonprofit and an affiliated organization regarding how the affiliate can most effectively serve its supporting role. Diplomacy may be required when a supporting nonprofit's leaders seek to have their supporting affiliate change long-standing routines and events in favor of new alternatives.

Orientation for New Directors

An orientation program or process can help new directors become effective more quickly. Often the Board Chair or the governance committee oversees such orientation and requests key staff members to participate in providing information about different aspects of the organization. In some cases, the Executive Officer may take the lead in organizing a group orientation session, or provide one-on-one orientation to a new board member if no group orientation is planned at the time the individual joins the board. Often orientation sessions include the opportunity to meet informally with other board members at a reception or dinner following the formal orientation program.

Written orientation materials, including board member contact information, copies of board and committee charters and calendars, year-end audit reports, and copies of governing documents, are often distributed to new board members as part of orientation sessions. Often these materials are included in a binder known as a "Directors' Manual" (see below) which may be in hard-copy or electronic form. When the press of business or difficulties in scheduling make it difficult or impossible to conduct in-person orientation programs, written materials can be expanded to help provide additional information that might otherwise have been covered in an in-person orientation.

Directors' Manual. Many organizations provide new board members with a "Directors' Manual," containing important legal and informational documents such as articles, bylaws, a roster of board members, often with pictures and biographies as well as contact information, a copy of the organization's mission statement, recent financial statements or annual reports, minutes of recent board and committee meetings, copies of committee charters, and perhaps a glossary of terms and acronyms in common usage at the organization. The contents of the manual may be determined by the Executive Officer, the Board Chair, the nominating or governance committee, or some combination of these individuals and groups. Often the Directors' Manual is in a paper binder or notebook, but increasingly it is in electronic form which can be provided to directors via computer disk or posted on a secure website with access restricted to directors. Staff usually prepares and revises the information contained in the manual, but it is important for the Executive Officer, the Chair, or another board member or committee to review material and help determine whether additional or different material should be included within the manual from time to time.

Appendix 23 has a sample table of contents for a director manual.

In-Person Orientations and Tours. As noted above, in-person orientations provide new directors with the opportunity to ask questions and hear directly from one or more experienced board and/or staff members. At such an orientation session, a new board member may be given a brief overview of the entity's history, mission, and current programs and an opportunity to ask questions about the materials in the orientation package that he or she received. Board matters emphasized in the orientation session would usually include the contents of the manual given to board members, if there is one; conflict of interest rules; the schedules of board and committee meetings and any other activities, including fund-raising events, that may be scheduled for the near future; review of the nature and activities of board committees; discussion of the scope of responsibilities of key staff members; key aspects of board or organizational culture or traditions; and any matters specifically requested by the new board member.

Often the orientation includes a tour of the organization's principal physical location and introductions to key staff members, who may give brief descriptions of their respective areas of responsibility. New board members may also be introduced to key support staff, such as the administrative assistant to the Executive Officer or other administrative staff who are likely to be those with whom the board member has the most frequent contact. Depending on the capabilities of the organization and the number of board members to be provided an orientation session at one time, the program may be tailored to the particular talents and experience of the new director. For example, if an individual was selected because of his or her knowledge about a particular program of the nonprofit, that individual may need less detail about that program, but more orientation on other aspects of the organization. A person who has been chosen because of his or her financial expertise may need more information about the nonprofit's programs and mission and less guidance in understanding financial information.

Appendix 24 has an outline of a possible orientation program for new directors.

Mentoring. Some nonprofit organizations have mentoring programs under which each new director is assigned to a veteran board member. Mentors can be a valuable asset in helping a new board or committee member become comfortable with the board, shortening the time within which the new person becomes a knowledgeable and valuable board member.

Orientation for Non-Board Members. An orientation program can also be useful for non-board members who serve on ad hoc or other committees with board members.

Ongoing Education of the Board

Continual education of the board about the affairs of the nonprofit and the environment in which it operates is also important to developing and maintaining an effective board. The Board Chair and the Executive Officer can greatly assist ongoing education efforts for board members by routinely scheduling time on agendas for important background/educational briefings. Unfortunately, because agendas may be tight, it can be tempting to replace educational presentations at board and committee meetings with more immediate matters. Scheduling stand-alone education sessions at convenient times during the year, such as periodic lunches or dinners or board retreats, can help relieve some of the pressure on agendas, but intermittent educational efforts may not be as effective in the long run as focusing on educating the board at every meeting.

Some organizations encourage attendance at outside educational programs and may pay for certain board members to attend seminars or programs hosted by other organizations on issues of importance to the organization. In some cases, the organization's outside consultants, such as attorneys, accountants, or insurance brokers, may provide complimentary seats at programs they are hosting on current business trends or legal developments that may be of interest to board or committee members.

Education on the Nonprofit's Affairs. Because nonprofit board members are volunteers and not necessarily familiar with the nonprofit's mission, they frequently need ongoing education about the nonprofit's operations and focus in order to be effective directors. Board Chairs and Executive Officers want to be sure that board members have a basic knowledge about the organization's programs and affairs so that board members can ask pertinent questions and contribute useful ideas without wasting valuable board time. Failure to provide such education can lead to frustration for the Executive Officer, who may feel the board does not understand either the organization's accomplishments or its challenges. Board members may feel they are being kept in the dark and that they must ask many questions to understand the information they are receiving. Worse, they may feel the Executive Officer is actually withholding valuable information. Executive Officers and Board Chairs can help address such issues in part by making sure the board routinely receives background information relating to key areas and issues that are reported on at board meetings. Such background information helps ensure that all board members, regardless of tenure on the board, have the same basic knowledge.

Education on the Law and External Developments. Beyond general education about the work of the nonprofit and its environment, it is important for board and committee members to be updated on a regular basis on significant changes in the law and other developments that affect the nonprofit's mission or operations and the board's governance and legal responsibilities. Such developments might be one of the regular items on the agenda for discussion between the Board Chair and the Executive Officer, so they can make sure that such items are included on board and committee agendas at appropriate times or intervals.

Evaluating and Improving Board Effectiveness

Effective nonprofit boards, no matter how different in style or approach, generally have several things in common: they understand the programs or mission of the organization, they help advance the organization's mission, and they understand and operate in accordance with legal and fiduciary responsibilities. Effective nonprofit boards typically utilize a number of governance practices adapted from the for-profit arena to help them maintain or improve their effectiveness. While governance practices used by for-profit organizations cannot assure nonprofit board or organizational effectiveness, many of them can help increase the likelihood that the nonprofit's activities are well-managed. Board and board member self-evaluations and board effectiveness surveys may be particularly useful in this regard.

Board Effectiveness Surveys

Comprehensive Surveys. For boards that have never examined their own operations in depth, a comprehensive board effectiveness survey can be a useful starting place, regardless of whether the board appears to be functioning well or whether there are obvious problems or perceptions of ineffectiveness. A board effectiveness survey:

- Polls the board on a wide array of issues related to the effective operation of the board, focusing on both substance and process;
- Provides a base line for looking at how the board itself believes it is doing, and for comparing board practices to those of other boards and to governance trends; and
- Becomes a starting point for making adjustments and improvements to governance structures, board processes, and when necessary, personnel.

Cooperation and Support of the Board Required. Any board effectiveness review requires the cooperation of board members, which can sometimes be difficult to obtain. Questionnaires must be filled out, or time reserved for responding to questions if the questions are asked face-to-face. Board members must be candid and feel comfortable that their confidences will be respected. Board members who recognize that an effectiveness review may be helpful or needed may first need to convince their fellow board members of the value of the review. This process can be delicate, as it often means convincing board members of the need to address a problem without alienating those on the board or otherwise involved with the nonprofit who may be resistant to considering needed change. It may be necessary to discuss the process at length until board members become comfortable with the idea, or perhaps to expose board members to members of other boards who have engaged in the process and can attest to its value.

Process. Once agreement to conduct an effectiveness survey is reached, the Executive Officer and the Board Chair work together to determine the best process for the organization to use in developing and managing the overall project and then assign responsibility to an individual director or a committee. The director or committee appointed to lead the project develops a series of questions with input from management and other board members, and, if desired, with assistance from an outside consultant. Often the nominating committee or the governance committee will have the responsibility for conducting a board effectiveness review. However, because such reviews are often conducted in conjunction with or as part of strategic planning efforts, other committees may also be involved. It is important to consider the scope of the survey before assigning responsibility to a specific committee.

Use of Outside Consultants. Whether to hire an outside consultant or facilitator for a board effectiveness review is an important initial consideration. That decision may depend on finances as well as the perceived ability of the board and its individual members to be rigorous in conducting the study and reaching what may be difficult conclusions themselves. If the board has not previously conducted such a study, use of an outside consultant may be particularly helpful in bringing credibility, as well as expertise and efficiency, to the process. To help offset costs or help determine the appropriate scope of review, sample effectiveness review documents may be available through a state or federal trade association or from governance-related publications or organizations.

Types of Questions. Questions included in a board effectiveness survey typically range from the level of "housekeeping" (e.g., time, place, and length of meetings) to the more substantive (e.g., the critical issues facing the organization in the next two years). Even when the exercise is conducted apart from a strategic planning effort, questions may still focus on issues related to strategy and performance of the organization as well as on matters more closely related to board composition and operations. At a minimum, these types of studies are designed to reveal the answers to questions such as:

- Is the board effective in its oversight duties?
- Is the board sufficiently supportive of the nonprofit?

- Are there backgrounds and talents that might be of benefit to the non-profit that are not represented in the present board composition?
- Does the board understand, support, and believe in the organization's mission and how it is being executed?
- Does the board adequately represent the nonprofit's constituencies?
- Is the Board Chair providing effective leadership?
- Is the board supportive of the Executive Officer?
- Is the board performing the functions or achieving the goals that it has previously determined for itself?
- Are meeting attendance and participation adequate to enable the board to perform its functions?
- Are there individual board members who are not adequately meeting the responsibilities expected of them?

Appendix 25 has sample board effectiveness questionnaires.

Obtaining the Answers. The questions developed are used as the basis for eliciting information from board members, although it is common for the answers to raise issues beyond the questions asked. Questions may be distributed in written form and answers provided either in writing or orally. Surveys also can be conducted electronically, which may improve the efficiency of the entire process.

More detailed and representative results are often obtained by using face-to-face or telephone interviews rather than relying on written or electronic responses to questions, although a telephonic or face-to-face process can be quite time consuming when the number of board members to be interviewed is large. Face-to-face interviews or telephone interviews are particularly important if there are perceived problems with board or organizational leadership. Board members are often reluctant to express negative opinions about individuals in writing. Use of a third party to conduct the survey and analyze responses allows the process to be done on a confidential basis, which may also be important to some directors.

Summarizing and Analyzing. Once the survey is completed, the board member or committee in charge of the process analyzes and summarizes the responses in a format that is useful to the board and protects the confidentiality of those who participated.

Summarized results are shared with the board and a process created for follow-up and adjustments to board procedures and organization. Most effectiveness surveys are not self-executing, but require changes in how the board or committees operate, who is on the board, and what is expected of board members, among other things. Issues raised in the survey may need to be addressed by a variety of board committees. Some problems related to board effectiveness are relatively easy to address—for example, those which indicate a need to change topics discussed at the board or to rotate committee membership more frequently. Others are more difficult—for example, a need for changes in board leadership, general dissatisfaction with the Executive Officer's relationship with the board or leadership of the organization, or concerns about individual directors. These types of issues may, and usually do, require considerable time to address and may call for considerable skill in dealing with interpersonal relationships.

Follow-up with the Board. Whatever the issues raised and conclusions reached, it is important that the issues be fully discussed and considered and that the ultimate decisions as to needed actions or changes have board support. It is also important that changes found advisable are not ignored. Once concerns and expectations of board members have been raised, they will expect action. Failure to follow through risks increasing disaffection and unhappiness of board members, as well as continuing ineffectiveness at the board level.

Building Consensus. Occasionally, there may be dissension among directors as to the conclusions to be drawn from the study. In this event, it may be necessary to enlist the services of a governance or organizational development expert to assist the board in determining how to proceed. At the very least, the Board Chair and Executive Officer will need to work together to help bring about consensus or move beyond the areas of disagreement so that changes can be agreed to and implemented. Sometimes major disagreements can lead to the resignation of dissenting board members.

Frequency. Board effectiveness studies typically require significant time and effort, and if outside consultants are used, expense. Such factors can make them impracticable to conduct annually. Nonetheless, the discipline of conducting regular reviews at least every three years, if not more often, provides an important mechanism for boards to better understand how board members view board operations and to make adjustments as needed before any significant problems occur.

The Practical Advice Section of this Chapter has additional information on issues to consider and actions needed to conduct a board effectiveness survey. See pages 209–210.

Ongoing Board Self-Evaluations

After a major effectiveness study has been completed, or when it is impractical to conduct a comprehensive study, conducting regular shorter form board self-evaluations can be useful. Board self-evaluations are usually shorter and less comprehensive than effectiveness reviews, and they focus more on issues related to operation of the board itself, with few or no questions on organizational or strategic issues, although such questions can also be included. Board self-evaluations can also be used to collect information on how board members feel changes have been implemented after a broader board effectiveness study. Board self-evaluations are typically compiled by the committee charged with governance responsibilities and are less likely to require the use of an outside consultant. They usually take the form of short questionnaires which board members fill out and return to the Governance Committee, or sometimes to the Board Chair. Results of these questionnaires also need to be summarized and presented to the full board and matters that surface in the questionnaires addressed, or again, the board risks increasing dissatisfaction from board members.

Appendix 26 has a typical short form board effectiveness self-evaluation.

Individual Director Evaluations

Developing a mechanism for evaluating individual director performance is another governance practice that can help build the effectiveness of nonprofit boards. When effective board members perceive that their fellow board members are weak or not pulling their weight, board and committee discussions and actions can be hampered, enthusiasm can dwindle, and, ultimately, the most effective board members may decide to leave the board. Additionally, if board-established criteria and expectations for membership are inconsistently applied, it becomes difficult to ask any board member to adhere to them.

Types of Individual Evaluations. There are two types of evaluations that may be helpful, either individually, or in combination: board member self-evaluations and peer evaluations. The prerequisite for both is establishment and approval of criteria for board membership. If none have been established or such criteria have not recently been reviewed and modified or reconfirmed, setting these criteria is a necessary first step in any board member evaluation process.

Director Self-Evaluations

As the name suggests, self-evaluations ask each board member to rate him or herself in specific areas, based on previously established criteria, and to respond to various questions related to board service.

Conducting Self-Evaluations. Self-evaluations are usually conducted by questionnaires distributed to each board member, which are returned to the nominating committee or governance committee, or perhaps to an outside consultant.

Types of Questions. Following are a few sample questions that might be used in a self-evaluation:

- Please rate yourself on a scale of 1-5 with 5 being the highest/best, with respect to the following :
  — Attendance at board and assigned committee meetings;
  — Understanding of the organization's mission;
  — Understanding of the organization's operations and financial situation;
  — Degree of participation in board and committee activities;
  — Understanding of the role of the board;
  — Personal degree of participation in fund-raising; and
  — Level of personal financial contributions to the organization.
- Has your participation increased or decreased in the past year, and if so, what are the reasons?
- Is there something management or the board could do to help you maintain or increase your effectiveness as a board member?

The inclusion of open-ended questions can be particularly helpful in eliciting useful information.

Benefit of Self-Evaluations. Self-evaluations help directors think about their own contributions to the work of the board and can serve as a catalyst for improvement, or sometimes for a decision to step down from the board. Self-evaluations are rarely threatening to board members or to the collegiality of the board, since board members only rate themselves.

Sharing Results. Results may be distributed to the committee conducting the survey, with or without summary. Following discussion in committee, and based on the information elicited in the evaluation, the Board Chair or chair of the nominating or governance committee may decide to follow up with various directors on issues raised in their responses or recommend changes to board practices to address issues that have surfaced in a number of questionnaires.

The Practical Advice Section of this Chapter has additional suggestions for developing and conducting director evaluations. See pages 190–192.

Peer Evaluations

Peer evaluations are a frank look, by board members, at each board member's contribution to the work of the board based on previously approved criteria, such as attendance and participation in board and committee meetings and activities, understanding of the mission and the organization's operations and financial situation, participation in fund-raising, personal contributions, understanding the role of the board, and advocacy in the community. Peer evaluations can be perceived as threatening to the collegiality of the board, but they have the benefit of more objectivity than self-evaluations.

Conducting a Peer Evaluation. Peer evaluations are often conducted by the governance committee or nominating committee with only committee members participating. They are perhaps most often conducted in connection with decisions as to whether a board member should be renominated for another term. However, there is also a benefit in conducting the evaluation annually, so that if one of more board members are not meeting expectations, the Board Chair or a member of the nominating or governance committee can speak to them and encourage them to improve their participation.

Peer evaluations can also be conducted by asking board members to rate each other, using confidential questionnaires that are based on previously established criteria. This type of peer evaluation is less common because board members often feel uncomfortable explicitly rating each other, even on a confidential basis. Questionnaires are often returned to an outside consultant because of board member concerns about confidentiality. If concerns about a particular board member surface, the nominating or governance committee, together with the Board Chair, will need to determine whether discussion with such director or directors might help in addressing the concerns raised or whether rotation off the board is more appropriate.

Types of Questions. The types of questions included in a peer evaluation questionnaire would usually be quite similar to those in a self-evaluation, or in a reappointment evaluation by the Board Chair or a governance committee, for example:

- Rate each board member with respect to the following factors on a scale of 1-5 with five being the highest/best possible rating:
  — Attendance at board and assigned committee meetings;
  — Understanding of the organization's mission;
  — Understanding of the organization's operations and financial situation;
  — Thoughtful participation in board and committee meetings;
  — Understanding the role of the board;
  — Respect for board processes and fellow board members;
  — Financial support to the organization consistent with expectations;
  — Participation in fund-raising activities; and
  — Advocacy for the organization in the community.

Benefit of Peer Evaluations. Peer evaluations can be particularly helpful when there is a perceived lack of collegiality on the board or during times of transition on the board (for example, when a board moves from being an operating board to a governance board). Peer evaluation can help management and the Chair better understand how perceptions among board members affect individual board member performance and willingness to participate in board activities or carry out certain responsibilities. They may raise issues and comments that some individuals would be reluctant to raise on a face-to face basis with fellow board members. Nonetheless, other board members may feel uncomfortable actually rating their fellow board members in any way, regardless of whether there are issues with collegiality, board effectiveness, or board member performance. Some may feel they should not rate fellow board members because they have insufficient information on their participation with the organization.

Sharing Results. The results of peer evaluations are usually discussed in the nominating committee or the governance committee and used to help make determinations about renominations, or to provide a basis for discussion with individual board members about how they might increase their own effectiveness in light of comments from their peers. Usually, the results of these individual peer evaluations are not shared with the full board, although general statistics that do not include individual names or attributes may be shared. For example, ten board members were rated 4 or higher for attendance at board meetings; three were rated 3 for attendance; and two were rated 1 for attendance. Ten members were rated 4 or higher for understanding the role of the board; three were rated 3; and two were rated 1 for understanding the role of the board.

The Practical Advice Section of this Chapter has additional suggestions for developing and conducting director self-evaluations. See page 192.

Comparing Governance Practices

It can be helpful to compare an organization's governance practices not only with those of similar organizations, but also with practices suggested by governance commentators and governance organizations. Such a comparative review may be undertaken by a governance committee of the board, but Executive Officers and Board Chairs may also find it helpful to conduct their own inquiries into governance trends. The Internet has become a useful tool for exploring governance concepts and commentary. There are also many books available on the topic of governance, both for nonprofits and for for-profit organizations. Many associations also have developed suggested or best practices or even created governance standards for their member organizations.

Process. One way to begin a comparison process is to create a spreadsheet listing in abbreviated form suggested governance practices from a variety of sources. These can then be compared to the nonprofit's current practices, and any differences or gaps can then be discussed to determine if changes might be helpful to the organization.

Governance Practices. Many commentators and some regulators, such as the IRS, believe that nonprofits should consider and follow many of the governance trends and practices typically followed by or required by law for for-profit companies. Set forth below is a list of issues and practices that are increasingly considered by both for-profit companies and nonprofit organizations when reviewing their board governance practices.

- *Director Independence*—the trend is for a majority or substantially all board members to be independent of management.

- *Conflict of Interest Policy*—the trend is for adoption of conflict of interest policies and procedures and for documenting in appropriate records, such as minutes, that there is effective implementation of such policies and procedures.

- *Code of Conduct for Directors*—governance commentators/activists often recommend adoption of board codes of conduct.

- *Term Limits*—many commentators/activists support term limits.

- *Age Limits*—some commentators/activists support age limits.

- *Diversity of Directors*—commentators/activists often recommend diversity of board membership, including age diversity and representation of the organization's target audience or beneficiary groups.

- *Director Orientation*—the trend is to provide more orientation and continuing education.

- *Engagement of Directors*—the trend is to encourage greater engagement, especially in the board's oversight role and through active committee participation.

- *Board Size*—the trend is to encourage smaller-sized boards (e.g., from nine to fifteen directors).

- *Subjects Covered at Board Meetings*—the trend, often encouraged or mandated by various laws, is to increase the types of subjects needing board oversight and attention, either at the board or committee level.

- *Advance Distribution of Materials*—the long-term practice is to send materials well in advance of meetings.

- *Increased Clarity of Material*—commentators/activists often recommend that board material be evaluated to assure that it is neither too dense nor too summary and is readily comprehensible.

- *Executive Sessions*—the trend is for increasing regular use of executive sessions.

- *Committee Structure and Membership*—commentators/activists often recommend continual review of committee structure and rotation of committee members.

- *Board Self-Evaluations*—the trend is for boards to conduct such evaluations.

- *Director Evaluations*—the trend is for boards to conduct such evaluations.

- *Executive Officer Evaluations*—the trend is for written evaluations.

- *Succession Planning*—commentators/activists encourage succession planning.

- *Greater Transparency in Dealing with Stakeholders*—the trend is for greater transparency generally with respect to a nonprofit's revenues, expenditures, and overall operations and effectiveness. To a considerable extent for tax-exempt nonprofits, this is mandated by the IRS Form 990 as revised in 2008.

- *Accessibility of the Board to Stakeholders and Other Constituencies*— often recommended by commentators/activists.

Practical Advice on Governing Documents, Board Structure, and Operations

Matters to Keep in Mind When Creating, Reviewing, or Amending Articles of Incorporation

The following suggestions may be helpful to consider in creating, reviewing, or amending articles of incorporation of nonprofit organizations:

- *Consult Legal Counsel.* While there are forms and templates available for nonprofit articles, it is prudent to consult legal counsel for advice and assistance in preparing articles of incorporation and any amendments to the articles to assure compliance with applicable state law and federal tax law. Nonprofit or tax-exempt status may be denied if articles are not properly drafted.

- *Check Name Requirements and Availability.* Names of nonprofits often are descriptive of their purpose, or reflect the origin of their formation or names of founders. Depending on state law, a corporation may need to include "Corporation," "Inc.," "Limited," or "Ltd." as part of its name as an indicator of the limited liability associated with this type of organization. However, some states and nonprofit organizations consider the use of appellations such as "Inc." and "Corporation" to signify more of a for-profit, as opposed to mission-oriented, organization; therefore, many nonprofits avoid such terms in their legal names.

Because it may be difficult or impossible to use a particular name if that name, or one very similar, is already in use by another corporation in the jurisdiction, it is important to check the availability of the name in state records and also to make sure it does not conflict with a trademark or service mark owned and used by another person or entity.

- *Pay Particular Attention to the Purpose Clause and Related Provisions.* The purpose clause is one of the most critical provisions of non-profit corporation articles. The organization's mission is derived from its purpose. If the purpose clause is drafted too narrowly, it may restrict the organization's mission and operations, unless subsequently amended. If drafted too broadly (e.g., allowing operations "for any legal purpose") it is unlikely to be sufficient for the organization to receive tax-exempt or nonprofit status. Not only must the purpose stated be consistent with the status desired, but certain additional provisions will need to be included in the articles in order to obtain tax-exempt status, or to comply with requirements for the type of nonprofit being created.

- *Adhere Closely to Language Used in State Statutes and Federal Laws and Regulations.* Articles are reviewed by state and federal officials before they are accepted for filing. Staying close to statutory and regulatory language may facilitate faster review and eliminate the need for changes in order for filing to be permitted.

- *Keep Track.* Keep track of all changes to the articles by filing the articles and all amendments in a separate book or folder. Tracking changes chronologically helps ensure an accurate historical record of changes. The Secretary of State will also have a record of amendments, but it is easier to access a file held at the organization if any questions arise about the date or contents of the articles or any amendments. If there are numerous amendments, the nonprofit may find it useful to file restated articles that incorporate all prior changes into one document.

Matters to Keep in Mind When Creating, Reviewing, or Amending Bylaws

The following suggestions may be helpful to consider in creating, reviewing, or amending bylaws of nonprofit organizations:

- *Use Plain English When Possible.* Writing bylaws in plain English makes them easier to read and understand. Bylaws that are hard to follow, or are written in an excessively formal or legalistic style, are less likely to be understood or consulted, often leading to deviations in board practice from what is provided in the bylaws. If particular provisions or language of the bylaws do not seem to make sense, ask legal counsel to explain them, and to delete or redraft provisions that are obsolete or confusing.

- ***Recognize that Some Statutory or Legal Language May Be Either Unavoidable or Helpful in Some Cases.*** Bylaw provisions relating to indemnification of board members often track specific statutory or other legal language so as to be sure the provision offers the maximum protection available. Simplification of such provisions to, for example, a more general statement permitting indemnification "to the maximum extent permitted by law" can avoid lengthy legal language and may help avoid problems if the bylaws are not updated to reflect state law changes to such provisions. On the other hand, such general statements may not be helpful to directors and officers trying to understand what protections they have.

  Many states have "default" provisions for some of the matters generally addressed in nonprofit bylaws, but allow organizations to reject such provisions and adopt other provisions not inconsistent with state law. When electing to follow the default provisions, some organizations choose to repeat such provisions verbatim in their bylaws. While duplication of these provisions in the organization's bylaws may provide a convenient reference to the specific desired provisions, such inclusion may also result in these provisions continuing to have effect even if the state law provision is subsequently changed, whether or not the board intended such a result.

- ***Control Placement of Legal Citations.*** Legal citations are generally not needed in bylaws, but, if such references are desired, they can easily be put into a parenthetical or an addendum at the end of the document, so as not to interrupt the flow of the text.

- ***Consider Provisions Carefully, with Assistance of Legal Counsel.*** There are a number of potential governance problems that inclusion of certain bylaw provisions and careful drafting may help avoid. Experienced legal counsel can help organizations understand the value of certain provisions as well as the importance of careful wording. Consider, for example, the following types of issues:

  — ***Term Limits.*** Will set term limits for Board Chairs and directors help revitalize the board or limit continuity and institutional knowledge?

  — ***Removal of Directors.*** Is a mechanism for removing board members before their term ends advisable in certain instances, such as in the case of criminal activity or other significant problems that may harm the organization or in the case of continuous absence from board meetings? If so, how will the removal be accomplished and who must initiate the procedure?

— *Role of the Chair and Other Officers.* Are roles and responsibilities of the Board Chair and other officers clear so as to avoid misunderstandings as to responsibilities?

— *Undue Influence.* Are provisions in place to help avoid concentration of power or undue influence by the Chair on certain board processes, such as nomination of new directors?

— *Supermajorities.* Is it desirable to limit the board's ability to change certain provisions of the bylaws by requiring a supermajority vote to do so, or is such a provision too limiting and impractical, if a supermajority can almost never be obtained in practice?

— *Designation of the CEO and CFO.* Is it clear who serves as the Chief Executive Officer or Chief Financial Officer of the organization?

— *Notice Provisions.* Are notice provisions for board and committee meetings or other matters realistic?

— *Use of Technology.* Is it useful for notices to be sent by e-mail or fax, if permitted by state law? Would it be helpful if meetings could be held by telephone or using video conferencing? Is it useful for consents or other documents to be approved by e-mail or signed electronically?

— *Committee Charters.* Are committee charters contained in the bylaws? If not, is board approval of charters required?

— *Flexibility.* How much flexibility is desirable and how will such flexibility be managed? For example, may the powers of officers or committees be modified by the board by resolution or approval of committee charter amendments rather than amendment to the bylaws? Can the board determine board size within a specified range? What practical problems will such flexibility create?

- *Use Style and Format to Help Readability and Prevent Confusion.* Consistency in format and style throughout the document not only helps make bylaws easier to read, but also helps prevent differences in such matters from being construed as a difference in intent or interpretation. Use a Table of Contents and section headings to make it easier to locate particular provisions. Numbering each paragraph of the bylaws makes it easier to find and refer to various provisions. A reference, for example, to "paragraph 3.2" leaves less possibility for confusion than merely a reference to "Section 3." Clearly identifying the current bylaws date on the cover page or in page footers and providing a summary list of the dates of prior bylaws at the end of the bylaws document facilitates tracking of changes over time and helps assure that the correct, most recent copy of the bylaws is being consulted.

- *Make Someone Responsible for Being Familiar with Bylaw Provisions.* Lack of familiarity with bylaw provisions is a common problem at nonprofits, particularly those without a Corporate Secretary. The problem can be reduced or eliminated by the Board Chair assigning a director or officer responsibility for understanding the contents of the organization's bylaws and alerting the Chair, the Executive Officer, and the board to instances in which the bylaws are not being understood or followed by the board. The chair of the governance committee, or the board member holding the position of Secretary, may be a logical choice for this task. Nonetheless, it is advisable for the Board Chair and Executive Officer to be familiar with basic bylaw provisions, especially those establishing quorums and voting rights.

- *Make Changes to Bylaw Provisions or Change Practices and Procedures.* When an organization's bylaws do not reflect its actual governance practices and procedures, either the bylaws need to be changed, or the board's practices and procedures need changing. Failure to change either the provisions or the practices can easily result in confusion and unintended consequences. When such differences are noted, action to amend the bylaws or to alter board practices is best taken immediately.

- *Conduct Regular Reviews of Bylaws.* Assigning responsibility for periodic (preferably at least every three years) review of the bylaws to a board committee, such as a governance committee or other committee charged with governance oversight, helps assure that bylaws remain consistent with state law requirements, evolving governance standards, and actual board practices. It is also useful to ask legal counsel to alert the organization to changes in law or governance practice that might require more frequent updates to bylaws.

- *Keep Track.* Maintaining a "bylaw book" or folder, which tracks all amendments to bylaws chronologically, helps ensure an accurate historical record of changes. This may be important in a variety of circumstances, including litigation. Tracking changes by subject matter may facilitate understanding the evolution of certain provisions.

- *Create a Conformed Copy of Amended Bylaws.* For ease of reference, it is helpful to create what is known as a conformed copy of the bylaws. A conformed copy is a duplicate of the original bylaws but includes the latest amendments. For example, if a few provisions have been amended, the conformed copy contains the amended provisions, not the original ones. To avoid confusion, the title page usually indicates that the document is a conformed copy as of a specific date. If many provisions are changed, bylaws can be readopted or restated in their entirety. In such cases, the restated bylaws are identified on the title page as being "Amended and Restated" as of a specific date. Ideally, a history of prior amendments is shown on the cover or end page.

- *Notify Appropriate Agencies and Others of Bylaw Changes.* Significant changes to bylaws and articles need to be reported to the IRS on Form

990 and in some circumstances may need to be reported earlier than the Form 990 filing date. State agencies and other organizations (such as major funders) may require notice of major changes as well. Legal counsel can advise when such notifications or filings are necessary.

- *Posting on the Intranet.* If board members have access to the organization's intranet or a "board only" section of the website, posting a conformed copy of bylaws there rather than providing a copy in paper form usually facilitates ease of access and also helps ensure that directors have access to the most recent version of the bylaws.

Clarifying Expectations for Directors

While nonprofits want many things from their directors, they often fail to make directors fully aware of what is expected of them. Developing and disseminating a list of expectations and responsibilities for directors can facilitate effective communication of these matters and the list may also be useful when recruiting new board members.

Create a List of Expectations and Responsibilities. The following steps might be followed in developing and using a list of board expectations and responsibilities:

- *Determine Project Leadership.* Assign responsibility for developing the list to a nominating or governance committee or other committee that has responsibility for oversight of board membership and recruitment.

- *Identify the Benefits.* Identify what board service offers to individuals who join the board (e.g., opportunity to help with its mission, knowledge of important developments in the field, access to leaders in the field, personal satisfaction from helping the organization grow).

- *Identify the Legal Responsibilities.* Identify the legal responsibilities the board and individual directors have and how these responsibilities translate into what the board expects of directors (e.g., attendance at board meetings, orientations, educational programs, retreats, and other events; service on one or more committees; advance preparation before meetings; advice and counsel; sharing of expertise; confidentiality regarding the organization's affairs; and disclosure of any conflicts or potential conflicts of interest).

- *Identify Expectations.* Identify what additional formal or informal expectations the nonprofit has for directors (e.g., helping the organization with fund-raising; making personal financial contributions; serving as an advocate in the community; introducing key staff to government officials, business executives, or community leaders; participating in important organizational events).

- *Create a Document.* Record board expectations and responsibilities in a document that lists all the benefits of board service and the responsibilities and expectations of directors.

- *Be Clear and Direct.* Make sure the description of responsibilities and expectations is explicit. For example, if the expectation is that each director will donate at least $10,000 a year, say so. If the expectation is that each director will serve on at least one committee, will personally visit at least one site annually where the organization's programs are provided, and will attend at least 75 percent of all board and committee meetings, say so. When expectations are clear, misunderstandings are reduced because staff and directors have a shared understanding of what is expected of all board members. In addition, board members who fail to live up to expectations can more easily be approached about correcting the problem or resigning.

- *Obtain Input from Others.* Circulate the draft board expectations and responsibilities document to officers, the Executive Officer, and senior management to make sure all key expectations and responsibilities of board members have been included.

- *Request Board Approval.* Ask the board to approve the document, so that it serves as a statement of expectations and responsibilities for existing directors as well as for potential board candidates.

- *Periodically Review and Update.* Ask the board and management staff to review the board expectations and responsibilities document periodically and modify it as necessary to ensure that it stays current.

Maintain Flexibility. There might be slightly different expectations for certain directors. For example, certain board members may not be expected to make the same level of personal financial contribution to the organization as other board members, and some may not be expected to make any personal financial contribution. Such differing expectations might apply to board members representing the beneficiary group being served by the organization or to board members who are public officials or members of religious organizations. When such exceptions exist, it is helpful to document them so there is no misunderstanding.

Appendix 14 has sample statements of expectations/ job descriptions for directors.

Board Committees and Committee Membership

A substantial amount of a board's work is often accomplished in board committees. Determining what types of committees a board needs is a board decision, but the Executive Officer and Board Chair are well-positioned by virtue of their leadership roles, as well as their continual interaction with board committees, to make recommendations to the board or a board governance committee with respect to committee structure. Here are some issues to keep in mind:

- Without regular review of committee structure, it is easy for a committee to continue in existence because of tradition or inertia, or for a committee's duties to expand incrementally over time such that its written charter becomes out-of-date and does not reflect the actual work of the committee.

- While changes in an organization's strategic plan may often signal the need for changes in committee structure, there are many other factors that can be helpful to consider on a regular basis, for example:
  - Is the function the committee was created to serve still important?
  - Is the work being done by the committee helpful to the board and the organization?
  - If the committee is not functioning well, is the problem one of leadership, membership, or staff support, or is the charter unclear or the role of the committee outdated?
  - Is a committee closely aligned with and supported by a particular internal staff division (e.g., a marketing committee aligned with the work of the marketing division)? Is this helpful or would a more cross-divisional alignment be useful (e.g., an external affairs committee aligned with marketing, communications, and development);

- Changes in committee structure can be disruptive, particularly if directors have a particular interest in the work of a committee on which they serve, or have served on a particular committee for a considerable time, or if supporting staff perceives a change as a loss of connection to the board.

- Establishing a process for regular review of committee functions by a board governance committee and for discussion of committee structure with the board may help establish a culture that accepts change as a matter of course.

Rotation of Committee Members and Chairs. Rotation of committee membership and chairs can be helpful in developing organizational expertise among directors as well as positioning individuals for future leadership positions. Here are some factors to keep in mind in thinking about rotation:

- Committee chairs and members often become quite attached to their roles with particular committees and may resist changes.

- Often particular expertise is needed on individual committees, making rotation more difficult. For example, audit committees and finance committees need members with financial expertise.

- As committees usually have only a small number of members, personality traits of individual members can play a significant role in committee effectiveness.

- There is a risk of loss of interest in board activities in general if board members are assigned to a committee working in an area in which they have no interest; conversely, appointing board members to a committee that they enjoy may heighten their interest in board activities in general.

- Failure to rotate committee membership and chair positions can result in lack of new ideas or enthusiasm and contribute to committee stagnation, and failure to rotate committee membership on the major governance committees (executive, finance, audit, nominating/governance) may contribute to the feeling that certain board members are more (or less) valued or part of important work of the board.

- Frequent changes in committee chairs may significantly increase the work of staff and also result in loss of consistency in committee work or loss of "institutional memory."

Board and Committee Meeting Materials

Materials given to boards and committees may come from different parts of a nonprofit organization. The larger the organization, the more likely it is to have a standardized format for materials presented to the board, strict parameters for who must review and/or approve materials, and deadlines by which they must be disseminated.

Steps to Improve the Distribution Process. Regardless of the size of the organization, several steps can improve not only the distribution process but also the usefulness of the material to the board. For example:

- ***Clarify Board Chair and Executive Officer Expectations.*** Agree on a process for the Board Chair and Executive Officer to consult on what each wants to see in a board package or wants distributed to board members.

- ***Set a Timetable.*** Set and publish reasonable dates by which material must be ready for distribution.

- *Assist Directors.* Assign staff to assist directors with drafting of reports or information being sent to the board (e.g., committee reports).

- *Use Templates.* Define standards for and, when feasible, create and consistently use a template for all board resolutions, reports, charts, cover letters, and other materials sent to the board.

Appendix 27 has sample cover letter formats for board materials.

- *Provide Information, Not Data.* Structure staff and board reports to provide concise information and analysis that makes sense of the relevant facts and data and that advances the board's understanding of the issue at hand without requiring board members to digest large volumes of information.

- *Use Executive Summaries.* Start reports or presentation slides with an executive summary or overview, with an explanation of the goal of the document (such as updating the board on issues, requesting approval, or providing background information).

- *Name a "Last Reviewer."* Assign someone in the organization the responsibility of ensuring that materials are consistent in format and substance and have been approved by the Executive Officer and Board Chair for inclusion in the board package or packet of information sent to directors.

- *Use Cover Letters to Highlight Important Matters.* Include a cover letter from the Chair or Executive Officer with every distribution, indicating what material is enclosed and why, and summarizing key points.

- *Number Pages, Items, Rows, and Columns for Ease of Reference.* Numbering each document and agenda item; numbering each page of each document; and, particularly with financial information, numbering or lettering each row or column greatly facilitates the ability of board members to find information and follow along in presentations.

- *Limit Distributions of Materials at Meetings.* Distribution of materials at meetings reduces the time board and committee members have to read and understand the substance of materials and is a practice best limited strictly to instances in which an important issue or fact has arisen since the board packet for the meeting was initially distributed; and

- *Label Amended or New Material.* When material must be distributed at a meeting, clearly label each item so it is easy to ascertain how the material fits with previously distributed material, or which previously distributed material it replaces.

Collect Confidential Material at the End of Meetings. To help prevent the inadvertent disclosure of confidential information, it is useful to establish the practice of collecting confidential board and committee materials at the end of each meeting.

Board and Committee Files. It can be important (especially if there is a challenge to a board action or litigation) to retain materials distributed at each board or committee meeting or between meetings in files that are easily accessible and identified by date the materials were distributed. Such files have traditionally been maintained in binders or other hard copy formats. Due to space constraints, more organizations are moving to electronic storage in a designated site on the organization's computer system, with appropriate back-up.

These board and committee meeting materials are typically referenced in, but not attached to, the official minutes and provide context for the minutes that may prove useful in the future as background and to establish the basis of certain board or committee decisions. In addition, board or committee members may request copies of such material at a later date or remember something in a prior report which may be relevant to current discussions. Having the material readily at hand in a meeting file enhances the ability of the organization to be responsive to any such request. These files are also a useful way for management to have access to the specific version of materials actually distributed to directors, as opposed to earlier or later versions that may have been developed within the organization.

Attendance

Making meetings interesting and providing ways for directors to feel that their participation is important and valued are two good ways to achieve regular attendance by a high percentage of board members.

Provide Special Presentations. Providing board members with information and presentations they cannot receive except by participation in meetings is an effective way to achieve strong attendance. An arts organization might include presentations from artists, a social service organization might invite beneficiaries of the organization's services to describe their experiences with the organization, or a research institute might invite specialists to talk about their findings. Passion for the organization's mission is a major factor in attracting individuals to the board, so giving board members greater access to mission-related aspects of the organization's operations is generally greatly appreciated as well as interesting to board members.

Seek the Board's Advice. Creating meetings where board members' advice and expertise is routinely both sought and listened to is another important factor in building regular attendance. If board or committee meetings consist primarily of reports, or it appears that the board or committee is simply expected to rubber-stamp a decision already made by management without engaging in robust discussion and questions, board members may feel that their individual presence is not needed or that they will not be missed if they do not attend; their participation levels may suffer accordingly. Conversely, agendas that contain both matters of interest and the opportunity for meaningful discussion on important issues encourage active participation.

Another approach to achieve regular attendance by a high percentage of board members is to establish a policy that attendance at a specified number of meetings is required to remain on the board or the committee. This approach requires enforcement and may require a mechanism for granting exceptions from time to time to individual board members.

Room Arrangements

One aspect of conducting effective meetings that is often overlooked is the arrangement of the meeting room itself (including provision of amenities and use of technology). Selection of rooms, furniture placement and suitability/comfort, availability of food and drink, control of room temperature, and effective use of technology (including microphones, slides, computers, and teleconferencing equipment) can all facilitate or interfere with the effective functioning of boards and committees. Use of name plates for board members is helpful, particularly with large boards where board members may not know each other well. Name plates can also be used to help facilitate changes in habitual seating arrangements, and to help facilitate small group discussions at a certain point during a meeting. Often something as simple as rearranging the seating among board members can positively affect the workings of a board or committee. Board Chair and Executive Officer attention to these kinds of practical meeting arrangements can be important to the successful conduct of meetings.

Inclusion of Staff

Boards are always interested in the level of competence of management, and one way for a board to become familiar with the senior management team is for members of the team to be included regularly in all or part of board and committee meetings. Some organizations include the entire senior management team in board meetings. Others limit participation to only a few key members of the team. Still others include only the Executive Officer (who may or may not be a board member). There is no common practice across all nonprofits with respect to including members of management in, or excluding them from, board and committee meetings. Each organization needs to consider what works best for it. However, once staff is invited to attend board meetings, it can become politically sensitive to change that practice, whether for some or all staff. Proximity or access to the board is generally perceived as an important indicator of status.

Potential Benefits of Including Staff. From the perspective of board or committee members, receiving information directly from responsible staff and observing the interaction of staff at board and committee meetings can provide valuable perspective on senior managers' strengths and weaknesses and allow board members to more effectively evaluate staff comments and recommendations. From the perspective of staff, having the opportunity to see the board and committees in action provides perspective on the role and concerns of the board and its individual members, as well as an appreciation for the kind of information board members need and the scope of the issues with which the board is dealing.

Potential Drawbacks of Including Staff. Including senior managers below the Executive Officer level in board or committee meetings may affect the quality of discussions. Board or committee members may not feel as free to criticize or to make certain suggestions when staff is present. This concern can at least partially be addressed by regular executive sessions during which management is excused from the meeting. But executive sessions usually only occur once during a meeting, and board members may have to defer discussion of questions and issues that might be better dealt with when they arise.

For effective board-management dialogue, Board Chairs and Executive Officers may need to make it clear that candid but respectful comments regarding management performance are welcome and that management can use future meetings to discuss progress or changes made in response to concerns expressed by directors.

Perspective of the Executive Officer. From the perspective of the Executive Officer, including staff at board or committee meetings carries some risk that staff members may overreact to (or possibly be disappointed by) board deliberations, causing the Executive Officer to have to spend time dealing with staff on such matters after the board meeting. On the other hand, the effectiveness of other management leaders may be enhanced by understanding the board's role and expectations. Staff presence at board meetings may also be used as a staff development tool and support succession planning for the Executive Officer or other management leaders.

Keeping the Meeting on Track

Keeping meetings on time and moving expeditiously through the agenda can be difficult for a Board Chair. Individuals making presentations often exceed the time allotted to them. Discussions can veer off course, or focus on minutiae rather than critical issues. Certain board members may dominate the meeting with their questions or perspectives. Sometimes board members seem uninterested or unengaged so that there is no meaningful discussion. Here are some suggestions that have proven useful in helping to assure that meetings run effectively:

- *Cover Letters.* Include a cover letter from the Chair or the Executive Officer with the agenda and board and committee materials signaling the focus and scope of the meeting and perhaps providing answers to anticipated questions, with routine offers of the opportunity to call the Chair or Executive Officer in advance of the meeting with questions.

- *Advance Distribution.* Send materials sufficiently in advance so that board and committee members have a chance to read them.

- *Number Items.* Number or otherwise identify materials so board members can easily find the agenda item to which they relate.

- *Mission-Related Presentation.* Routinely include presentations on the substance of the organization's mission of the kind that board and committee members would not have access to were it not for their participation on the board. This not only helps engage the board and increase board member commitment, but also educates board members and facilitates their understanding of actions to be taken by the board.

- *Tie Agenda to Strategic Issues or Plan.* Tie major items on the agenda to the organization's critical issues or strategic plan.

- *Front-Load Important Items.* Put the most important items for discussion at the beginning of the agenda.

- *Limit Items.* Limit the number of items on agendas so there is a reasonable possibility for real discussion.

- *Time Frames.* Include an indication of the anticipated discussion time for each agenda item.

- *Specify Action Required.* Indicate on the agenda and in materials what action is required of the board or committee (review, recommend, discuss, approve).

- *Handle Routine Items Quickly.* Use a consent agenda to speed up handling of routine matters.

- *Use Written Reports.* At board meetings, use written rather than oral reports from committee chairs and limit comments on committee work to matters not covered in the written reports or to significant aspects of the matters included in the reports.

- *Control Multiple Comments from Same Person.* Allow all those who wish to speak to do so before calling on someone a second time.

- *Provide an Opportunity for Suggestions.* Provide an opportunity at the beginning of the meeting for board or committee members to suggest issues they would like to have discussed during the meeting. Or, before adjournment, ask board and committee members if they would like to remain after the meeting to discuss issues or questions that were not addressed in the meeting and/or to include them on the following meeting's agenda.

- *Touch Base Before the Meeting.* Before the meeting, but after materials have been sent out, call or meet with a number of board or committee members to determine what issues they might want to have discussed in more depth and what questions they might have or what other issues they particularly want discussed. This practice can be particularly useful with new board or committee members, who may be reluctant to ask questions in meetings, and with board or committee members who have a tendency to dominate meetings, as certain of their issues can be anticipated in presentations that will be made at the meeting.

- *Ask Specific Board Members to Participate.* To help move the discussion along on complex issues and in order to counterbalance comments from board or committee members with a tendency to dominate, alert several board or committee members in advance that their active participation would be appreciated in order to facilitate discussion; call on such members to elicit their comments.

- *Exercise the Chair's Prerogative.* If discussion becomes prolonged or unwieldy, exert the prerogative as Chair to:
  — Reorder the agenda mid-meeting;
  — Declare a short break or recess the board or committee meeting to change its rhythm or close off discussion that has become repetitive or unproductive; or
  — Propose deferral of action to a subsequent meeting to allow staff to address issues that have been raised.

Handling Questions and Requests

Responding to board member questions or requests for additional information or suggestions can occupy considerable time at meetings and also create difficulties of time management for staff between meetings. In dealing with questions or requests for information, it can be helpful to keep in mind the following:

- *Questions May Indicate a Need for Further Staff or Board Committee Work.* One role of the Chair is to help make sure that board or committee members feel prepared to take requested actions. If directors or committee members have many questions or requests for additional information or seem hesitant to approve a requested action, it does not necessarily mean that the board will decline to take the action requested. It may, however, be a sign that the advance materials or the presentation at the meeting were deficient and that the board or committee is not sufficiently informed to take the requested action. In such cases, the Chair may decide to take the lead in requesting that action be deferred and steps be taken by staff or perhaps a board committee to help assure that information is supplied before a subsequent discussion.

- *Certain Questions May Be Better Handled Outside of the Meeting.* The Chair always has the prerogative to suggest that certain questions or requests be handled one-on-one between the Executive Officer or the Board Chair and the board member making the request or asking the question, particularly if the matter does not seem of general interest or significance to the matter at hand.

- *Questions Often Generate Unintended Work for Staff.* Board and committee members are sometime oblivious to the fact that their requests may have the effect of creating substantial additional staff work, upsetting priorities, or adding to the workload of employees trying to be responsive. The Executive Officer and Board Chair can help minimize disruption and unintended consequences of board member inquiries and suggestions by simply reminding board and committee members of this fact and also by setting parameters with staff on how such requests are to be handled.

Executive Sessions During Board and Committee Meetings

Executive sessions provide a convenient forum for boards to discuss matters outside the presence of staff, or with specific members of staff whom the board invites to the executive session. The following suggestions may assist in managing the process of holding executive sessions:

- *Schedule Regularly.* Hold executive sessions regularly, perhaps even at every board meeting or major committee meeting. This practice may facilitate surfacing issues of concern to board members earlier than might otherwise be the case and can also help prevent sending a signal that seems to imply that something critical or sensitive has arisen. Regular executive sessions may also reduce any anxiety of the Executive Officer with such sessions as they become a matter of routine.

- *Calendar Certain Topics for Discussion Over the Course of the Board Year.* Maximize the potential benefit of executive sessions by developing a list of topics that might be helpful to discuss in executive session over the course of a board year. Such topics might include performance of the Executive Officer, performance of other senior staff, comments from auditors and accountants, board member concerns about performance of the organization or of particular programs, or concerns about board functioning.

- *Opportunity for Open Discussion Can Be Helpful.* Even if there is no specific agenda for a particular executive session, use the time to ask board members for general comments on how they think the organization or the board are functioning or their impressions of the board meeting.

- *Minimize Staff and Guest Disruption.* If possible, hold executive sessions either first or last on the agenda to minimize disruption to the meeting and having to request staff or guests to exit and then rejoin a meeting.

- *Decide If or How Discussions Will be Reflected in Minutes.* Establish a policy on whether minutes will reflect only the fact that an executive session was held or the general topics discussed, and be consistent in following that policy. If more detailed minutes of the executive session are needed (for example, if a resolution is adopted during the executive session or a personnel action is taken), it is important to maintain a separate minute book or folder for these minutes and to make sure that they are approved by the board or committee that held the executive session. The minute book or folder for these minutes may need to be stored separately from other minute books or folders to protect the confidentiality of information in these minutes. Personnel records may also need to be updated if personnel actions are taken during an executive session.

Minutes

Minutes are not intended to be a verbatim report and need not report what was said (rather than done). Recognition of the proper function of minutes may eliminate the inclination to tape record meetings—a practice that generally serves only to extend the time it takes to prepare a draft and which can create legal issues when such tapes are not routinely destroyed. When drafting minutes, the following guidelines may be helpful:

- *Identify Topics Discussed.* Minutes may describe simply what topics were covered, rather than summarize what was actually said. For example, "The committee discussed the size of the staff in relation to available space, future staff needs, the possibility of reconfiguring space, and the feasibility of renting additional space or of implementing telecommuting."

- *Exercise Care with Characterizations and Opinions.* To avoid creating inadvertent legal problems, experienced minute drafters typically avoid characterizations and adjectives, either favorable or unfavorable, and make every effort to stick to facts and avoid characterizations and opinions. "The board reviewed the report," rather than "The board reviewed the report in detail." "The board listened to comments on the success of the exhibit," rather than "The board listened to comments on the tremendous success of the exhibit." In the event that an adjective or other characterization may seem appropriate, make it clear that it is a characterization or adjective used by the speaker, e.g., "Mr. X characterized the exhibition as a tremendous success."

- *Be Careful About Naming Names.* Boards and committees take action as a group. It is usually not important to identify individuals or to specify who said what in summarizing discussions. However, minutes typically list which board members were present and which were absent for the meeting. Particularly when a major action is taken, it may be useful to note whether a board member was actually present at the time the specific action was taken. Also, in situations involving a potential conflict of interest, it is important to note whether the board member with the conflict was "present but did not vote," or "was not present and did not vote." If a board or committee member dissents or abstains from an action, it is important to note his or her dissent or abstention in the minutes, since if the action is ever challenged, the dissent or abstention could be relevant to the director's defense against claims of director wrongdoing. In addition, frequent dissents or abstentions by one or more directors may signal the need to address problems in board function or director conduct.

- *Note General Basis for Action.* When action is taken, minutes generally indicate the general basis for the action—e.g., after discussion, after review of material, after the presentation, following questions.

- *Be Specific Regarding Actions Taken.* When reporting action taken, be as specific as possible. Include the text of any resolutions adopted either in the body of the minutes or as an attachment.

- *Repetition Is Fine.* It is fine to be repetitious in style. Minutes are meant to be a record, not literature.

- *Length Is Something to Consider.* In general, shorter or medium length minutes are likely to generate less legal risk than detailed long minutes, especially if counsel is not involved in reviewing them. More concise minutes are also more likely to be read, understood, and appreciated by board and committee members.

- *Subheadings May Be Helpful.* Using subheadings for each section is a helpful organizing device and can also be useful as an assistance in indexing and looking for particular information from past meetings.

- *Executive Sessions.* Minutes are not usually taken at executive sessions, although it can be helpful to list the general topic(s) discussed. If a resolution is adopted during the executive session, it may be included in separate minutes for the executive session. If the subject matter is sensitive, it may be appropriate to include a general resolution and refer to specifics in other documents retained in a confidential meeting file.

Prepare Minutes as Soon as Practicable. It is helpful if a draft of minutes is produced as soon as practicable after a meeting. This practice facilitates review by the board Secretary and others while memory of the meeting is still fresh, making it easier to remember key points.

Disposition of Notes. Once minutes are approved, most Secretaries in the for-profit sector dispose of handwritten notes, any prior drafts, and, if used, any tapes of the meeting. This is also a good practice to follow in nonprofit organizations. The approved minutes are the official record of the meeting and it is better practice not to retain prior drafts or notes that might be confusing if records are ever subpoenaed or otherwise subject to litigation or controversy.

Minutes Book. Minutes are usually kept in a binder or a folder titled Minutes (and known as the Minutes Book), and organized by date of meeting. Committee minutes are usually filed in a separate notebook or folder for each committee. Any resolutions or other actions taken by written consent are also kept in the minute book.

Index and Copies of Resolutions. It is helpful to keep a separate list or folder of resolutions adopted and, particularly, of policies adopted, so they are easier to find when someone needs to refer to them.

Reports of Meetings

Often committee chairs report to the board orally on committee activities. This practice can take up considerable time at board meetings and also may result in inconsistent or incomplete reporting on committee activities. Written reports to the board help ensure more accurate and efficient reporting.

Forms of Committee Reports. One common approach to written committee reports is simply to use committee minutes themselves as the form of report to the board. Another approach is to shorten committee minutes to remove language that is not relevant for a report to the board, such as the call to order, motions to adjourn, and similar administrative matters that are important for the committee minutes themselves, but not necessarily for a report to the board. This practice can reduce the volume of paper sent to the board while still preventing inadvertent discrepancies between committee minutes and reports.

In lieu of traditional narrative minutes and reports, some committees use a template prepared in advance of the meeting that lists topics to be discussed in accordance with the agenda, and leaves space for the secretary to insert a description of the action taken once the committee meeting is over. With this approach, care needs to be taken that the description of the action taken is consistent with the language used in the committee's minutes.

Another effective but time-saving approach to committee minutes and reports is to use a table format that lists each topic in one column, provides a brief summary of the matters discussed in the second column, notes actions taken (e.g.., resolutions adopted or the outcome of matters subject to committee vote) in a third column and, if desired, includes a final column noting action to be taken after the committee meeting either by the committee chair, other committee members, or organization staff. This column can also include actions to be discussed at future committee meetings.

Evaluating and Improving Board Effectiveness

Good governance involves attention to both process and substance and requires careful thought as well as tailoring to the organization. Board effectiveness studies can help to make the process and substance relevant to the particular organization, particularly for larger or complex organizations. Smaller organizations with smaller-sized boards may be able to address effectiveness issues without the need for a formal effectiveness study.

Comprehensive Effectiveness Studies

A comprehensive board effectiveness survey enables organizations to take a close look at how the board is functioning, how up-to-date its governance practices are, and whether these practices are serving the board and the organization well. Such a study may be most useful if the following are considered:

- *Leadership.* Appoint a director to lead the project. Results will improve if the board owns the project.
  - Choose someone other board members respect but do not resent or fear.
  - If possible, choose someone other than the Chair, since the study will probably consider the effectiveness of the Chair.
  - If possible, select a leader with some governance expertise and familiarity with evolving governance trends and practices to help ensure that the survey addresses not only the board's current practices but also current thinking on governance issues.

- *Consultants.* Consultants offer expertise, impartiality, and confidentiality and some directors feel more comfortable talking to a third party, but outside parties often charge for their services.
  - Many consulting firms have board effectiveness practices.
  - There are individuals, including retired corporate secretaries, retired attorneys, and others who may offer such services.

- — Retired board members, former chairs, and former Executive Officers may also be good choices to help lead or consult on this sort of project.
- — Many law firms can help, especially on legal issues related to governance structures, fiduciary duties, and good governance recommendations from the IRS, other governmental agencies, public officials, and governance experts.

- *Getting Started.* In creating a board effectiveness survey:
  - — Keep questions simple, avoiding two- or three-part questions.
  - — Focus on process as well as substance.
  - — Review governance literature to be sure the questions address key governance trends.
  - — Involve executive staff in design of the questions to make sure their issues/questions are covered as well.

- *In-Person Interviews.* Individual in-person or phone interviews can take from 20 to 60 minutes, depending on the issues discussed, concerns raised, and willingness of board members to speak honestly. So for a large board, the time required to complete the survey can be substantial.

- *Limits of Written Questionnaires.* Written questionnaires may be a practical necessity for organizations with large boards, but often they do not provide as much helpful information as interviews, even when questions are open-ended, and the responses often are not as clear or as thoughtful as with in-person interviews.

- *Summaries.* Try summarizing the results in several ways, as different patterns may emerge, e.g., summarizing answers to each question and then trying to summarize by topic mentioned, regardless of which question was being answered.

- *Comparison to Trends.* Compare the issues identified to trends in corporate governance, either through review of literature or discussion with an outside consultant or law firm.

- *Recommendations.* Make recommendations based on responses as well as governance trends.

Ongoing Board and Director Self-Evaluations and Peer Evaluations

Because board effectiveness may change with staff, officer, and board member changes, retaining a board's effectiveness requires constant attention. Annual shorter form reviews of board effectiveness can be helpful in maintaining effectiveness of the board and of individual directors. These reviews can be handled by short written questionnaires that are developed and reviewed by a board committee.

Getting Started. The following are principles that may assist in developing these shorter form evaluations:

- *Keep the Questions Simple.* Avoid two- and three-part questions and lengthy questions that might be subject to various interpretations.

- *Consider Mixing Up the Format.* Using a mix of yes/no, number ranking, and open-ended questions may help make the questionnaire easy to complete and more informative. Questionnaires that are entirely open-ended may deter some individuals from responding. Questionnaires that use only numerical rankings may not provide sufficient information.

- *Keep Scales and Rankings Similar Throughout.* Multiple scales (1-10, 1-5, etc.) in the same questionnaire can lead to anomalous results, or may imply differences that do not really exist. When using scales, remind people frequently throughout the questionnaire of which end of the scale is for High (or Good) or Low (Bad) ratings, and make sure the questions are phrased so they are easily compatible with the ranking scale.

- *Leave Space for Comments.* Comments can be very informative and help clarify rankings.

- *Adapt from Prior Surveys.* If the self-evaluation follows a comprehensive effectiveness study, consider using or adapting questions from that study, or at least creating questions on similar topics covered in that study.

- *Ask for Additional Comments.* Include a question asking directors to identify and add comments on issues that might not have been covered in the questionnaire. Often such comments help provide perspective on previous comments on the same questionnaire and raise issues of concern to board members that may not have been included in the questionnaire.

Technology Is Available to Help. There are now many online tools available that greatly simplify the process of distributing and summarizing shorter form board or board member self-evaluations. Many of these services are available at no cost. The questionnaire may be uploaded to the nonprofit's site so that board members can log on and fill out the questionnaire. When the time for completion of questionnaires is over, the site displays answers in aggregate as well as by individual respondent. It also computes percentages, such as 97 percent of respondents indicated they were "Highly Satisfied" with the performance of the Executive Officer, or "50 percent of respondents indicated a need for increased explanation of the organization's financial accounting practices." The sites generally allow comments to be printed out either in aggregate or by board member. With care in setting up the site, it is possible to allow for anonymity in responses if that seems desirable, and use of a third party to review responses can further enhance confidentiality. A variety of online survey tools can be found by searching online using the key words "online survey tools."

Risks of Annual Written Questionnaires. While short form annual questionnaires can be useful, there is a risk that the questionnaires and the process become so routine that the value is lost. Reviewing and revising the questionnaire annually is critical, so the questions remain relevant. Additionally, it can be helpful to alternate between a process that relies solely on written responses to a questionnaire and one that involves either small group discussions of the questionnaire (for example, at committee meetings) or individual face-to-face or phone interviews. Discussions often surface information or generate suggestions that might not be included in written responses.

Appendices: Sample Forms and Guidelines

APPENDIX 1

SAMPLE BYLAW PROVISION SETTING FORTH FUNDAMENTAL DIRECTOR DUTIES

Practical Advice Note: Not all organizations specifically list director duties in their bylaws. However, including such a provision can be a helpful reminder to directors as well as a way for the organization to highlight in an important governance document the legal standard of conduct expected of directors.

Article ____ — Directors

Section ___ – Standards of Conduct for Directors

a. Each member of the Board of Directors, when discharging the duties of a director, shall act in good faith, and in a manner the director reasonably believes to be in the best interests of the nonprofit corporation.

b. The members of the Board of Directors or a committee of the board, when becoming informed in connection with their decision-making function or devoting attention to their oversight function, must discharge their duties with the care that a person in a like position would reasonably believe appropriate under similar circumstances.

c. In discharging his or her duties as a board member, a director may rely on the following persons, unless the director has knowledge that makes such reliance unwarranted:

   1. One or more officers or employees of the nonprofit corporation whom the director reasonably believes to be reliable and competent in the functions performed or information, opinions, reports, or statements provided;

   2. Legal counsel, public accountants, or other persons retained by the corporation as to matters involving skills or expertise the director reasonably believes are matters: (i) within the particular person's professional or expert competence or (ii) as to which the particular person merits confidence; and

   3. A committee of the board of which the director is not a member if the director reasonably believes the committee's determinations merit confidence.

APPENDIX 2

INTERNAL REVENUE SERVICE (IRS) SAMPLE CONFLICT OF INTEREST POLICY AND SAMPLE BYLAWS PROVISION ON CONFLICT OF INTEREST PROCEDURES

Document 1
Sample Conflict of Interest Policy

Practical Advice Note: The sample conflict of interest policy below is provided by the IRS as guidance for organizations seeking to obtain tax-exempt status by completing IRS Form 1023. The sample may be useful for existing nonprofits to consider as well. Note that the reference to "Schedule C" in the bracketed language directed to hospitals refers to a schedule in the Form 1023.[1]

IRS Sample Conflict of Interest Policy

Note: Items marked *Hospital insert – for hospitals that complete Schedule C* are intended to be adopted by hospitals.

Article I
Purpose

The purpose of the conflict of interest policy is to protect this tax-exempt organization's (Organization) interest when it is contemplating entering into a transaction or arrangement that might benefit the private interest of an officer or director of the Organization or might result in a possible excess benefit transaction. This policy is intended to supplement but not replace any applicable state and federal laws governing conflict of interest applicable to nonprofit and charitable organizations.

Article II
Definitions

1.   Interested Person

Any director, principal officer, or member of a committee with governing board delegated powers, who has a direct or indirect financial interest, as defined below, is an interested person.

[Hospital Insert—for hospitals that complete Schedule C

---

1. This sample conflict of interest policy is available at Appendix A to Instructions For IRS Form 1023 (Application for Recognition of Exemption Under Section 501(c)(3) of the Internal Revenue Code). Form 1023 is updated periodically. Check the Internal Revenue Service website for the most up-to-date version. www.irs.gov.

If a person is an interested person with respect to any entity in the health care system of which the organization is a part, he or she is an interested person with respect to all entities in the health care system.]

2. Financial Interest

A person has a financial interest if the person has, directly or indirectly, through business, investment, or family:

a. An ownership or investment interest in any entity with which the Organization has a transaction or arrangement,

b. A compensation arrangement with the Organization or with any entity or individual with which the Organization has a transaction or arrangement, or

c. A potential ownership or investment interest in, or compensation arrangement with, any entity or individual with which the Organization is negotiating a transaction or arrangement. Compensation includes direct and indirect remuneration as well as gifts or favors that are not insubstantial. A financial interest is not necessarily a conflict of interest. Under Article III, Section 2, a person who has a financial interest may have a conflict of interest only if the appropriate governing board or committee decides that a conflict of interest exists.

**Article III
Procedures**

1. Duty to Disclose

In connection with any actual or possible conflict of interest, an interested person must disclose the existence of the financial interest and be given the opportunity to disclose all material facts to the directors and members of committees with governing board delegated powers considering the proposed transaction or arrangement.

2. Determining Whether a Conflict of Interest Exists

After disclosure of the financial interest and all material facts, and after any discussion with the interested person, he/she shall leave the governing board or committee meeting while the determination of a conflict of interest is discussed and voted upon. The remaining board or committee members shall decide if a conflict of interest exists.

3. Procedures for Addressing the Conflict of Interest

a. An interested person may make a presentation at the governing board or committee meeting, but after the presentation, he/she shall leave the meeting during the discussion of, and the vote on, the transaction or arrangement involving the possible conflict of interest.

b. The chairperson of the governing board or committee shall, if appropriate, appoint a disinterested person or committee to investigate alternatives to the proposed transaction or arrangement.

c. After exercising due diligence, the governing board or committee shall determine whether the Organization can obtain with reasonable efforts a more advantageous transaction or arrangement from a person or entity that would not give rise to a conflict of interest.

d. If a more advantageous transaction or arrangement is not reasonably possible under circumstances not producing a conflict of interest, the governing board or committee shall determine by a majority vote of the disinterested directors whether the transaction or arrangement is in the Organization's best interest, for its own benefit, and whether it is fair and reasonable. In conformity with the above determination it shall make its decision as to whether to enter into the transaction or arrangement.

4. Violations of the Conflicts of Interest Policy

a. If the governing board or committee has reasonable cause to believe a member has failed to disclose actual or possible conflicts of interest, it shall inform the member of the basis for such belief and afford the member an opportunity to explain the alleged failure to disclose.

b. If, after hearing the member's response and after making further investigation as warranted by the circumstances, the governing board or committee determines the member has failed to disclose an actual or possible conflict of interest, it shall take appropriate disciplinary and corrective action.

Article IV
Records of Proceedings

The minutes of the governing board and all committees with board delegated powers shall contain:

a. The names of the persons who disclosed or otherwise were found to have a financial interest in connection with an actual or possible conflict of interest, the nature of the financial interest, any action taken to determine whether a conflict of interest was present, and the governing board's or committee's decision as to whether a conflict of interest in fact existed.

b. The names of the persons who were present for discussions and votes relating to the transaction or arrangement, the content of the discussion, including any alternatives to the proposed transaction or arrangement, and a record of any votes taken in connection with the proceedings.

Article V
Compensation

a. A voting member of the governing board who receives compensation, directly or indirectly, from the Organization for services is precluded from voting on matters pertaining to that member's compensation.

b. A voting member of any committee whose jurisdiction includes compensation matters and who receives compensation, directly or indirectly, from the Organization for services is precluded from voting on matters pertaining to that member's compensation.

c. No voting member of the governing board or any committee whose jurisdiction includes compensation matters and who receives compensation, directly or indirectly, from the Organization, either individually or collectively, is prohibited from providing information to any committee regarding compensation.

[Hospital Insert-for hospitals that complete Schedule C]

d. Physicians who receive compensation from the Organization, whether directly or indirectly or as employees or independent contractors, are precluded from membership on any committee whose jurisdiction includes compensation matters. No physician, either individually or collectively, is prohibited from providing information to any committee regarding physician compensation.]

Article VI
Annual Statements

Each director, principal officer, and member of a committee with governing board delegated powers shall annually sign a statement which affirms such person:

a. Has received a copy of the conflict of interest policy,

b. Has read and understands the policy,

c. Has agreed to comply with the policy, and

d. Understands the Organization is charitable and in order to maintain its federal tax Exemption, it must engage primarily in activities that accomplish one or more of its tax-exempt purposes.

Article VII
Periodic Reviews

To ensure the Organization operates in a manner consistent with charitable purposes and does not engage in activities that could jeopardize its tax-exempt status, periodic reviews shall be conducted. The periodic reviews shall, at a minimum, include the following subjects:

a. Whether compensation arrangements and benefits are reasonable, based on competent survey information, and the result of arm's length bargaining.

b. Whether partnerships, joint ventures, and arrangements with management organizations conform to the Organization's written policies, are properly recorded, reflect reasonable investment or payments for goods and services, further charitable purposes, and do not result in inurement, impermissible private benefit, or in an excess benefit transaction.

Article VIII
Use of Outside Experts

When conducting the periodic reviews as provided for in Article VII, the Organization may, but need not, use outside advisors. If outside experts are used, their use shall not relieve the governing board of its responsibility for ensuring periodic reviews are conducted.

APPENDIX 2 (CONT'D)

Document 2
Sample Bylaws Provision: Conflict of Interest Procedures

Article _____
Conflicts of Interest

Section __.1 – Disclosure of Interests

Any Director, Officer, employee, or committee member having a financial or other personal interest, including a conflicting fiduciary interest (due to status as an officer or director of another organization), in a transaction, contract or other matter presented to the Board of Directors or a committee thereof for authorization, approval, or ratification shall provide prompt, full, and frank disclosure of such interest to the Board or committee prior to its acting on such contract or transaction.

Section __.2 – Evaluation of Conflict of Interest Matters

The body to which such disclosure is made (i.e., the Board or applicable committee) shall determine, by a majority vote, whether a conflict of interest (due to a personal financial or other interest, including any conflicting fiduciary interest) exists or can reasonably be construed to exist, which would reasonably be expected by an objective third party to affect the Director's ability to make an unbiased decision in the best interest of the Corporation and the System.

Section ___.3 – Appropriate Action when a Conflict of Interest Is Determined to be Present

If a conflict of interest is deemed to exist, such person shall not vote on, or use his or her personal influence on, or be present for or participate (other than to present factual information or to respond to questions) in the discussions or deliberations with respect to, such contract or transaction. Such person may be counted in determining the existence of a quorum at any meeting where the contract or transaction under discussion is being voted upon.

Section ___.4 – Record in Minutes

The minutes of the meeting shall reflect the disclosure made of any conflict or potential conflict of interest, the vote thereon, and, where applicable, the abstention from voting, presence, and participation, and whether a quorum is present.

Section ___.5 – Conflict of Interest and Other Policies

The Corporation shall also adopt policies from time to time regarding conflicts of interest, including requirements regarding disclosure of such interests.

APPENDIX 3

ADDITIONAL SOURCES OF INFORMATION ON GOVERNANCE STANDARDS AND PRACTICES FOR NONPROFITS

There are a multitude of organizations that gather, recommend, or report on specific governance practices or standards for nonprofits. Below is a list of some of these organizations and one or more examples of their publications on governance principles and practices.

American Bar Association

Guide to Nonprofit Governance in the Wake of Sarbanes-Oxley. ABA Coordinating Committee on Nonprofit Governance, 2005

American Management Association

Good Governance for Nonprofits, Developing Principles and Practices for an Effective Board, Laughlin, Fredric, and Andringa, Robert, AMACOM, a Division of the American Management Association, 2007

BoardSource

The Source, Twelve Principles of Governance that Power Exceptional Boards, BoardSource, 2005

Independent Sector

Compendium of Standards, Codes, and Principles of Nonprofit and Philanthropic Organizations, Independent Sector

www.independentsector.org/compendium_of_standards

Principals for Good Governance and Ethical Practice, A Guide for Charities and Foundations, Panel on the Nonprofit Sector convened by Independent Sector, 2007   www.nonprofitpanel.org/report/principles/Principles_guide.pdf

Internal Revenue Service

IRS Form 990 Part VI. IRS website www.irs.gov

Governance and Related Topics – 501(c)(3) Organizations. IRS publication. IRS website www.irs.gov

International Center for Not-For-Profit Law

Ten Emerging Principles of Governance of Nonprofit Corporations and Guides to a Safe Harbor, Silk, Thomas, International Journal of Not-For-Profit Law, November 2004 www.icnl.org

Minnesota Council of Nonprofits

Principles and Practices for Nonprofit Excellence, Minnesota Council of Nonprofits, 2005 www.mncn.org

Standards for Excellence Institute

Standards for Excellence ® : An Ethics and Accountability Code, Standards for Excellence Institute, 2004 www.standardsforexcellenceinstitute.org

The Society of Corporate Secretaries and Governance Professionals

Governance for Nonprofit Organizations from Little Leagues to Big Universities, Society of Corporate Secretaries and Governance Professionals, 2008

Urban Institute

Nonprofit Governance in the United States, Findings on Performance and Accountability from the First National Representative Study, Francie Ostrower, Urban Institute, 2007 www.urban.org/publications/411479.html

See also the Bibliography to this publication.

APPENDIX 4

SAMPLE JOB DESCRIPTIONS FOR THE BOARD CHAIR

Document 1
Role of the Chair

The Chair presides at meetings of the board and the executive committee and has oversight responsibility for the development of board and executive committee agendas.

The Chair has primary leadership responsibility for all matters related to board and board committee governance, oversight, and effectiveness, including oversight of the process for establishing board and committee goals and priorities.

The Chair is the board's principal liaison with the Executive Officer and other executive management and has primary responsibility for oversight of the performance evaluation process for the Executive Officer.

The Chair is the board's principal representative with external constituencies and at public functions.

The Chair generally performs all acts incident to the office of Chair, except those specifically delegated to or shared with other officers as specified by the board or in the bylaws.

APPENDIX 4 (CONT'D)

Document 2
Board Chair Job Description

I Position Summary

1. The Board Chair is a volunteer position.

2. The Chair is responsible for leading the [Nonprofit Corporation] [(NPC)] board of directors in the board's oversight of the operations of NPC.

3. The Chair shall be appointed by and from among the directors, for a three (3) year term and may be appointed for up to two (2) consecutive, full three (3) year terms as Board Chair.

4. The Chair will have an equal vote with other members of the NPC board on matters presented to the NPC board for determination.

5. The Chair will elicit and encourage the active participation of the other NPC board members in NPC board activities.

II Responsibilities

The Board Chair shall be responsible for the following:

1. **Board Meetings.** Preside over all meetings of the board and set the board's agenda, in consultation with NPC's President and Chief Executive Officer.

2. **Board Structure; Director Roles.** Periodically review the board's organizational and committee structures, and individual director committee assignments, to assure that such structures and assignments are effective in supporting the board's priorities.

3. **Board Education.** Provide input to NPC Senior Management and the Governance Committee regarding the quality and nature of the information presented to, and the continuing education opportunities provided for, the board and its individual members.

4. **Director Conduct.** Evaluate board and director conduct for consistency with NPC's bylaws and policies.

5. **Board Self-Evaluation.** Assure the completion of a periodic board self-evaluation process, as conducted by the Governance Committee.

6. **Director Recruitment.** Engage in regular communications with the Governance Committee and the President and Chief Executive Officer, as applicable, regarding the recruitment and orientation of new board members.

7. **Board Management Relations.** Foster mutually supportive relationships between the board and management.

8. **Board Deliberation.** Facilitate informed board review and candid board-management discussions of significant aspects of System operations.

9. **Evaluation of the President/CEO.** Participate in and direct the annual evaluation of the President and Chief Executive Officer.

10. **Meetings with President/CEO.** Meet at least once every month with the President and Chief Executive Officer.

11. **Committee Membership.** Serve as a voting member and Chair of the Executive Committee. Serve as an ex officio member with voice but not vote of all other NPC Board Committees.

12. **Other Duties.** Carry out all other duties assigned by the board.

EFFECTIVE DATE: _____

APPENDIX 5

SAMPLE MISSION STATEMENTS

As available at guidestar.org

1. **American Bar Association, Chicago, IL**
   Mission Statement: Promote Administration of Justice, Professional Excellence and Respect for the Law

2. **American Cancer Society, Nationwide**
   Mission Statement: The American Cancer Society is the nationwide, community-based, voluntary health organization dedicated to eliminating cancer as a major health problem by preventing cancer, saving lives, and diminishing suffering from cancer, through research, education, advocacy, and service.

3. **African American Arts Alliance of Chicago, Chicago, IL**
   Mission Statement: Professional service organization which includes theater, dance, music, literature, visual arts groups and individual artist [sic] to increase public awareness, interaction, communication and development of African American arts organizations and artists within the city of Chicago.

4. **Amnesty International, New York, NY**
   Mission Statement: To undertake research and action focused on preventing and ending grave abuses of the rights to physical and mental integrity, freedom of conscience and expression, and freedom from discrimination, within the context of our work to promote all human rights.

5. **Autism Society of America, Bethesda, MD**
   Mission Statement: The mission of the ASA is to promote lifelong access and opportunities for persons within the autism spectrum and their families, to be fully included, participating members of their communities through advocacy, public awareness, education, and research related to autism.

6. **Bill and Melinda Gates Foundation Trust, Seattle, WA**
   Mission Statement: Our belief that every life has equal value is at the core of our work at the foundation. We follow 15 guiding principles, which help define our approach to our philanthropic work, and employ an outstanding leadership team to direct our strategies and grant-making.

7. **BoardSource, Washington, D.C.**
   Mission Statement: BoardSource is dedicated to advancing the public good by building exceptional nonprofit boards and inspiring board service.

8. **Boys & Girls Clubs of America, Nationwide**
   Mission Statement: To enable all young people, especially those who need us most, to reach their full potential as productive, caring, responsible citizens.

9. **Funkanometry San Francisco Dance, San Francisco, CA**
   Mission Statement: The Funkbrella is a professional dance company dedicated to serving youth and young adults in the performing arts. We work to provide high quality dance training, present innovative artistic works, and cultivate a diverse community of leaders.

10. **The Hispanic Business Association, Cleveland, OH**
    Mission Statement: The Hispanic Business Association is a not-for-profit organization devoted to development of Hispanic businesses in order to strengthen and stabilize commercial districts within the city of Cleveland, the organizations focus [sic] on providing technical assistance to start-up and existing companies.

11. **Museum of Modern Art, New York, NY**
    Mission Statement: Founded in 1929 as an educational institution, The Museum of Modern Art is dedicated to being the foremost museum of modern art in the world. Through the leadership of its Trustees and staff, The Museum of Modern Art manifests this commitment by establishing, preserving, and documenting a permanent collection of the highest order that reflects the vitality, complexity and unfolding patterns of modern and contemporary art; by presenting exhibitions and educational programs of unparalleled significance; by sustaining a library, archives, and conservation laboratory that are recognized as international centers of research; and by supporting scholarship and publications of preeminent intellectual merit.

12. **National Association of Sports Commissions, Cincinnati, OH**
    Mission Statement: to provide to members information regarding selection of sporting events, to raise the level of professionalism and participation in the sports commission industry, to foster and promote amateur sports competitions, and to support amateur sports and the Olympic movement in the United States.

13. **National Conference for Community and Justice, Inc., Willowbrook, IL**
    Mission Statement: The National Conference for Community and Justice, founded in 1927 as The National Conference of Christians and Jews, is a human relations organization dedicated to fighting bias, bigotry and racism in America. NCCJ promotes understanding and respect among all races, religions and cultures through advocacy, conflict resolution and education.

14. National Underground Railroad Freedom Center, Inc., Cincinnati, OH

Mission Statement: We reveal stories about freedom's heroes, from the era of the Underground Railroad to contemporary times, challenging and inspiring everyone to take courageous steps for freedom today.

15. Society of Corporate Secretaries and Governance Professionals

Mission Statement: Professional education and networking with peers

16. St. Jude's Children's Research Hospital, Memphis, TN

Mission Statement: To find cures and means of prevention for childhood catastrophic diseases through research and treatment.

17. Smithsonian Institution, Washington, D.C.

Mission Statement: The Smithsonian's mission is "the increase and diffusion of knowledge". It was established in 1846 with funds bequeathed to the United States by James Smithson. The Institution is as an independent trust instrumentality of the United States and holds more than 137 million artifacts and specimens in its collections. It is a center for scientific research and scholarship in the arts, history, and culture.

18. West Des Moines Little League, Inc., West Des Moines, IA

Mission Statement: To provide healthy activity for children using the ball field as a classroom to instill discipline, team work, sportsmanship and fair play, and to establish a set of values to guide them into adulthood.

APPENDIX 6

Document 1
Part III of IRS Form 990

Form 990 (2010)   Page **2**

Part III   **Statement of Program Service Accomplishments**

Check if Schedule O contains a response to any question in this Part III   .   .   .   . ☐

1   Briefly describe the organization's mission:

----

2   Did the organization undertake any significant program services during the year which were not listed on the
prior Form 990 or 990-EZ?   .   .   .   .   ☐ **Yes**   ☐ **No**

If "Yes," describe these new services on Schedule O.

3   Did the organization cease conducting, or make significant changes in how it conducts, any program
services?   .   .   .   .   ☐ **Yes**   ☐ **No**

If "Yes," describe these changes on Schedule O.

4   Describe the exempt purpose achievements for each of the organization's three largest program services by expenses. Section
501(c)(3) and 501(c)(4) organizations and section 4947(a)(1) trusts are required to report the amount of grants and allocations to
others, the total expenses, and revenue, if any, for each program service reported.

4a   (Code: _____) (Expenses $ _____ including grants of $ _____) (Revenue $ _____)

4b   (Code: _____) (Expenses $ _____ including grants of $ _____) (Revenue $ _____)

4c   (Code: _____) (Expenses $ _____ including grants of $ _____) (Revenue $ _____)

4d   Other program services. (Describe in Schedule O.)
(Expenses $ _____ including grants of $ _____) (Revenue $ _____)

4e   **Total program service expenses ▶**

Form **990** (2010)

APPENDIX 6 (CONT'D)

Document 2
Part VI of Form 990

Form 990 (2010)   Page **6**

Part VI   **Governance, Management, and Disclosure** *For each "Yes" response to lines 2 through 7b below, and for a "No" response to line 8a, 8b, or 10b below, describe the circumstances, processes, or changes in Schedule O. See instructions.*

Check if Schedule O contains a response to any question in this Part VI . . . . ☐

Section A. Governing Body and Management

			Yes	No
1a	Enter the number of voting members of the governing body at the end of the tax year . .	**1a**		
b	Enter the number of voting members included in line 1a, above, who are independent .	**1b**		
2	Did any officer, director, trustee, or key employee have a family relationship or a business relationship with any other officer, director, trustee, or key employee?	**2**		
3	Did the organization delegate control over management duties customarily performed by or under the direct supervision of officers, directors or trustees, or key employees to a management company or other person? . .	**3**		
4	Did the organization make any significant changes to its governing documents since the prior Form 990 was filed?	**4**		
5	Did the organization become aware during the year of a significant diversion of the organization's assets? .	**5**		
6	Does the organization have members or stockholders?	**6**		
7a	Does the organization have members, stockholders, or other persons who may elect one or more members of the governing body?	**7a**		
b	Are any decisions of the governing body subject to approval by members, stockholders, or other persons?	**7b**		
8	Did the organization contemporaneously document the meetings held or written actions undertaken during the year by the following:			
a	The governing body?	**8a**		
b	Each committee with authority to act on behalf of the governing body?	**8b**		
9	Is there any officer, director, trustee, or key employee listed in Part VII, Section A, who cannot be reached at the organization's mailing address? *If "Yes," provide the names and addresses in Schedule O*	**9**		

Section B. Policies *(This Section B requests information about policies not required by the Internal Revenue Code.)*

			Yes	No
10a	Does the organization have local chapters, branches, or affiliates?	**10a**		
b	If "Yes," does the organization have written policies and procedures governing the activities of such chapters, affiliates, and branches to ensure their operations are consistent with those of the organization? .	**10b**		
11a	Has the organization provided a copy of this Form 990 to all members of its governing body before filing the form?	**11a**		
b	Describe in Schedule O the process, if any, used by the organization to review this Form 990.			
12a	Does the organization have a written conflict of interest policy? *If "No," go to line 13*	**12a**		
b	Are officers, directors or trustees, and key employees required to disclose annually interests that could give rise to conflicts?	**12b**		
c	Does the organization regularly and consistently monitor and enforce compliance with the policy? *If "Yes," describe in Schedule O how this is done*	**12c**		
13	Does the organization have a written whistleblower policy?	**13**		
14	Does the organization have a written document retention and destruction policy?	**14**		
15	Did the process for determining compensation of the following persons include a review and approval by independent persons, comparability data, and contemporaneous substantiation of the deliberation and decision?			
a	The organization's CEO, Executive Director, or top management official	**15a**		
b	Other officers or key employees of the organization	**15b**		
	If "Yes" to line 15a or 15b, describe the process in Schedule O. (See instructions.)			
16a	Did the organization invest in, contribute assets to, or participate in a joint venture or similar arrangement with a taxable entity during the year?	**16a**		
b	If "Yes," has the organization adopted a written policy or procedure requiring the organization to evaluate its participation in joint venture arrangements under applicable federal tax law, and taken steps to safeguard the organization's exempt status with respect to such arrangements?	**16b**		

Section C. Disclosure

17   List the states with which a copy of this Form 990 is required to be filed ▶ --

18   Section 6104 requires an organization to make its Forms 1023 (or 1024 if applicable), 990, and 990-T (501(c)(3)s only) available for public inspection. Indicate how you make these available. Check all that apply.

☐ Own website   ☐ Another's website   ☐ Upon request

19   Describe in Schedule O whether (and if so, how), the organization makes its governing documents, conflict of interest policy, and financial statements available to the public.

20   State the name, physical address, and telephone number of the person who possesses the books and records of the organization: ▶ --

Form **990** (2010)

APPENDIX 7

SUMMARY OF STATE CHARITABLE SOLICITATION AND REGISTRATION REQUIREMENTS AND FORMS

Laws regarding solicitation of funds from residents vary from state to state, but most often states require the charitable organization to register before engaging in any solicitation. In an effort to consolidate the information and data required by the various states, the National Association of State Charities Officials and the National Association of Attorneys General created the Unified Registration Statement (URS).[1] Three of the forty states that require registration, specifically Colorado, Oklahoma, and Florida, do not accept the URS.[2] The other thirty-seven states and the District of Columbia accept the URS as an alternative to several required forms, but thirteen jurisdictions require supplemental forms as well.[3] In addition, while many states accept the URS for an initial charitable solicitation registration, they require state-specific forms for annual registration renewals. Initial filing fees vary by state, from a nominal amount to several hundred dollars.

While the URS has created a convenient form consolidating much of the requested information, it is very important that organizations confirm what documents are required by the specific state they wish to solicit funds within before engaging in any such activities. Because many significant differences remain among various state requirements, organizations that need to register in multiple states may wish to engage specialized counsel or consultants to assist them with charitable solicitation registrations.

---

1. Available at http://www.multistatefiling.org/.

2. The URS also provides information on how to register in these states at http://www.multistate-filing.org/ (by clicking on the "Other States that Require Registration" link towards the bottom of the web page, under Appendix).

3. Arkansas, California, District of Columbia, Georgia, Maine, Minnesota, Mississippi, North Carolina, North Dakota, Tennessee, Utah, Washington, West Virginia, and Wisconsin require supplementary forms which can be found at http://www.multistatefiling.org/e_tpforms.htm.

ORGANIZATIONS THAT RATE NONPROFITS ON FUND-RAISING EFFICIENCY AND OTHER CRITERIA

The American Institute of Philanthropy produces a Charity Rating Guide covering a variety of criteria. Neither the ranking criteria nor the publication are available online, but may be purchased at minimal cost. www.charitywatch.org

The BBB Wise Giving Alliance ranks nonprofits based on a variety of criteria, including fund-raising efficiency. Criteria and rankings are available for free on the BBB Wise Giving Alliance website: www.bbb.org/us/Charity-Standards

Charity Navigator ranks nonprofits based on a variety of criteria, including fund-raising efficiency. Criteria and rankings are available for free on the Charity Navigator website: www.charitynavigator.org

MinistryWatch.Com provides free rankings on a variety of criteria for nonprofits engaged in Christian ministries. www.ministrywatch.com

APPENDIX 9

SAMPLE EXECUTIVE OFFICER EVALUATION FORM

Practical Advice Note: There is no universal template for Executive Officer evaluations. Evaluations need to be tailored to specific organizations and to the goals and priorities established by the board and the Executive Officer. Nonetheless, it may be helpful to consider the following areas when developing a format for evaluating an Executive Officer. Bracketed language contains suggestions for the types of matters to be evaluated/discussed under each general heading.

Evaluation of Executive Officer
[Date]

1.   Advancement of Mission of the Organization. [Specific areas for comment might include one of more of the following:
    a.   Vision for the organization
    b.   Strategic plan development/implementation
    c.   Program oversight and implementation
    d.   Outreach to community, donors, and other constituents
    e.   Status of the organization relative to peers in same field of endeavor]

2.   Management of Organization Administratively. [Specific areas for comment might include one or more of the following:
    a.   Implementation of specific administrative tasks previously identified by board
    b.   Oversight of the financial/accounting reporting process and internal controls
    c.   Focus on general administrative matters, including
        i.   Communication with staff
        ii.   Staff assessment and development, staffing levels, HR policies and staff morale
        iii. Interdepartmental cooperation/coordination]

3.   Relationship with Board as a whole and specifically with Chair and Committee Chairs. [Specific areas for comment might include one or more of the following:
    a.   Communications
    b.   Cultivation
    c.   Sensitivity to specific concerns of board leadership/members]

4.   Accomplishment of Other Specific Goals. [For matters not encompassed elsewhere in review]

5.   Areas for Future Focus or Attention. [To identify specific areas of weakness, or areas that need to be prioritized for greater attention or focus.]

APPENDIX 10

SUMMARY: HUMAN RESOURCES AND EMPLOYMENT-RELATED LAWS

(Adapted with permission from *Guide to Representing Religious Organizations*, published by the American Bar Association in 2009 from material written by Ann T. Stillman, Esq.)

I.   Laws Relating to Employment Discrimination

A.   Title VII of the Civil Rights Act of 1964 (Title VII)

Title VII makes it illegal to fail or refuse to hire or to discharge any individual, **or otherwise to discriminate** against any individual with respect to his compensation, terms, conditions, or privileges of employment, based on such individual's race, color, religion, sex (including based on pregnancy), or national origin. Title VII applies to employers engaged in any industry affecting interstate commerce, which have fifteen or more employees (including part time employees). Title VII also bans retaliation against any individual for exercising his or her Title VII rights.

Prohibited discrimination includes harassment because of race, color, religion, sex, or national origin. Two types of harassment are prohibited by Title VII: 1) quid pro quo and 2) hostile environment. Quid pro quo may be translated as "this for that," which means that this type of harassment occurs when employment decisions or expectations are based on an employee's submission to or rejection of unwelcome conduct. Hostile environment harassment consists of "comments or conduct that has the purpose or effect of unreasonably interfering with an individual's work performance or creating an intimidating, hostile or offensive working environment. The conduct is judged from the perspective of a reasonable person, by judging whether the conduct would substantially affect the work environment of such a person.

Title VII permits hiring on the basis of religion, sex, or national origin if such status is a bona fide occupational qualification (BFOQ) reasonably necessary to the normal operation of a particular business or enterprise. A BFOQ is one that affects an employee's ability to do the job and relates to the "essence" or the "central mission" of the employer's business.

Virtually every state has a statute that is similar to Title VII, although some state statutes are more comprehensive, including other categories for which employment discrimination is prohibited, such as sexual orientation. Additionally, many larger localities have civil rights ordinances.

B.   Age Discrimination in Employment Act (ADEA)

The ADEA prohibits discrimination in employment of persons forty years of age or older. The ADEA applies to entities with twenty or more employees.

Under the ADEA it is unlawful to: 1) fail or refuse to hire, to discharge or to otherwise discriminate against any individual with respect to compensation, terms, conditions, or privileges of employment, because of such individual's age; 2) limit, segregate, or classify employees in a way that would deprive an individual of employment opportunities or adversely affect his employee status, because of such individual's age; or 3) to reduce the wage rate of any employee in order to comply with the ADEA. The ADEA contains an exception applicable if age is a bona fide occupational qualification reasonably necessary to the operation of the employer's business. However, this exception is interpreted very narrowly.

ADEA prohibition against age discrimination includes a ban on harassment based on age, against employees forty years of age or older. The ADEA also prohibits retaliation for exercising rights protected by the ADEA.

C.   Americans with Disabilities Act (ADA)

Title I of the ADA prohibits employment discrimination against a qualified individual with a disability. The ADA generally applies to employers with fifteen or more employees.

The term disability is defined as (A) a physical or mental impairment that substantially limits one or more major life activities of such individual; (B) a record of such an impairment; or (C) being regarded as having such an impairment. The definition of disability is construed broadly in the ADA. A "qualified individual with a disability" is defined as a disabled person "who, with or without reasonable accommodation, can perform the essential functions of the employment position that such individual holds or desires."

Under the ADA, "major life activities" include "caring for oneself, performing manual tasks, seeing, hearing, eating, sleeping, walking, standing, lifting, bending, speaking, breathing, learning, reading, concentrating, thinking, communicating, and working. Major life activities also include the operation of a major bodily function, such as the immune system; normal cell growth; and digestive, bowel, bladder, neurological, brain, respiratory, circulatory, endocrine, and reproductive functions. Other activities may also be deemed major life activities. In addition, an impairment that is episodic or in remission is a disability if it would substantially limit a major life activity when the impairment is active.

The determination of whether a person has a disability must be made on a case-by-case basis. Even if an individual has a disability, to be protected by the ADA, the individual must be otherwise qualified to perform the **essential functions** of the job. Some of the factors considered in making an "essential function" determination are: 1) the employer's judgment; 2) a written job description; 3) time spent on the job performing the function; and 4) the consequences of not requiring the employee to perform the function.

Discrimination under the ADA includes the failure to make "reasonable accommodations" (e.g., the failure to allow use of a service dog in the workplace) to the known physical or mental limitations of an otherwise qualified applicant or employee with a disability, unless the employer can demonstrate that the accommodation would impose an undue hardship on the operation of the business. The ADA also prohibits retaliation for the exercise of rights protected by the Act.

An undue hardship may not be claimed simply because the cost of an accommodation is high in relation to an employee's salary or because other employees complain. However, if the accommodation requires a heavier workload for other employees, an undue hardship may be found.

D. Equal Pay Act

The Equal Pay Act of 1963 requires employers to provide "equal pay" for men and women who perform equal work unless the difference in pay is based on seniority, a merit system, or some factor other than sex. The Act applies to employees who are: 1) engaged in commerce or in the production of goods for interstate commerce, 2) employed in an enterprise with employees engaged in commerce and that has a gross volume of business (sales or receipts) of at least $500,000, and 3) employed by health and educational institutions, including hospitals, pre-schools, elementary and secondary schools, and nursing homes.

E. Genetic Information Nondiscrimination Act (GINA)

GINA prohibits failing to hire, discharging, or discriminating against any employee with respect to compensation, terms, conditions, or privileges of employment because of the employee's genetic information. GINA generally applies to employers with fifteen or more employees. GINA also prohibits limiting, segregating, or classifying employees in any way that would adversely affect the status of an employee because of the employee's genetic information. GINA requires employers to keep confidential any genetic information that they have acquired, and generally prohibits requesting or disclosing such information, except under limited circumstances. The term "genetic information" includes information about an employee's genetic tests, the genetic tests of family members of the individual, and the manifestation of a disease or disorder in family members of the individual, but excludes information about the sex or age of an individual.

Under GINA, an employer may not request, require, or purchase genetic information with respect to employees or their family members, except in limited circumstances such as when an employee's family medical history is being requested or required by the employer to comply with certification provisions of the Family and Medical Leave Act or similar laws. Since "genetic information" includes the manifestation of a disease in family members, employers generally should avoid even casually requesting information about a disease afflicting an employee's family member.

Employers must maintain an employee's genetic information on separate forms and in separate medical files, to be treated as a confidential medical record. Disclosure of such information by an employer may be done only in limited situations, such as: at the employee's written request; in response to certain court orders, or government investigations; and in connection with the employee's compliance under the Family and Medical Leave Act or similar laws. The requirements applicable to those limited situations are specific and employers should carefully follow the requirements before disclosing employee genetic information.

An employee who has suffered retaliation, been discriminated against or been subject to another "unlawful employment practice" in violation of GINA may be entitled to compensatory and punitive damages.

II. Other Federal Employment Laws

A. Family and Medical Leave Act (FMLA)

The FMLA requires employers to provide twelve work weeks of unpaid leave within a twelve-month period to an eligible employee for one or more of the following reasons: 1) the birth of a son or daughter or in order to care for such a newborn child, 2) the placement of a son or daughter with the employee for adoption or foster care, 3) a serious health condition of the employee, 4) to care for the employee's son, daughter, parent, or spouse who has a serious health condition, or 5) due to a "qualifying exigency" arising out of an employee's spouse, son, daughter, or parent being on active duty (or having been notified of an impending call or order to active duty) in the Armed Forces in support of a contingency operation. A serious health condition is an illness, injury, impairment, or physical or mental condition that involves one of two conditions: 1) inpatient care at a hospital, hospice, or residential medical care facility, or 2) continuing treatment by a health care provider.

The FMLA also provides that an eligible employee who is a spouse, son, daughter, parent, or next of kin of a "covered service member" is entitled to a total of twenty-six work weeks of leave within a twelve-month period to care for the service member. The covered service member must be a member of the Armed Forces who is undergoing medical treatment, recuperation, or therapy, is otherwise in outpatient status, or otherwise on the temporary disability retired list for a serious illness or injury.

The FMLA applies to employers of fifty or more employees in twenty or more calendar work weeks, in an industry affecting commerce. In addition, elementary and secondary schools, without regard to the number of persons employed, also generally are covered by the FMLA.

An employee is eligible to take FMLA leave if the employee: 1) has been employed by the employer for at least twelve months, 2) has worked at least 1,250 hours during the twelve-month period immediately preceding the commencement of the leave, and 3) is employed at a worksite where fifty or more employees are employed by the employer within seventy-five miles of that worksite. Special rules apply to the instructional employees of elementary and secondary schools that have employees who are eligible for FMLA leave. Instructional employees are "those whose principal function is to teach and instruct students in a class, a small group, or an individual setting."

The critical aspect to FMLA leave is not the unpaid leave—it is the right of the employee to be reinstated to his or her position (or an equivalent position) upon return from leave. If an employee was receiving group health benefits at the commencement of the leave, the organization must maintain those benefits at the same level as if the employee had continued to work. An employer may deny job restoration to certain key employees, if necessary, to prevent "substantial and grievous economic injury" to the employer's operations. According to the FMLA, a "key employee" is a "salaried FMLA-eligible employee who is among the highest paid ten percent of all the employees employed by the employer within seventy-five miles of the employee's work site."

Employees may take FMLA leave intermittently or on a reduced leave schedule when medically necessary or for leave due to a "qualifying exigency." However, leave taken intermittently or on a reduced leave schedule for the placement, adoption, or foster care of a healthy child or for the birth and care of a healthy child is subject to the organization's approval, except for pregnancy-related leave that qualifies as leave for a serious health condition. Employees must provide thirty days' or other advance notice of FMLA-eligible leave events, when such leave is foreseeable.

Information about FMLA coverage must be placed in the employee handbook, if there is one, or in other written materials on employee leave and benefits. Employers must also provide individualized notices containing certain information to employees under circumstances specified by regulation, including when the employee informs the employer of the need or intent to take FMLA leave, or when the employer acquires knowledge that an employee's leave may qualify as FMLA leave. Prototype notices are available from local offices of the Department of Labor's Wage and Hour Division or at http://www.dol.gov. If an employer fails to provide adequate and timely notice, the employer may be liable for actual monetary losses sustained by the employee as a direct result of the failure, and/ or for other appropriate relief, including reinstatement.

An organization may require the employee to provide a medical certification of a serious health condition from his or her health care provider or the health care provider of the relative for whom the employee is caring. The Department of Labor provides optional forms (Form WH-380-E, WH-380F and WH-385) that may be used for the certification. In addition, the organization may require periodic reports as to the employee's status and intent to return to work, as well as a fitness-for-duty certification upon return to work (unless such a fitness-for-duty certification is disallowed pursuant to regulation, collective bargaining agreement, or state or local law). An organization may require that leave for a "qualifying exigency" be supported by a certification meeting regulatory requirements (Form WH-384).

B.   Fair Labor Standards Act (FLSA)

The FLSA requires that all employees, except those who are exempt, be paid at least the federal minimum wage for all hours worked, and be paid overtime pay at time and one-half the regular rate of pay for all hours worked in excess of forty hours in a work week. The FLSA also requires that a record be kept of each employee's wages and hours. The FLSA restricts work for youths less than sixteen years of age and prohibits workers under eighteen from performing jobs declared hazardous by the Secretary of Labor. Finally, the FLSA prohibits retaliation for exercising rights protected by the FLSA.

The Act applies to employees: (1) who are engaged in commerce or the production of goods for interstate commerce; 2) who are employed in an enterprise with employees engaged in commerce and that has a gross volume of business (sales or receipts) of at least $500,000; and 3) employees of health and educational institutions, including hospitals, pre-schools, elementary and secondary schools, and nursing homes.

There is an exemption from the FLSA for bona fide executive, administrative, professional, and outside sales employees. For this exemption to apply, an employee generally must be paid on a salaried basis of no less than $455 per week, and perform a type of work that: 1) is directly related to the management of his or her employer's business, 2) is directly related to the general business operations of his or her employer or the employer's clients, 3) requires specialized academic training for entry into a professional field, 4) is in the computer field, 5) is making sales away from his or her employer's place of business, or 6) is in a recognized field of artistic or creative endeavor. Teachers are exempt as learned professionals, regardless of their salary.

The minimum wage and overtime requirements are inapplicable to certain religious workers, including nuns, monks, priests, lay brothers, ministers, deacons, and other members of religious orders who serve pursuant to their religious obligations in the schools, hospitals, and other institutions operated by their church or religious order. This exemption has been narrowly construed by courts.

C. Worker Adjustment and Retraining Notification Act (WARN)

WARN applies to employers with 100 or more full-time employees. Such employers must provide their employees with at least sixty calendar days' notice before closing a facility or conducting a "mass layoff." A facility is considered closed when its shutdown results in an employment loss for fifty or more employees during a thirty-day period. A mass layoff is a reduction in force (other than a plant closing) resulting in an employment loss for at least one-third of the employer's workforce, numbering at least fifty employees, or at least 500 employees. An "employment loss" generally means (A) an employment termination, other than a discharge for cause, voluntary departure, or retirement; (B) a layoff exceeding six months; or (C) a reduction in hours of work of more than 50 percent during each month of any six-month period."

D. Sarbanes-Oxley Act of 2002 (SOX): Application to Nonprofit Organizations

SOX is a law that was adopted in 2002 in response to a number of corporate and accounting scandals affecting public companies. SOX generally imposes requirements only on for-profit public companies. However, two provisions of SOX apply to nonprofits.

One of the provisions, the "whistleblower protection provision," can limit employment actions taken by a nonprofit organization against an employee. This provision prohibits retaliation, in the form of any harmful action, including interference with a person's employment or livelihood, "for providing to a law enforcement officer any truthful information relating to the commission or possible commission of any federal offense."

The second SOX provision applicable to nonprofits prohibits actual or attempted: 1) record alteration, destruction, or concealment with the intent to impair the object's integrity or availability for use in a federal proceeding; and 2) any other obstruction, influencing, or impeding of a federal proceeding.

E.   Uniformed Services Employment and Reemployment Rights Act (USERRA)

USERRA protects the job rights of individuals who leave their jobs for military service or certain types of service in the national disaster medical system. USERRA also prohibits employment discrimination against past and present members of the uniformed services, including veterans and members of the Reserve and National Guard and applicants to the uniformed services. Regulations under USERRA require employers to post a notice of the above rights for their employees. The Act applies to employees of any type of private sector employer, regardless of size.

USERRA requires reemployment if the employee: 1) leaves his or her job to perform service in the uniformed service; 2) ensures that his or her employer receives advance written or verbal notice of the service; 3) had five years or less of cumulative service in the uniformed services while with the employer; 4) returns to work or applies for reemployment in a timely manner after conclusion of service; and 5) has not received a less than honorable discharge. Employees must generally be restored to their job and to the benefits they would have attained if they had not been absent due to military service.

USERRA prohibits discrimination in initial employment, reemployment, retention in employment, promotion, or any benefit of employment because of an employee's application for membership in the uniformed service, membership or prior membership in the uniformed service, or obligation to serve in the uniformed service. Employers may not retaliate against anyone assisting in the enforcement of rights under USERRA, even if that person has no service connection.

While employees are on leave for military service, they have the right to continue their existing employer-based health plan coverage both for themselves and for their dependents for up to twenty-four months. Even if such coverage is not elected, the employees have the right to reinstatement in the employer's health plan when reemployed, generally without any waiting period or exclusions, except for service-connected illnesses or injuries.

APPENDIX 11

INTERNAL REVENUE SERVICE REBUTTABLE PRESUMPTION CHECKLIST

Practical Advice Note: *Satisfying the Internal Revenue Service's rebuttable presumption procedures becomes important when nonprofits are entering into a transaction with, or the payment of compensation to, a disqualified person as defined under the "intermediate sanction rules" (Section 4958 of the Internal Revenue Code) imposing sanctions for excess benefit transactions involving such a person.*

A disqualified person includes any person who was, at any time during the preceding five-year period, in a position to exercise "substantial influence" over the affairs of the organization, family members of such persons, and corporations, partnerships or trusts or estates in which such persons and their family members own more than 35 percent of the total combined voting power, 35 percent of the profits interest or 35 percent of the beneficial interest, respectively. Those persons deemed to have "substantial influence" and therefore subject to the intermediate sanctions rules generally include:

(a) voting directors,

(b) presidents, CEOs or COOs, and

(c) treasurers and CFOs.

Other persons may have substantial influence depending on the facts and circumstances. These persons include, among others, founders, substantial contributors, and individuals who manage a discrete segment or activity of the organization that represents a "substantial portion" of its activities, assets, income, or expenses.

Rebuttable Presumption Checklist[1]

1.   Name of disqualified person. _____

2.   Position under consideration: _____

3.   Duration of contract (1 yr., 3 yr., etc.): _____

4.   Proposed Compensation:

Salary: _____

Bonus: _____

Deferred compensation: _____

---

1.   This form is available online at www.irs.gov/pub/irs-utl/m4958a2.pdf.

Fringe benefits (list, excluding Sec. 132 fringes):

_____   _____   _____   _____

_____   _____   _____   _____

_____   _____   _____   _____

Liability insurance premiums: _____

Foregone interest on loans: _____

Other: _____

5.   Description of types of comparability data relied upon (e.g., association survey, phone inquiries, etc.):

   a) _____

   b) _____

   c) _____

   d) _____

6.   Sources and amounts of comparability data:

Salaries: _____   _____   _____

Bonuses: _____   _____   _____

Deferred compensation: _____   _____   _____

Fringe Benefits (list, excluding Sec. 132 fringes)

_____   _____   _____   _____

_____   _____   _____   _____

_____   _____   _____   _____

Liability insurance premiums: _____   _____   _____

Foregone interest on loans: _____   _____   _____

Others: _____   _____   _____

7.   Office or file where comparability data kept: _____

8.   Total proposed compensation: _____

9.   Maximum total compensation per comparability data: _____

10.   Compensation package approved by authorized body:

Salary: _____

Bonus: _____

Deferred compensation: _____

Fringe benefits (list, excluding Sec. 132 fringes):

_____ _____ _____ _____

_____ _____ _____ _____

_____ _____ _____ _____

Liability insurance premiums: _____

Foregone interest on loans: _____

Other: _____

11. Date compensation approved by authorized body: _____

12. Members of the authorized body present (indicate with X if voted in favor):

_____

_____

_____

_____

_____

13. Comparability data relied upon by approving body and how data was obtained:

_____

_____

_____

_____

14. Names of and actions (if any) by members of authorized body having conflict of interest:

_____

_____

_____

15. Date of preparation of this documentation (must be prepared by the later of next meeting of authorized body or 60 days after authorized body approved compensation): _____

16. Date of approval of this documentation by Board (must be within reasonable time after preparation of documentation above): _____

APPENDIX 12

SAMPLE EMERGENCY BYLAW PROVISION

Article____
Emergency Governance Provisions

Section ___.1 – Definitions

1. A "Major Emergency" means a major national or local emergency caused by a natural disaster, terrorist, or other significant event resulting in serious disruption in normal life over multiple days or an extended period of time; including but not limited to the declaration of a civil defense emergency by the U.S President or concurrent resolution of the U.S. Congress, or a proclamation of a civil defense emergency by the Governor of the State of [insert name of state] that relates to an attack on the United States or any of its possessions.

2. "Necessary emergency action" means action that is deemed by the Board of Directors, during a State of Emergency, to be necessary to be taken by such body immediately, under circumstances in which it is not reasonable to wait until normal conditions have returned. All necessary emergency actions taken by the Board of Directors pursuant to this Article _____ shall be deemed duly authorized and approved.

3. "State of Emergency" means the period of time during which Major Emergency conditions exist in the [state/city] area.

Section ___.2 – Emergency Quorum, Notice, and Meeting Provisions

If as a result of a Major Emergency, a sufficient number of persons then constituting the Board of Directors are not available or cannot be located in order to satisfy the quorum requirements otherwise set forth in these Bylaws, then the number of the available members of the Board shall be deemed a quorum for purposes of a meeting and for due authorization of any necessary emergency action. The available members of the Board of Directors shall determine reasonable notice for a meeting pursuant to this Section.

Section ___.3 – Emergency Representation and Actions in the Absence of Members of the Board of Directors

If during a State of Emergency no available members of the Board of Directors are able to be located to appoint interim or replacement Board Members, the Board of Directors shall consist of the most senior executive officers of [Nonprofit Corp.] or its Affiliates, in the following order:

- [NONPROFIT CORP.] Treasurer; Secretary; and

- [NONPROFIT CORP.] Treasurer; and

- [NONPROFIT CORP.] Executive Vice Presidents; and

- If there are less than five persons in the combined groups above, all Senior Vice Presidents of [NONPROFIT CORP.]; and

- If there are less than five persons in the combined groups above, all Vice Presidents of [NONPROFIT CORP.].

APPENDIX 13

SAMPLE DOCUMENT RETENTION POLICY AND SCHEDULE

Record Retention and Destruction Policy

This Record Retention and Destruction Policy of _____ ("Nonprofit") sets forth the record retention responsibilities of the staff, members of the Board of Directors, committee members, volunteers, and others for the maintenance and destruction of the Nonprofit's records.

1.   **Record Retention and Destruction.** It is Nonprofit's policy to maintain complete and accurate records. Nonprofit's staff, members of the Board of Directors, committee members, volunteers, and others contracting with Nonprofit shall transfer to Nonprofit for maintenance all paper and electronic records of Nonprofit not already maintained by Nonprofit. The records shall be maintained in accordance with the attached schedule. All other records are to be destroyed after three years. No staff member, member of the board of directors, committee member, volunteer or other party contracting with the Nonprofit shall knowingly destroy a record (regardless of form) with the intent to obstruct or influence the investigation or proper administration of any matter within the jurisdiction of any government department or agency or in relation to any such matter.

2.   **Conversion of Records to Electronic Form.** Paper records may be converted to electronic form for ease of access and storage, as approved by the Executive Director.

3.   **Exceptions to Policy.** Exceptions to the rules and terms for retention may be made only by the Nonprofit's Executive Director or Chair of the Board of Directors.

4.   **Responsibility for Administration of Policy.** The Executive Director shall be responsible for administering this Policy. As part of such administration, the Executive Director shall, in consultation with legal counsel, take steps to ensure that Nonprofit records are stored and destroyed (on at least an annual basis) in a manner consistent with this Policy.

5.   **Distribution of Policy.** A copy of this Policy will be distributed annually to all staff, members of the Board of Directors, committee members, volunteers, and others who handle Nonprofit records.

Record Retention Schedule

Practical Advice Note: *Retention periods of a certain length may be required by state or federal law or regulations or based on statute of limitations and audit periods for specific kinds of activities or records. In some cases, if no law or regulation clearly applies, the retention period should be based on what is useful for the organization.*

Type of Record	Retention Period*
Accounts receivable and payable ledgers and schedules	7 years
Annual audited financial statements	Permanent records
Articles of Incorporation, bylaws, Minutes, and other governance records	Permanent records
Bank statements, deposit records, electronic fund transfer documents, reconciliations	7 years
Contracts	10 years after termination
Tax returns	Permanent records
Litigation documents	10 years after termination

APPENDIX 14

WRITTEN STATEMENT OF EXPECTATIONS/JOB DESCRIPTION FOR BOARD MEMBERS

Practical Advice Note: Most nonprofit boards have expectations for directors related to board and committee meeting attendance, personal financial contributions, committee service, and advocacy for the organization within the community. Putting such expectations in writing helps reduce the opportunity for confusion and misunderstanding. The contents of these types of documents can be tailored to fit the needs of the organization. Some documents may include a summary of the legal duties and responsibilities of directors. Others may focus more on matters that are in addition to or that arise out of these legal duties and responsibilities.

Example 1
Expectations for Directors of XYZ Nonprofit

1. **Board Attendance, Committee Work, and Sharing of Expertise.** The XYZ Nonprofit board is a governance board, dealing with issues central to XYZ's long term success.

   Consistent board meeting attendance helps provide critical governance oversight by the board and is required. Meeting dates and times for the year are attached.

   Much of the work of the board is accomplished in committees. Directors are encouraged to join and attend meetings of at least one committee. Committee membership is rotated. A list of committees is attached.

   In addition to board and committee work, directors contribute significantly to XYZ through their work on special projects or by making themselves available on a regular basis for consultation with management or the board on issues on which they have special knowledge, experience, or expertise.

   Many directors help arrange for donation of resources or management time from their companies or their network to assist management on particular issues or problems.

2. **Annual Fund.** All directors are expected to give generously to XYZ's annual fund each fiscal year (July to June).

   The minimum annual expected contribution is $xxx, but most directors contribute at higher levels, if personal circumstances permit. Matching gift programs may be used to meet contribution levels.

   XYZ should be one of the highest priorities of a director's individual charitable giving.

3. **Endowment Campaign.** Directors are expected to support XYZ's endowment campaign with a substantial personal contribution, preferably at the $xxx figure level, if personal circumstances permit. While not all directors will

be able to give at that level, it is expected that whatever contribution is made will be a stretch gift for the director. Endowment contributions may be paid over a three-to-five-year period.

4. **Fundraisers.** Directors are expected to attend and contribute to one or more XYZ fundraisers. XYZ hosts one major annual fundraiser and several smaller donor events during the year.

5. **Solicitation of Others.** All directors should be prepared to solicit contributions on behalf of XYZ from sources identified by the board or the development department as prospects. Fundraising is critical to XYZ Nonprofit and is a board responsibility.

6. **Advocacy and Networking.** Directors are expected to be strong advocates for XYZ within the community. Advocacy and networking are especially important when XYZ launches a new program.

7. **Showcasing XYZ in the Community.** XYZ wants to showcase its staff and its programs as widely as possible. Directors are expected to help with this effort by identifying groups and events at which XYZ staff might speak on behalf of XYZ.

8. **Donor Cultivation Events.** XYZ's directors all participate in donor cultivation events sponsored by XYZ. We have a number of cultivation events annually and directors are requested to attend at least ___ such events each year.

9. **Building Support.** Directors are expected to help identify potential new donors and to help build support for XYZ Nonprofit in the community, especially the corporate giving community.

10. **Building the Board.** Building the board is a continual process. Directors are expected to help XYZ find new directors who support XYZ's mission, are willing to advocate on behalf of XYZ, who will work well with other members of the board, and who will contribute generously to the annual fund and endowment. New directors are nominated by the Committee on Directors and Governance, but helping to build the board is everyone's responsibility.

Approved by the Board of XYZ on _____

APPENDIX 14 (CONT'D)

Example 2
Board Member Job Description (Approved_____)

A. Length of Term

1. Each board member shall serve a three-year term from the effective date. A board member may serve up to three successive three-year terms.

B. Time Commitment Required

1. The board of directors meets every other month for an average of 3.5 hours per meeting.
2. Committees of the board meet four to six times a year, depending on the committee.
3. Directors are expected to attend an annual board retreat, of one to three days in length, including a board dinner.
4. Board members are encouraged to attend the [Major Fundraising Event Name] and other events featuring the system or individual sites or service lines, as appropriate and within the director's available time.

C. General Qualifications

Each board member should have each of the skills or attributes described below:

Organizational History and Mission; Ethics

1. Possess an understanding and appreciation of, or a willingness to learn, the history and mission of [Nonprofit Name].
2. Demonstrate high ethical standards and integrity in his or her personal and public conduct.

Knowledge and Experience

1. Possess experience in and knowledge of (or willingness and ability to obtain knowledge of) the _____ industry sufficient to enable the individual to be an effective board member, including the ability to comprehend and ask relevant questions regarding materials routinely provided to the board on [Nonprofit Name] operations and plans.
2. Possess experience in mission, business, professional, or volunteer positions that will enable him or her to provide useful insights into various matters addressed by the board.
3. Have current or recent prior service on other nonprofit or for-profit boards; service in a management position of an organization of comparable size or with other characteristics similar to [Nonprofit

Name]; other comparable experience; or the willingness and ability to quickly learn and apply principles and practices of corporate governance as required to be an effective board member.

D. General Expectations and Responsibilities

Each board member is expected to:

1. Have the ability to participate effectively in board meetings, including articulating and responding to alternative viewpoints through effective communication.
2. Be willing and have the ability to devote the time required to be an effective board member, including serving on one or more board committees; preparing for board and committee meetings through advance review of meeting materials; and attending at least 75 percent of all board and committee meetings, in person or by phone (if necessary).
3. Commit to attend annual events designated for board members, such as the annual board retreat, social functions designed to integrate the board and acquaint board members with one another, and other special functions as requested.
4. Be willing to participate in periodic board member self-evaluations and annual board evaluations, and be open to constructive criticism on performance as a board member.
5. Adhere to [Nonprofit Name] policies applicable to board members, including maintaining the confidentiality of [Nonprofit Name] information and conflict of interest disclosure procedures.
6. Support the philanthropic goals of the [Nonprofit Name].
7. Be willing to consider new ideas and changes in historic practices, consistent with the mission, principles, and values of [Nonprofit Name].
8. Possess the ability to make independent decisions, unencumbered by material conflicts of interest.
9. Be committed to understanding the needs and diversity of the communities served by [Nonprofit Name] facilities and programs.
10. Commit to active participation in board work, meaning preparing for each meeting and actively engaging in discussion at board meetings.
11. Stay informed about the organization and keep abreast of recent developments pertaining to [Nonprofit Name] and in the _____ industry in general.
12. Consistently act in good faith and in a manner which reflects the best interests of [Nonprofit Name] and the communities it serves.

APPENDIX 15

SAMPLE CONTENTS FOR INFORMATION PACKETS PROVIDED TO PROSPECTIVE DIRECTORS

1.   Mission Statement

2.   Summary information on history of the organization

3.   Latest annual report on Form 990

4.   Latest "glossy" annual report given to donors and other constituents, if the organization has one

5.   Latest annual audit report

6.   List of current directors

7.   List of the organization's expectations for trustees

8.   List of board committees

9.   Biographical information on executive officer and other senior staff

10.   Summary information on programs offered by the organization

11.   Major marketing/advertising brochures

12.   Meeting dates and dates of major events directors are expect to attend

APPENDIX 16

SAMPLE FORM OF ACTION BY UNANIMOUS WRITTEN CONSENT

Practical Advice Note: *There is no universal format for an action by written consent, but many such documents follow the format and contain provisions similar to the sample below.*

Action by Written Consent

[Name of Organization]   [Date]

Pursuant to the provisions of Section __ of [Name of State Nonprofit Law] and consistent with the bylaws of [Name of Organization], we, the undersigned directors of [Name of Organization] adopt the following resolution in this action by written consent without a meeting:

[Insert Resolution]

This action by written consent may be executed in counterparts and each such counterpart shall be considered an original and all counterparts together shall be considered one document. The effective date of the above resolution is [_____, 20__, irrespective of the date of signing][1] [the latest date on which this consent shall have been executed by any director].

_____   _____
[Signature of Director]   [Signature of Director]
[Name of Director]   [Name of Director]
Dated: _____   Dated:_____

_____   _____
[Signature of Director]   [Signature of Director]
[Name of Director]   [Name of Director]
Dated: _____   Dated: _____

_____   _____
[Signature of Director]   [Signature of Director]
[Name of Director]   [Name of Director]
Dated: _____   Dated: _____

---

1. In most states actions taken by unanimous written consent may have retroactive effective dates—i.e., prior to the date by which all directors have signed. Such consents therefore operate similar to ratifications of prior actions.

APPENDIX 17

SAMPLE FORM OF WAIVER OF NOTICE

Practical Advice Note: *There is no universal format for a waiver of notice. Waivers may be executed in advance, or more typically, after a meeting. Most such documents follow the format and contain provisions similar to the sample below. Such waivers are only required for directors who do not attend the meeting. Attendance at a meeting is deemed a waiver unless the director attends solely for the purpose of objecting to the holding of the meeting due to the lack of required notice.*

Waiver of Notice and Consent to Meeting

[Name of Organization]

The undersigned, a director of [name of organization], does hereby waive, pursuant to section __of the bylaws, notice of the time, date, and purpose of the [insert date] meeting of the directors.

Dated: _____

_____

Signature

Printed Name of Director:_____

APPENDIX 18

AGENDA SAMPLES

Practical Advice Note: *There are no universal formats for agendas. Following are two possible agenda structures. Agendas that provide guidance as to what is required of the board or how much time is anticipated to be necessary for each item can be helpful to directors.*

Sample 1

Agenda
[Insert Name of Organization]
Board of Directors Meeting
[Insert date]
[Insert location of meeting]

1.	Call to Order and Introductions	
2.	Executive Officer's Report	For Information/Discussion
3.	Financial Report	For Information/Discussion
4.	Presentation on _____	For Information/Discussion
5.	Presentation on _____ and adoption of resolution to _____	Action Required (approval)
6.	Committee Chair Reports	For Information (and action if applicable)
7.	General Announcements	For Information
8.	Consent Agenda (for matters requiring little or no discussion)	Action Required
	a. Minutes of [insert date] board meeting	(Approval)
	b. Written committee reports	(Acknowledge Receipt)
	c. Routine or other resolutions not requiring board discussion	(Approval)
9.	Executive Session	

Next Meeting: [insert date and location]

APPENDIX 18 (CONT'D)

Sample 2

Agenda
[Insert Name of Organization]
Board of Directors Meeting
[Insert date]
[Insert location of meeting]

1.	Call to Order and Introductions	1 minute
2.	Minutes of [insert date] meeting	1-2 minutes
3.	Financial Report	30 minutes
4.	Executive Officer's Report	30 minutes
5.	Presentation on _____	45 minutes
6.	Committee Reports	10 minutes
7.	Old Business, if needed	
8.	New Business, if needed	
9.	Executive Session	15 minutes
10.	Adjournment	

Note: The next meeting is to be held on _____, _____, 20__
at _____.

APPENDIX 19

SAMPLE EXECUTIVE SESSION AGENDA

Practical Advice Note: Often there is no need for a separate agenda for an executive session of the board. However, if there is more than one important item for discussion, or if a resolution needs to be adopted during the session, it may be useful to create an agenda for distribution during the executive session.

Agenda for Executive Session

[Insert date]
Confidential
Return this document at the end of the meeting.

1.   Discussion of Executive Officer Performance (see attached draft performance evaluation)

2.   Approval of Executive Officer compensation (see attached resolution)

3.   Discussion of possible opportunity to acquire facility

4.   Opportunity for directors to express comments or concerns on other matters pertaining to the organization

Please remember that all matters discussed in the executive session are confidential and not to be reported to or discussed with anyone not in attendance at the meeting. The Chair will brief directors who are unable to attend the executive session.

Please return all materials distributed during the executive session to the Chair.

APPENDIX 20

SAMPLE SECRETARY'S CERTIFICATE AND FORMATS FOR RESOLUTIONS

Practical Advice Note: *There is no universal form of Secretary's certificate. However, most such certificates would be similar in format and contain similar provisions to those indicated below.*

Document 1
Sample Secretary's Certificate

Secretary's Certificate

I, _____, Secretary of [Insert name of organization], a [insert name of state] corporation, do hereby certify that the resolution [select: set forth above, set forth below or attached hereto as Exhibit A] is a true and accurate copy of a resolution adopted by the board of directors of [insert name of organization] [select: at a duly called meeting of the board on [insert date], or in a duly executed action by written consent without a meeting effective [insert date]].

I further certify that said resolution has not been rescinded, amended, or modified and is in full force and effect as of the date hereof.

In witness whereof, I have executed this certificate this _____ day of _____ [and affixed the organization's seal].

[Signature]
[Name], Secretary
[Name of Organization]

APPENDIX 20 (CONT'D)

RESOLUTION FORMATS

Practical Advice Note: There is no universal standard for when formal resolutions are required or for the format they should take. Resolutions are typically used in connection with approvals of large expenditures, real estate, brokerage and banking matters, major acquisitions and dispositions of assets, amendments to an organization's governing documents, or other substantial matters, and particularly in connection with any matter for which it is expected that a third party will want evidence of specific board approval.

Resolution Format without "Whereas" clauses

Resolution re Banking Authority

RESOLVED, that _____, the Executive Director of _____ (the "Organization"), together with _____, Director of Finance, are authorized on behalf of the Organization to open and maintain such bank accounts as they may deem advisable, and are:

(A) Authorized to [jointly] [individually] (i) sign, whether manually or by facsimile signature, in the name of this Organization, checks, drafts, or other written orders for the payment of money now or hereafter in said respective accounts; (ii) issue written, telephonic, electronic, or oral instructions with respect to the transfer of funds now or hereafter on deposit in said respective accounts by wire, automated clearinghouse, or other electronic means of transfer, without any written order for the payment of money being issued with respect to such transfer, provided that telephonic or oral instructions are confirmed in writing; and

(B) Enter into such agreements with banks with respect to any noncredit banking services (including, without limitation, electronic services) as such individuals in their sole discretion deem advisable or in the best interests of this Corporation; and

RESOLVED, FURTHER, that any and all checks, drafts, notes, or other orders of every kind deposited or to be deposited for the accounts of this Organization with any banking depository of this Organization or for collection or otherwise, requiring endorsement in the name of this Organization, shall be sufficiently endorsed when there appears such name stamped or in written endorsement thereon, without any signature or countersignature affixed.

Format which uses "Whereas" clauses

Resolution re Purchase of Property Located at
[Insert street address]

WHEREAS, _____(the Organization) requires additional facilities in which to conduct its operations, and

WHEREAS, the Board of Directors of the Organization has determined it is preferable for the Organization to own rather than rent such additional premises, and

WHEREAS, the Board of Directors has reviewed the information provided by management regarding a certain property recommended to be purchased and the Board has determined that such property is suitable for the Organization and that the terms and conditions proposed, including the purchase price, are reasonable and appropriate;

NOW THEREFORE,

BE IT RESOLVED that the Organization purchase the real estate commonly known as [insert name and/or street address] in the city of [insert city], county of [insert county], state of [insert state] for a purchase price not to exceed [insert price] and on the terms of the purchase agreement attached hereto; and

BE IT FURTHER RESOLVED that the Executive Officer and the Finance Officer of this Organization are authorized to sign said purchase agreement on behalf of this organization and any other documents or instruments required in connection with and to effectuate said purchase in accordance with the terms specified in the purchase agreement.

Format which does not use "Whereas" or "Resolved"

Resolution re Election of Directors

The board of directors of _____ authorizes and determines:

1. The number of directors constituting this board is set at 10.

2. The following individuals are elected as directors of _____ until the next annual meeting of this organization or until their earlier resignation, retirement, or removal.

[List directors individually]

APPENDIX 21

MINUTES GUIDELINES AND TEMPLATES

Practical Advice Note: *Minute writing is an art and the level of detail and format of minutes will vary based on a variety of factors. Following are some guidelines that may be helpful.*

Document 1
Guidelines

What to include:

1. Meeting Details, including:
   a. Type of meeting (regular/special, committee/board)
   b. Date and location
   c. Who attended (directors/staff/guests)
   d. Directors who did not attend or who arrived late after substantive discussion
   e. Who presided
   f. Who kept the minutes (served as secretary)

2. Meeting Substance
   a. Specify issues discussed, including names of presenters
      i. Note materials distributed, if any
      ii. List major points of discussion or matters considered, in summary form
   b. Clearly state decisions/actions taken
      i. Include resolutions adopted, if any
      ii. Indicate names of directors voting against or abstaining on resolution, or not present at the time of the vote
      iii. When a conflict of interest situation is being dealt with by the board, indicate whether the director with the conflict was present for some or all of the discussion or action.
      iv. If no resolution adopted, indicate if there was consensus on the topic, or if matter was deferred or informally tabled
   c. Identify information items and reports received
      i. Include name of report or item and topics covered
      ii. Include list of materials distributed, if any
      iii. Include names of individuals (and if applicable, their position, such as committee chair) giving oral reports
   d. Indicate whether executive session was held

What to avoid:

1. At the Meeting
   a. Tape recording
   b. Taking notes that attempt to capture every word

2.   When Writing Minutes
     a.   Waiting for weeks to do initial drafts or to send out for review
     b.   Using characterizations and adjectives
     c.   Including verbatim or lengthy descriptions
     d.   Using language that isn't clear as to what specific action was taken and by whom
     e.   Indicating time spent on particular items

APPENDIX 21 (CONT'D)

Practical Advice Note: *Formats for minutes vary among organizations based on tradition, preferences of board leadership, recommendations from legal counsel, and, in some cases, as a result of legal or regulatory concerns. Although there is no universal template for minutes, consistency in format is generally considered advisable. Following is a template that may be helpful to officers or staff charged with drafting minutes.*

Document 2
Templates for Minutes

Minutes of the Regular Meeting of the Board of Directors of
[Insert Name of Organization]
Held [Insert Date]
At [Insert Location]

The following directors were present/absent (* indicates absence)
[List all directors. Place * after the names of those not present]

The following members of management were present:

The following guests were present:

Call to Order and Introductions

[Insert name of Chair], Chair called the meeting to order at _____ [a.m. or p.m.] and introduced the members of staff and guests in attendance.

Approval of Minutes

On motion made, seconded, and carried, the board approved the previously distributed minutes of the meeting of the board held [insert date].

Report of the Executive Officer

[Insert name of Executive Officer], Executive Officer, reviewed and responded to director questions on the following matters:

[List matters discussed and brief summary of what presented]

Financial Report

[Insert name and title] reviewed and responded to director questions on the previously distributed financial statements [including the [insert date] income statement and the balance sheet. He/She also reviewed and responded to questions on the status of the organization's performance in comparison to the budget approved on _____. It was the consensus of the board that management [e.g., needed to take steps to reduce expenses in connection with _____]. The Executive Officer indicated that he/she would discuss potential options for [e.g., expense reduction] with the Executive Committee at its next meeting.

Presentation on Programming

The Executive Director introduced [Insert name and, if applicable, title], who manages the organization's community outreach programs. Mr./Ms. [insert name] reported on recent efforts to [e.g., expand/revamp] certain programs, including [name of programs]. He/she responded to director questions on [e.g., costs and effectiveness of] the various programs, [e.g., actions being taken to train staff and plans to make constituents aware of changes to programming].

Presentation on Banking/Brokerage Relationships

The Executive Director and the Treasurer reviewed the organization's banking and brokerage relationships and requested board approval of a resolution to open a new brokerage account at [insert name of institution] to facilitate handling of donations of stock by individuals through that institution. Following discussion, on motion made, seconded, and carried, the board adopted the following resolution in the format requested by [name of brokerage institution]:

[Insert text of resolution]

Committee Reports

The board acknowledged receipt of the following previously distributed committee reports
> Report of the [Insert Date] Meeting of the Committee on Governance
> Report of the [Insert Date] Meeting of the Nominating Committee
> Report of the [insert Date] Meeting of the Executive Committee

[Insert Name], Chair of the [Insert Committee Name] responded to director questions on [insert as appropriate, e.g., the process that committee was using to survey governance practices of other nonprofit organizations].

Announcements

The Chair reminded directors of the [insert date] board offsite planning meeting and requested directors who had not already done so to confirm their attendance at the meeting.

Executive Session

All staff and guests left the meeting at this time and the board then met in executive session.

Adjournment

There being no further business, the meeting was adjourned at _____[a.m. or p.m.]

_____
[Insert Name]
Secretary

APPENDIX 22

SAMPLE GENERAL DELEGATION OF AUTHORITY AND DELEGATION FOR SPECIFIC TRANSACTION

Practical Advice Note: Delegations of management authority to the Executive Officer and other organization leaders or managers often occurs through the organization's bylaws. The samples below provide both short-form and long-form examples of such delegation.

Document 1
General Delegations

SAMPLE 1: SHORT-FORM MANAGEMENT DELEGATION IN BYLAWS

SECTION ___ – President

The President shall be the Chief Executive Officer of the Corporation. The President shall be the direct executive representative of the Board of Directors in the management of the Corporation and shall have all the duties and authority such position customarily requires. The President shall hire and appoint, subject to approval of the Board, Vice Presidents and other senior officers of the Corporation. The President shall have authority to sign all contracts and other legal instruments on behalf of the Corporation, except as otherwise provided by the Board of Directors.

SAMPLE 2: LONG-FORM MANAGEMENT DELEGATIONS IN BYLAWS

SECTION ____ – Chief Executive Officer (CEO)

The Chief Executive Officer (CEO) of the Corporation shall be appointed from among qualified professional candidates to serve as the chief executive officer of the Corporation. Subject to these Bylaws and such orders as may be issued by the Board, the CEO shall have the responsibility for the administration of the day-to-day affairs of the Corporation. Specifically, the CEO shall:

a. Advise and make recommendations to the Board relating to the operation of the Corporation and long-range planning.

b. Act to implement and further Corporation goals, policies, and procedures, and make recommendations to the Board regarding material goals, policies, and procedures.

c. Prepare and submit to the Board an annual operating budget for the Corporation and a long-term capital plan.

d.   Serve as an ex officio, voting member on all committees established by the Corporation.

e.   Oversee the operations of the Corporation, including:

i.   Represent the Corporation with governmental and other organizations;

ii.   Support the activities of the Corporation and its employed staff in implementing the Corporation's mission.

f.   Sign any contracts or other instruments authorized to be executed by or on behalf of the Corporation.

g.   Perform such other duties as may be prescribed by the Board or the President and all duties incident to the office of senior executive officer.

The CEO shall be responsible for designating an appropriate officer to perform the duties of the CEO in the event of such officer's absence or disability and for performing such other duties as may be delegated by the Board or the President.

SECTION _____ – Vice President(s)

Any Vice President(s) shall perform such duties as are established from time to time by the CEO and shall report to such senior executive officer. In all other matters, the Vice President(s) shall function in accordance with the specific authorities that have been delegated by the President and the senior executive officer.

APPENDIX 22 (CONT'D)

Practical Advice Note: *Boards also delegate authority by adopting resolutions related to particular transactions or types of transactions. While such delegations are often quite specific as to the authority being delegated, it is also common practice to include a general authorization for designated officers to take other actions deemed necessary to carry out the intent of the resolution.*

Document 2
Delegation Related to Specific Transaction

[DATE]
RESOLUTION
TO APPROVE [TRANSACTION]

WHEREAS, the [Nonprofit Name] Board of Directors has considered the [describe relevant facts] and has determined that it is reasonable and appropriate, and in the best interests of [Nonprofit Name] and its stakeholders to evaluate a possible [Transaction], through execution of a nonbinding letter of intent and the commencement of full due diligence;

NOW, THEREFORE, BE IT RESOLVED that the [Nonprofit Name] Board of Directors hereby approves the execution of a nonbinding Letter of Intent in such form as the [Nonprofit Name] President deems reasonable and appropriate, and the associated commencement of full due diligence review, to evaluate the possible [Transaction]; and be it further

RESOLVED, that upon execution of a nonbinding Letter of Intent on behalf of [Nonprofit Name], the President and other executive officers of [Nonprofit Name] are hereby authorized and directed to take any and all such actions as are necessary and appropriate to conduct appropriate due diligence to assess the potential benefits and terms of a [Transaction]; and be it further

RESOLVED, that the [Nonprofit Name] President and other executive officers of [Nonprofit Name] are each hereby authorized and directed to take or cause to be taken any and all such other actions as they deem necessary or appropriate to effectuate the intent of the foregoing resolutions.

APPENDIX 23

SAMPLE TABLE OF CONTENTS FOR DIRECTORS' ORIENTATION MANUAL

[Name of Organization] Directors' Orientation Manual

Welcome Letter from Board Chair and Executive Officer

Overview of Director Responsibilities

List of Directors, Biographical Information, and Terms

Mission Statement and History of the Organization

Calendar
    Board Meetings
    Key Events

Committees
    Committee Assignments
    Committee Descriptions/Charters
    Committee Meeting Schedule

Contact Information
    Directors
    Senior Staff
    All Staff Directory

Financial Information
    Current Annual Report and Form 990
    Key Financial Facts
    Current Budget
    Most Recent Financial Statements
    Tutorial re Key Financial Indicators and Other Important
    Financial Issues

Glossary of Frequently Used Terms and Acronyms

Governing Documents
    Articles
    Bylaws
    Summaries or Explanation re Indemnification/Insurance Provisions

Organization Chart
    Legal Entity Structure (subsidiaries and joint venture organizations)
    Internal Organizational Structure (departments or divisions)

Minutes
>   Board Minutes for Past Twelve Months
>   Minutes of Assigned Committees for Past Twelve Months

Policies
>   Conflict of Interest Policy
>   Internet/Intranet Usage Policy
>   Media Policy

Strategic Plan

Website and, if Applicable, Intranet/Board Only Access Information

APPENDIX 24

SAMPLE OUTLINE OF DIRECTOR ORIENTATION PROGRAM

Practical Advice Note: The suggestions below assume a group orientation meeting for several directors. However, the topics could be covered with individual directors on a one-to-one basis. Matters may also be covered in more than one meeting, although the logistics of getting a group of directors together for more than one orientation meeting may be difficult.

Orientation Outline:

1.   Welcome from the Board Chair and the Executive Officer

2.   Introduction of board leadership, if present—Chair

3.   Introduction of senior staff and review of senior staff responsibilities, the organization chart, and work of the major departments—Executive Officer

4.   Mission and history of the organization—Executive Officer

5.   Current status of the organization, current priorities, major programs and activities, and strategic plan—Executive Officer and Chair

6.   Financial tutorial—Chief Financial Officer

7.   Board matters—Board Chair

    a.   Responsibilities of directors

    b.   Committees and committee assignments

    c.   Board goals and priorities

8.   Tour of facilities—Executive Officer

APPENDIX 25

SAMPLE BOARD EFFECTIVENESS QUESTIONNAIRES

Sample 1
Open-Ended Questionnaire

[Please provide your written comments on the issues listed below.] or [Please review the questions listed below and prepare your comments in advance of your scheduled interview with _____].

Your answers and comments will be kept confidential. They will be used to help the board assess its own effectiveness and to address concerns that directors may have about how we function as a board and an organization.

Please be as specific as possible in your assessment.

Board Composition and Knowledge

1. The skills/background/experience/diversity and number of directors

2. a) The board's understanding of [the organization's] mission, management/ positioning of the organization, the organization's competitive environment, and long-range needs;

    b) Your own personal understanding of these items

3. The board's knowledge of the [organization's] constituency and financial support base

Board Meetings

4. The number, location, and length of board meetings

5. The subjects covered at meetings

6. The time spent on particular subjects

7. The opportunity for discussion at board meetings

8. The directors' ability to suggest agenda items

9. The amount and quality of presentations and education on [the organization's mission or area of focus] at the board meetings

Information Flow

10. The quality, quantity, and method of delivery of information provided to directors:

    a) in connection with board meetings,

    b) unrelated to board meetings

Board Relationship to Management/Staff

11. Management's willingness to respond to director questions, requests for information, special reports, receptiveness to board suggestions, etc.

12. Director access to management; relationship with management and staff; and opportunity for input and feedback with management

Board Participation

13. Director participation

    a)   at board meetings,

    b)   at committee meetings,

    c)   outside of regular meetings
         (e.g., events related to the organization)

14. Deployment of the board in the community, with donors, constituents, and unrelated groups for advocacy, etc.

15. Opportunities for informal "get togethers" with other board members (e.g., dinners following board meetings, lunches, etc.)

16. Overall cohesiveness of the board (participation of the full board vs. individual director efforts)

Board Committees

17. Committee structure, mandate, and numbers of committees

18. Committee appointments

19. Committee agendas, information, and materials

General Questions on Board Effectiveness

20. Are there any factors that currently impede board/committee effectiveness?

21. Are there factors that currently enhance board/committee effectiveness?

22. How does the effectiveness of [this organization's] board compare to that of other boards on which you serve?

Questions About Your Service on the Board

23. How effectively is [this organization] using your talents?

24. What attracted you to board service at [this organization] in the first place and what keeps you interested as a director?

Strategic Issues and Goals for This Organization

25. What are the major strategic issues facing [this organization] over the next three years, in your opinion?

26. What goals would you like to see [this organization] accomplish in the next

   a) year

   b) three years?

What Else?

27. Are there any other issues you wish to raise or comment on?

APPENDIX 25 (CONT'D)

Sample 2
Effectiveness Questionnaire for Telephone Interview

Please review the listed items and prepare your responses in advance of your telephone interview with [_____] on [_____]

1.   What do you like most about being on the XYZ board?

2.   What do you like least about being on the XYZ board?

3.   Are we using your talents the way we should? If not, please give us suggestions.

4.   Please give us your views on the overall effectiveness of the XYZ board with respect to the following matters, suggesting any improvements you feel would be appropriate.

Board Meetings:

Time, place, length, etc.

Substance/topics covered

Opportunity for discussion/meaningful input

Opportunity to learn about XYZ (or some important aspect of mission)

Sufficiency and usefulness of materials

Value in attending

Committee Meetings:

Time, place, length, etc.

Substance/topics covered

Opportunity for discussion/meaningful input

Opportunity to learn about XYZ (or some important aspect of mission)

Sufficiency and usefulness of materials

Value in attending

Leadership provided to the organization by:

Chair of the Board

Officers/Committee Chairs

Managing Executive/CEO

_____(Other senior management leader)

5.   What do you think are the one or two most important strategic issues facing XYZ over the next several years? [OR: On a scale of 1 to 5, with 1 being most important and 5 being least important, please rank the strategic importance of the issues listed below:]

Here are some possibilities for you to consider in preparing your answer to this question.

Raising a meaningful endowment

Maintaining a balanced (deficit-free) operating budget

Increasing excellence in _____

Evolving the mission or type of work done by XYZ

Increasing contributed income

Increasing earned income

Managing expenses and finding ways to structurally reduce expense

Creating a long-term financial plan that eliminates the current "structural deficit"

Developing a successful _____ program

Obtaining a more permanent facility

Improving financial reporting and discipline

Developing management and board leadership succession programs

Improving the relationship of management to the board

Improving communications with the board

Improving communications with or outreach to the community or other major stakeholders

Maintaining good board governance/effectiveness

Board leadership development

Increasing the size and stature of the board

Improving the board's understanding of _____

Achieving better understanding of changing nature of environment in which XYZ operates and impact on strategy and mission

APPENDIX 26

BOARD EFFECTIVENESS SELF-EVALUATION FORM

Adapted with permission from *Governance for Nonprofits: From Little Leagues to Big Universities*, The Society of Corporate Secretaries and Governance Professionals, 2008

Yes   No

☐   ☐   Does the board get enough information of the right kinds, at the right time, from the right members of management?

☐   ☐   Is there an effective director orientation program?

☐   ☐   Does the board have active committees composed of a small, effective number of members to tackle audit, development/fund-raising, finance, governance, nomination, personnel, program, and other key matters?

☐   ☐   Are committee members and chairs rotated with appropriate intervals?

☐   ☐   Are meetings conducted effectively, with appropriate frequency, on time, and according to well-thought-out agendas circulated in advance?

☐   ☐   Are meetings characterized by open communication and diligent questions on point discussed in a collegial manner?

☐   ☐   Does the board meet regularly in private apart from the executive director and other managers?

☐   ☐   Are the board's actions motivated by and designed in furtherance of the mission?

☐   ☐   Does the board periodically review the mission statement and implementation strategy?

☐   ☐   Does the board act as if it is accountable to contributors and beneficiaries?

☐   ☐   Does the board communicate effectively on a regular basis with its stakeholders, contributors, and beneficiaries?

☐   ☐   Does the board establish goals for management and review their effectiveness and performance at least annually?

☐   ☐   Are there effective processes and structures to evaluate, communicate with, and counsel managers and staff?

☐   ☐   Are there guidelines/delegations that clearly specify managers' authority?

☐   ☐   Does the board micromanage operations or, at the other extreme, does it rubberstamp management decisions and let management handle everything with little board oversight?

☐   ☐   Does the board review the operation's significant legal exposures and assess the organization's legal compliance processes and record?

☐   ☐   Are there effective audit and financial oversight processes?

☐   ☐   Does the board review and adopt the organization's capital and operating budgets?

☐   ☐   Are there clear and effective procedures on handling funds, contributions, and assets?

☐   ☐   Are there effective standards and procedures to minimize and disclose potential conflicts of interest?

☐   ☐   Does the board governance or nominating committee: regularly assess board practices and structures for effectiveness; evaluate current directors and counsel those whose performance is less than ideal; and continually look for talented potential new directors?

☐   ☐   Does the board have an appropriate level of turnover in its membership—new members and ideas balanced with experience and continuity?

Practical Advice Note: *This format may easily be adapted to a numerical rating scale for each item. Just replace Yes and No with a line and instructions to provide a numerical 1-10 ranking for each item with, for example, 10 indicating that the organization is doing well in the category rated and a 1 indicating the organization is not doing well in the category rated, and numbers in between signaling some level of concern or need for improvement.*

APPENDIX 27

SAMPLE COVER MEMO FORMATS
RE BOARD MATERIALS

Practical Advice Note: Using a consistent format for materials distributed to board members helps prevent board members from being confused by multiple reports and documents. Consistency in format also helps board members track important information and be better able to understand trends. Summarizing important information in cover letters also helps officers focus their material and their presentations to the board.

Sample 1

Sample Format for Cover Memo to the Board
[to be included with board meeting materials]

[Date]

To: Board of Directors

From: Executive Officer

Re: Agenda for Board Meeting

At the upcoming board meeting, we have several important matters to discuss.

First: [insert description of the most important matter]. A draft resolution is included for your consideration as we need a board decision and vote on this matter at this meeting.

Second: [insert description of other important matter.] This matter will likely require several discussions at the board level and is currently under consideration by two of our board committees. The purpose of the presentation at this meeting is to bring the board up to date on our progress.

In addition to the above, we will have a presentation on _____ by _____. This presentation is designed to help you better understand the [economic environment in which we and other nonprofits providing similar services currently operate].

Finally, also included in your materials are our routine committee and other reports to help keep you informed of matters that do not generally require discussion at the meeting. However, please feel free to raise any questions during the meeting about any of these reports.

APPENDIX 27 (CONT'D)

Sample 2

Sample Format for Memo Describing Required Board Action re Resolution [to be included with board meeting materials]

[Date]

To: Board of Directors

From: Executive (or other) Officer

Re: Resolution re Bank Account

Action Requested:

Approval of the attached resolution [authorizing new signatories to our principal bank account and opening an additional account.]

Background:

As a result of several recent personnel changes in the Finance Department, we need to amend our signatories to our principal bank account with XYZ Bank. The Finance Department also has requested that we open a second account to assist with [_____]. Attached is the form of resolution that XYZ requires for both these matters. There is minimal opportunity to amend the language of this resolution as it is a standard form of XYZ Bank.

APPENDIX 27 (CONT'D)

Sample 3

Sample Format for Memo Accompanying Financial Information
[to be included with board meeting materials]

[Date]

To: Board of Directors

From: Chief Financial Officer

Re: Accompanying Financial Report

Action Requested:

Review the attached financial report for the month of _____.

Background:

In this report, there are a number of variances that reflect differences in timing rather than significant differences in performance in comparison to plan. Those include variance in the following: [   ]

Of particular note this month:

[Continued growth in revenue
Increases in personnel expense
Actions taken by management to improve budgeting expertise of department managers]

Each of the above will be discussed at the meeting, along with any other questions you may have.

BIBLIOGRAPHY

Publications from the American Bar Association and The Society of Corporate Secretaries and Governance Professionals

2008 Benchmarking Survey Report. The Society of Corporate Secretaries and Governance Professionals, 2008

Board Committees: Considerations, Structures and Uses in Effective Governance. The Society of Corporate Secretaries and Governance Professionals, 2008

Boyd, Willard L. III. *Lawyers' Service on Nonprofit Boards: Managing the Risks of an Important Community Activity.* ABA, Business Law Today, Vol. 18, No. 2, Nov/Dec 2008

Corporate Minutes: A Monograph for the Corporate Secretary. The Society of Corporate Secretaries and Governance Professionals, 2006

Current Board Practices, 6th Study. The Society of Corporate Secretaries and Governance Professionals, 2008

Developing a Web Portal for the Board. The Society of Corporate Secretaries and Governance Professionals, 2008

Directors: Selection, Orientation, Compensation, Evaluation and Termination. The Society of Corporate Secretaries and Governance Professionals, 2001

Futter, Victor and Lisa A. Runquist, eds. *Nonprofit Resources, 2nd edition, A Companion to Nonprofit Governance and Management.* American Bar Association and The Society of Corporate Secretaries and Governance Professionals, 2007

Guide to Nonprofit Corporate Governance in the Wake of Sarbanes-Oxley. ABA Coordinating Committee on Nonprofit Governance. American Bar Association 2005

Governance for Nonprofits: From Little Leagues to Big Universities. The Society of Corporate Secretaries and Governance Professionals, 2008

Logistical Arrangements for Board Meetings: A Guide for the Corporate Secretary. The Society of Corporate Secretaries and Governance Professionals, 2009

Model Nonprofit Corporation Act. American Bar Association, 2008

Overton, George W. and Jeannie Carmedelle Frey, eds., *Guidebook for Directors of Nonprofit Corporations, 2nd ed.* ABA Nonprofit Corporations Committee, American Bar Association, 2002

Records Retention. The Society of Corporate Secretaries and Governance Professionals, 1985

Runquist, Lisa. *The ABCs of Nonprofits.* American Bar Association, 2005

Tortorice, Donald, *Modern Rules of Order*, 3rd ed. American Bar Association, 2007

Varallo, Gregory V. and Daniel A. Dreisbach. *Fundamentals of Corporate Governance: A Guide for Directors and Corporate Counsel*, 2nd ed. American Bar Association, 2009

Other Publications

AIIM. *The ABCs of Records Retention Schedule Development.* May/June 2006 [available at www.aiim.org/infonomics/abcs-of-records-retention-schedule-development.aspx]

American Law Institute. *Principles of the Law of Nonprofit Organizations, Tentative Draft, No. 2.* 2009

Avner, Marcia. *The Lobbying and Advocacy Handbook for Non-Profit Organizations: Shaping Public Policy at the State and Local Level.* Amherst Wilder Foundation and Minnesota Council of Nonprofits, 2004

BBB Wise Giving Alliance. *Standards for Charity Accountability.* Better Business Bureau, 2003

Bell, Jeanne and Elizabeth Schaffer. *Financial Leadership for Nonprofit Executives: Guiding Your Organization to Long-term Success.* CompassPoint Nonprofit Services, 2005

Berger, Steven. *Understanding Nonprofit Financial Statements*, Third Edition. BoardSource, 2008

BoardSource. *Board Self-Assessment: Assess to Advance,* 2009

BoardSource. *The Handbook of Nonprofit Governance (Essential Texts for Nonprofit and Public Leadership and Management).* Jossey-Bass, 2010

BoardSource. *The Nonprofit Board Answer Book*, 2nd ed. Jossey-Bass, 2007

BoardSource. *Nonprofit Governance Index 2010*

Board Source. *The Source: Twelve Principles of Governance that Power Exceptional Boards.* 2005

Boffa, Alane L. *Disclaimers and Private Foundations.* 36 Tax Advisor 459 (2005)

Bryce, Herrington, J. *Financial & Strategic Management for Nonprofit Organizations: A Comprehensive Reference to Legal, Financial, Management, and Operations Rules and Guidelines for Nonprofits, 3rd ed.* Jossey-Bass Inc., 2000

Carlson, Mim and Margaret Donohue. *The Executive Director's Guide to Thriving as a Nonprofit Leader*, 2nd Ed. Jossey-Bass, 2010

Carver, John. *Boards That Make a Difference: A New Design for Leadership in Nonprofit and Public Organizations.* Jossey-Bass, 1997

Carver, John, and Miriam Carver. *Reinventing Your Board: A Step-by-Step Guide to Implementing Policy Governance.* Jossey-Bass, 2006

Chiat, Richard, and William Ryan and Barbara E. Taylor. *Governance as Leadership: Reframing the Work of Nonprofit Boards.* BoardSource and Wiley and Sons, Inc., 2005

Chasin, Cheryl, Susan Ruth, and Robert Harper. *Tax Exempt Organizations and World Wide Web Fundraising and Advertising on the Internet.* 2000 (available at www.irs.gov/pub/irs-tege/eotopici00.pdf.)

Connors, Tracy Daniel, ed. *The Nonprofit Handbook: Management,* 3rd ed. John Wiley & Sons, 2001

Dietel, J. Edwin, ed. *Designing an Effective Records Retention Compliance Program,* Vol 3. Corporate Compliance Series. West, 2010

DeMott, Deborah A. *Self-Dealing Transactions in Nonprofit Corporations.* 59 Brooklyn Law Review 131 (1993)

Drucker, Peter. *Managing the Nonprofit Corporation: Principles and Practices.* Harper Paperbacks, 2006

Graham, Andrew. *Measuring Board Effectiveness: Developing an Assessment Tool.* (available at post.queensu.ca/~grahama/specializedteachingareas/ MEASURINGBOARDEFFECTIVENESS.pdf)

Emil, Angelica. *The Wilder Nonprofit Field Guide to Crafting Effective Mission and Vision Statements.* Amherst H. Wilder Foundation, 2001

Fishman, James. *Improving Charitable Accountability.* 62 Md. L. Rev. 218 (2003)

Fishman, James. *Standards of Conduct for Directors of Nonprofit Corporations.* 7 Pace L. Rev. 389 (1987)

Fishman, James, and Stephen Schwarz. *Nonprofit Organizations: Cases and Materials,* 3rd ed. Foundation Press, 2006

Fishman, James and Stephen Schwarz. *Taxation of Nonprofit Organizations: Cases and Materials,* 3rd ed. Foundation Press, 2006

Floch, Julie L. *Not-for-Profit Governance: Too Much or Not Enough?* CPA J., Jan. 2006, at 80

Fremont-Smith, Marion, *Governing Nonprofit Organizations: Federal and State Law and Regulation.* Harvard Press, 2004

Fremont-Smith, Marion. *Is It Time to Treat Private Foundations and Public Charities Alike?* 52 Exempt Org. Tax Rev. 257 (2006)

Fremont-Smith, Marion. *Pillaging of Charitable Assets: Embezzlement and Fraud.* 46 Exempt Org. Tax Rev. 333 (2004)

Goldschmid, Harvey J. *The Fiduciary Duties of Nonprofit Directors and Officers: Paradoxes, Problems, and Proposed Reforms.* 23 Journal of Corporation Law 631 (1998)

Gottlieb, Hildy. *Board Recruitment & Orientation: A Step-by-Step, Common Sense Guide.* Renaissance Press, 2001

Grace, Kay Sprinkel. *The Ultimate Board Member's Book: A 1-Hour Guide to Understanding and Fulfilling Your Role and Responsibilities.* Emerson & Church, 2006

Herman, Melanie Lockwood. *Ready..... or Not: A Risk Management Guide for Nonprofit Executives.* Nonprofit Risk Management Center, 2009

Herman, Melanie L., George L. Head, Peggy M. Jackson and Toni E. Fogarty. *Managing Risk in Nonprofit Organizations.* Wiley, 2003

Renz, David O., & Associates, The Jossey-Bass Handbook of Nonprofit Leadership and Management, 3d ed. Jossey-Bass, 2010

Hopkins, Bruce. *The Law of Tax-Exempt Organizations*, 9th ed. John Wiley & Sons, 2010

Hirzy, Ellen Cochran. *Nonprofit Board Committees: How to Make Them Work.* National Center for Nonprofit Boards, 1993

Hirzy, Ellen Cochran. *The Nominating Committee: Laying a Foundation for Your Organization's Future.* National Center for Nonprofit Boards, 1994

Independent Sector. *The Basics of Nonprofit Advocacy.* 2010 [available at www.independentsector.org/ the_basics_of_nonprofit_lobbying]

Ingram, Richard T. *Ten Basic Responsibilities of Nonprofit Boards.* BoardSource, 2009

Izuel, Leeanna and Leslie Park. *Tax-Exempt Organizations and Internet Commerce: The Application of the Royalty and Volunteer Exceptions to Unrelated Business Taxable Income.* William Mitchell Law Review 245 (2004)

Jacobs, Jerald and Daniel Ogden. *Legal Risk Management for Associations.* American Psychological Association, 1995

Kurtz, Daniel. *Board Liability: Guide for Nonprofit Directors.* Moyer Bell, 1988

Kurtz, Daniel and Sarah E. Paul. *Managing Conflicts of Interest: A Primer for Nonprofit Boards*, 2nd ed. BoardSource, 2006

Lansdowne, David. *Fund Raising Realities Every Board Member Must Face: A 1-Hour Crash Course on Raising Major Gifts for Nonprofit Organizations.* Emerson & Church, 2006

Mancuso, Anthony. *The Corporate Records Handbook: Meetings, Minutes & Resolutions.* Nolo, 2010

Mathiasen, Karl. *Board Passages: Three Key Stages in a Nonprofit Board's Life Cycle.* Management Assistance Group, National Center for Nonprofit Boards (now BoardSource) 1990, 5th printing 1998 [available at http://www.managementassistance.org/ht/a/GetDocumentAction/i/5975]

McDowell, Suzanne Ross. *Nonprofits and the Internet: Tax and Other Legal Issues.* The Computer & Internet Lawyer (October 2004) [Available at www.steptoe.com/assets/attachments/2483.pdf]

McVeigh, Ellen W. and Eve R. Borenstein. *The Changing Accountability Climate and Resulting Demands for Improved "Fiduciary Capacity" Affecting the World of Public Charities.* 31 William Mitchell Law Review 119 (2004)

Nober, Jane C. *Legal Brief: Conflicts of Interest,* Foundation News & Commentary, Vol. 44, No. 4 July/August 2003 [Available at http://www.foundationnews.org/CME/article.cfm?ID=2561]

Nober, Jane C. *Legal Brief: Conflicts of Interest, Part II: May the Foundation's Lawyer Serve as a Trustee?* Foundation News & Commentary, Vol. 45, No. 1 Jan/Feb 2004 [Available at http://www.foundationnews.org/CME/article.cfm?ID=2747

Nober, Jane C. *Legal Brief: Conflicts of Interest, Part III (investment management),* Foundation News & Commentary, Vol. 45, No. 5 Sept/Oct 2004 [Available at http://www.foundationnews.org/CME/article.cfm?ID=3006]

Olson, John. F., Josiah O. Hatch III and Ty R. Sagalow, *Director and Officer Liability: Indemnification and Insurance.* West, 2009

O'Connell, Brian. *The Board Member's Book: Making a Difference in Voluntary Organizations.* The Foundation Center, 3rd ed., 2003

O'Regan, Katherine M. and Sharon M. Oster. *Does the Structure and Composition of the Board Matter? The Case of Nonprofit Organizations.* 21 J. L. Econ & Org. 205 (2005)

Powell, Walter W. and Richard Steinberg, eds. *The Nonprofit Sector: A Research Handbook,* Yale University Press, 2006

Principles for Good Governance and Ethical Practice: A Guide for Charities and Foundations, Panel on the Nonprofit Sector Convened by Independent Sector, October 2007 [available at http://www.nonprofitpanel.org/report/principles/Principles_Guide.pdf]

Reider, Rob. *Improving the Economy, Efficiency, and Effectiveness of Not-for-Profits: Conducting Operational Reviews.* Wiley, 2001

Report to the Blue Ribbon Commission on Board Evaluation: Improving Director Effectiveness. National Association of Corporate Directors, 2001

Report to Congress and the Nonprofit Sector on Governance, Transparency and Accountability: A Final Report to Congress and the Nonprofit Sector. Panel on the Nonprofit Sector, Independent Sector ed., 2005

Report to Congress and the Nonprofit Sector on Governance, Transparency and Accountability: A Supplement to the Final Report to Congress and the Nonprofit Sector. Panel on the Nonprofit Sector, Independent Sector ed., 2006

Richardson, Virginia G. and John Francis Reilly. *Public Charity or Private Foundation Status: Issues Under IRC 509(a)(1)-(4), 4942(j)(3), and 507.* Exempt Org. Continuing Professional Educ. Tech. Instruction Program for FY 2003 § B, 2002

Robert, Henry M., III, William J. Evans, Daniel H. Honemann, Thomas J. Balch, and Sarah Corbin Robert. *Robert's Rules of Order Newly Revised* 11th ed. Perseus Publishing, 2000

Robert, Henry M., III, William J. Evans, Daniel H. Honemann and Thomas J. Balch. *Robert's Rules of Order Newly Revised in Brief*, Perseus Publishing, 2004

Rowland, Cynthia R. *UPMIFA, Three Years Later, What's a Prudent Director to Do?* Business Law Today, July/August 2009

Salamon, Lester, ed. *The State of Nonprofit America.* Aspen Institute and Brookings Institution Press 2001

Samuels, David G., and Howard Pianko. *Nonprofit Compensation, Benefits, and Employment Law.* Wiley, 2002

Siebart, Patricia. *Corporate Governance of Nonprofit Organizations: Cooperation and Control.* 28 Int'l J. Pub. Admin. 857 (2005)

Siegel, Jack. *A Desktop Guide for Nonprofit Directors, Officers, and Advisors: Avoiding Trouble While Doing Good.* John Wiley & Sons, 2006

Silk, Thomas. *Ten Emerging Principles of Governance of Nonprofit Corporations.* 43 Exempt Org. Tax Rev. 35 (2004)

Strengthening the Transparency, Governance, and Accountability of Charitable Organizations: A Final Report to Congress and the Nonprofit Sector. Panel on the Nonprofit Sector, Independent Sector ed., 2005

Supplement: Strengthening the Transparency, Governance, and Accountability of Charitable Organizations: A Final Report to Congress and the Nonprofit Sector. Panel on the Nonprofit Sector, Independent Sector, ed., 2006

Tesdahl, D. Benson. *The Nonprofit Board's Guide to Bylaws: Creating a Framework for Effective Governance.* BoardSource, 2003

Vermeer, Thomas E. et. al. *The Composition of Nonprofit Audit Committees.* Acct. Horizons, Mar 2006, at 75

Waechter, Sue. *Driving Strategic Planning: A Nonprofit Executive's Guide.* BoardSource, 2010

Warren, Shelia and Rosemary E. Fei. *Politics and Lobbying: Lobbying Clauses in Grant Agreements with Organizational Grantees.* 19 Tax'n Exempts 236 (2006)

White, Mervyn F. *Essentials of Operational Risk Management, Risk Management Checklist.* November 10, 2004, [available at, http://www.carters.ca/pub/checklst/opriskman.pdf.]

Internet Sites

Alliance for Justice, www.afj.org/for-nonprofits-foundations

American Bar Association, www.americanbar.org

BoardSource, www.boardsource.org

Center for Lobbying in the Public Interest, www.clpi.org

Center for Nonprofit Management, www.cnmsocal.org

Community Resource Exchange, www.crenyc.org

Council on Foundations, www.cof.org

Free Management Library, managementhelp.org

Guidestar, www.guidestar.org

Idealist.org, www.idealist.org

Independent Sector, www.independentsector.org

Internal Revenue Service, www.irs.gov/charities

Form 990, available at, http://www.irs.gov/charities/article/

Maryland Nonprofits, www.marylandnonprofits.org

Minnesota Council of Nonprofits, www.mncn.org

National Council of Nonprofits, www.councilofnonprofits.org

Nonprofit Law Blog, www.nonprofitlawblog.com

Nonprofit Risk Management Center, www.nonprofitrisk.org.

Society of Corporate Secretaries and Governance Professionals, www.governanceprofessionals.org

The Chronicle of Philanthropy, www.philanthropy.com

The Nonprofit Times, www.nptimes.com

USA.Gov for Nonprofits, http://www.usa.gov/Business/Nonprofit.shtml

Wiley Online Library, www.onlinelibrary.wiley.com

INDEX

About the Editors

Cheryl Sorokin is a consultant on board governance issues, with emphasis on nonprofit board governance. Ms. Sorokin is the former Group Executive Vice President and Corporate Secretary of Bank of America NT&SA and BankAmerica Corporation. She holds both a bachelor's degree in Spanish and a master's degree in education from Indiana University, and a doctor of jurisprudence (Order of the Coif) from Northwestern University Law School. Ms. Sorokin is the former Chair of the Corporate Practices Committee of the Society of Corporate Secretaries and Governance Professionals, served as a director of the Society from 1991 to 1994 and is the recipient of the Bracebridge H. Young Distinguished Service Award, the Society's highest honor, given for extraordinary contributions to the Society and the governance profession. In addition to the Society, she is a member of the California Bar Association and the American Association of University Women. She is a director of Hispanic Connections, Vice Chair of the American Conservatory Theater and a member of the Advisory Council of Pocket Opera.

Judith A. Cion (1943–2011) was former President of The Governance Group, a consultant in the areas of corporate governance, the corporate secretarial process and securities practices and processes. She also served as General Counsel and Secretary of Hibernia Corporation and its commercial banking subsidiaries. Earlier in her career she was with Mellon Bank, The Coca-Cola Company, in private practice in New York City and managed capital markets, securities regulation and corporate governance development projects in the former Soviet Union and Eastern Europe. Ms. Cion was a past chairman of the Society of Corporate Secretaries and Governance Professionals and a former president of the Society's New Orleans Chapter and served as chairman of the Society's Education Committee. Ms. Cion was a graduate of Pomona College and the Harvard Law School.

Jeannie C. Frey is a health care attorney practicing in Chicago, IL. She is currently the Senior Vice President of Legal Services and General Counsel for Resurrection Health Care, a nonprofit health care system. Ms. Frey frequently speaks and writes on nonprofit governance issues, and served as the lead editor of the *Guidebook for Directors of Nonprofit Corporations* (ABA 2002); primary author of the *Guide to Nonprofit Governance in the Wake of Sarbanes-Oxley* (ABA 2005); and co-executive editor of the *Guide to Representing Religious Organizations* (ABA 2009). Ms. Frey is a former Chair of the Nonprofit Organizations Committee of the ABA Business Law Section. She received the Outstanding Nonprofit Lawyer Award from the ABA's Business Law Section in 2000. Ms. Frey is a graduate of Yale Law School and the University of Colorado, Boulder.

Richard L. Sevcik is a partner in the Chicago office of K&L Gates, LLP, where he leads the firm's exempt organizations group. He concentrates his practice in exempt organizations and health care law. He has extensive experience representing public charities, tax-exempt health care systems, private foundations and charitable trusts. He is a member of the ABA's Business Law Section and Section of Taxation, Exempt Organizations Committee, and has regularly participated in the providing of comments to the Internal Revenue Service on tax-exempt issues. He serves on the Board of the Trustees of the Ravinia Festival Association and the Board of Directors of the Lincoln Park Zoological Society, where he chairs its Planned Giving Advisory Council. He serves on the Professional Council for Philanthropy of Northwestern Memorial Foundation and the Planned Giving Advisory Council of the Ravinia Festival Association. He also serves as Secretary of the National Merit Scholarship Corporation. Mr Sevcik is a graduate of University of Chicago Law School and received his B.A. from the University of Iowa.